Cap. Horsley

Cap. Bolton

White Webbs Gate

Bulls

Cross

Bels

New River

Gur Brook

Tukey Str

Enfield Wash

Maden Br.

Forty Hill

10 Cap. Watts

Cap. Armstrong

Gough Esq

Pottash Hou.

Enfield

Highway

Mr Cull

Beaker

Street

Green Street

Windmill

Field

NFIELD

Dunnne

Mr Headley

Lincoln

House

Ponders End

Scotland Gr.

OuterField

Mr Porter

Bury Street

Cuckow Hall

Salmon Br.

Sadlers

Mill Br.

Marsh Side

LOWr EDMONTON

Piss Corner

Jeremys Hinn

Dunckes Lane

A DESIRABLE NEIGHBOURHOOD

April Showers

Enfield Preservation Society was set up in December 1935 (Gazette 1 May 1936)

A HISTORY OF ENFIELD

Volume Three - 1914 to 1939

A DESIRABLE NEIGHBOURHOOD

BY

David Pam

Enfield Preservation Society

1994

To all my loyal readers

ISBN 0 907318 12 6

Published by Enfield Preservation Society Ltd, 107 Parsonage Lane, Enfield, Middlesex EN2 0AB

Registered Charity No 276451

Designed and produced by J. A. Robey, Ashbourne, Derbyshire

Printed in the UK by
The Cromwell Press Ltd
Broughton Gifford, Wiltshire

Contents

Maps and Plans

Graphs

Illustrations

Acknowledgements

My thanks are again due to Valerie Carter who has patiently read every word of the text, the captions, the references and even the index, in order to eliminate my mistakes. My brother Charles has again relentlessly pointed out the places where my arguments appeared inconclusive and my explanations incomplete. Graham Dalling has been as reliable as in the previous volumes in indicating sources to fill gaps in the author's knowledge and in providing snippets of information which he produces like a conjurer, even on the most abstruse and unlikely subjects. Brian Warren and Terence Goulding have again produced the maps and they are of the same high quality as those with which they embellished my previous volumes. Andrew Combe has devised the graphs. My thanks are also due to Keri Davies and his staff in the Enfield reference library, to Kate Godfrey and to Christopher Simons. The book and its predecessors could scarcely have been published without the drive and energy of the secretary of the Enfield Preservation Society, Irene Smith.

Once again Enfield people, some of whom I had not previously met, have generously allowed me to use their memories to add humour and pathos to the picture. My thanks are offered to; Mrs Doris Shuttlewood, Richard Slater, Sid Robinson, Donald Payne, Miss Iris Mann, Miss Gertrude Williams, Michael Rye, Mrs Norah Clarke, Mrs D. Wright and Roy Tedscoe.

I have listed below those to whom my thanks are due for the loan of photographs, particularly Ken Jones, Peter Lister and Stephen Sellick.

Enfield Libraries photographs number: 1, 3, 4, 6, 7, 10, 16, 19, 28, 31, 32, 38, 39, 40, 41, 43, 53, 55, 58, 59, 60, 61, 62, 63, 64, 65, 75, 78, 90, 92, 98, 101, 114, 115, 120, 125, 126, 127, 133, 135, 139, 153, 168, 169, 202, 205, 212, 215, 216, 217, 221, 224, 225, 227.
Enfield Preservation Society: 5, 18, 22, 23, 24, 25, 42, 69, 81, 102, 104, 106, 107, 116, 117, 119, 121, 122, 124, 134, 161, 190, 191, 196, 197, 204, 208, 215.
Enfield Gazette. 207, 118.
John Newman: 193, 218, 219, 226.
David Hammond: 95, 108.
Furncrafts: 109.
Donald Payne: 14, 15, 57.
Sylvia Elmes: 56.
Stephen Sellick: 2, 11, 20, 21, 27, 29, 68, 77, 95, 99, 112, 163, 174, 195, 198, 220.
Sid Robinson: 34, 35, 182, 189.
Frederick Adams: 30, 128, 129.
Doris Shuttlewood: 214.

Richard Slater: 48.
Michael Rye: 8, 9, 17, 33.
Ken Jones: 12, 13, 36, 47, 49, 50, 54, 113, 123, 136, 142, 143, 212, 213.
Peter Hills: 188.
F. L. Oakman: 138.
David Pam: 67, 79, 82, 83, 85, 86, 87, 89, 93, 94, 100, 105, 145, 152, 160, 162, 167, 170, 173, 175, 178, 183, 187.
Marian Heather: 111.
Stanley Smith: 84, 144, 146, 179, 200.
Reg Williams: 103.
Ken Wright: 52.
Pamlin Prints: 130.
Greater London Record Office: 137, 147, 148, 150.
Alan Dumayne: 176, 177, 180.
Bob Mantle: 223.
Don Gresswell: 74.
A. E. Usher: 97.
Ralph Hutchings: 110.
Ronald Chapman: 149.
A. H. Sellick: 194.
H. A. Mabbott: 222.
Michael Whitman: 235.
Norah Read: (donated) 46.
Jean Cox: (donated) 184, 234.
Leggatt family scrapbook: 26.
Enfield Advertiser: portrait of the author.

   I have to thank Stanley Smith for the preparation of the very large number of photographs used in this volume, and to thank my wife Maisie for much more than merely typing the manuscript.

   I have also to thank Dr John Robey for having transformed my crudely prepared manuscripts into three volumes of the highest quality

Notes on References

The principal source for this volume has been the *Enfield Gazette* supplemented at times by other local newspapers. The classes, Education (ED) and Munitions (MUN) at the Public Record Office, have been used. All other materials noted in references are from the Enfield Local History Library.

Preface

The shape of a local history is inevitably distorted by the weight of the evidence presenting itself on each period. Thus while the first volume of my History of Enfield spanned some twenty centuries and the second covered seventy-seven years, this third volume relates the changes which took place during the quarter of a century from the outbreak of one world war to the onset of another.

Twenty-one years of uncertainty and unreality in politics followed the end of the First World War. Yet despite the fear and concern which the headlines brought into every home, despite the threats and ravings of Hitler, the bombast of Mussolini, despite the news of unemployment in the distressed areas of the north, despite even the suffering of north London neighbours without a job, seeking work with drawn, anxious faces, despite all this, a steady advance towards a better life continued locally.

The 1914-18 war saw, for the first time on a large scale, the intervention of the State in the lives of its citizens. Britain became the arsenal for all the allied armies; even the Americans, after they came into the war, were armed and supplied from British factories. Restrictive working practices were suspended, and wages and working conditions came under the control of the Ministry of Munitions. The State now regulated food and drink, public houses were placed under strict control and even nationalised. Rationing was introduced for tea, butter and sugar and price controls imposed on bread and potatoes. Factory canteens were introduced. Pauperism declined, the children were better fed than they had been before the war. Women left domestic service for well-paid work in war factories; their status rose and those over thirty were even given the vote in July 1918.

The lifting of government controls after the war brought about rapid price increases leading to industrial disputes. Wages lagged behind prices. Old age pensions had to be raised in 1919 to 10s a week. Nevertheless the post-war boom created temporary prosperity which lasted until the winter of 1920-21; by this time unemployment had reached two million. The unemployed and their dependents were now covered by the National Insurance Scheme introduced in 1911. Unemployed men received 15s a week, with 5s for a wife and 1s for each child; this was paid for up to fifteen weeks. Agricultural workers, domestic servants and the self-employed remained outside the scheme and dependent in adversity upon Boards of Guardians. Unemployment was endemic throughout the years between the wars. The number of those unemployed fell to little over a million in 1929 but from 1931-35 it remained above two million.

Boards of Guardians were abolished in 1930, their successors were the local public assistance committees where payment, 15s 3d for an adult male, was subject to a means test. The nineteenth century attitudes of the Poor Law often survived on these committees. They were abolished in 1934 when the Unemployment Insurance Act established the Unemployment Assistance Board, which became responsible for all insured workers who had exhausted their benefit after 156 days. It made benefit a statutory right so long as the applicant was genuinely seeking work.

The efficiency of much of the country's industry was improved with the establishment of the Central Electricity Board in 1926. By 1933 the National Grid was complete. The introduction of compact electrical motors facilitated the expansion of factories in places served by electric power. The output of electricity quadrupled between 1925 and 1939. The rapid extension of surburban house building in the 1930s provided the market for many light industries including the electrical industry.

The Addison Act 1919 established housing as a national responsibility and laid the emphasis on quality rather than cheapness; land for council housing was used lavishly. Rent controls on privately rented property had been imposed in 1915, although after 1923 rents could be raised with a change of tenancy. The 1933 Housing Act removed some controls but retained rent control on some four million lower-rated houses. One consequence was that the private rented sector became unprofitable and was virtually eliminated after 1945. The years between the two wars saw the advent of two new classes of householder; the owner-occupier and the council house tenant. People's lives from the 1920s were to be illuminated and warmed by electricity, and made cheerful by the wireless and the cinema. Their food was usually cooked by gas, the old solid fuel ranges were ripped out and taken away.

The 1919 budget had increased death duties to forty per cent on landed estates valued at £2 million or over, causing a widespread sale of land. The real losers were the landed gentry. In 1900 Enfield had been a patchwork of large estates. Many of them survived in 1918, especially in the western part of the parish, but today only a few, fossilised as large public parks or golf courses, remain to give an impression of the world we have lost.

The uncontrolled expansion of suburbia was halted in the Thirties. Raymond Unwin, in 1933, urged the creation of a 'green girdle' around London, and 25,000 acres were set aside as open country by the Green Belt Act 1938.

The period between the two wars was the heyday of local government. Local authorities were left to carry out the initiatives of central government in housing, education and poor relief. Local government expenditure in England and Wales rose from £140m in 1913 to £533m in 1939. Central government grants and sanctioned loans facilitated this great expansion in local authority spending which might not have been tolerated if it had had to come out of the pockets of the ratepayers. Government grants rose from 22 per cent of local spending in 1913 to 41 per cent in 1939, but power follows the purse and the years after 1950 saw the independence of local authorities further and further eroded.

Health improved between the wars, certainly among those in regular employment, both because families had fewer children and because men drank less. The National Insurance Act gave people access to free medical treatment through panel doctors, though hospital treatment had to be paid for according to means. A most important improvement in the years between the wars was the decline in infant mortality. The number of deaths through infectious diseases was also reduced through isolation, immunization, vaccination and cleanliness.

Houses built in the Twenties and Thirties had bathrooms with hot water. Hospitals and local authorities now provided maternity care, and the school medical service did what it could for the health of the children, despite reluctant co-operation from many parents.

The Education Act 1918 provided universal compulsory education up to the age of fourteen. Mostly it was elementary education; in 1923 only 7.5 per cent of children were educated in secondary schools. Following the Hadow Report in 1926 education was divided into primary and secondary, which was again sub-divided as modern and grammar. County grants for higher education enabled some of the brighter children of self-denying working-class parents to go to grammar school.

Religion declined in its influence, especially in urban and suburban areas. Working-class people found more time and money for leisure, which became rapidly commercialised. Cigarette smoking was promoted among both men and women by cigarette cards and gift coupons. Football pools became a national addiction. Almost everybody went regularly to the cinema, especially after the introduction of the 'talkies' in the late Twenties. Dance music was eagerly awaited on the wireless. The working class took a new pride in their gardens. Newspapers fought for mass circulation with gift offers and free insurance. Family holidays at the seaside became more common. Hitler, Mussolini and the Spanish Civil War could be ignored, both by the people and by their political representatives. The tragic nature of the First World War had given rise to a desperate yearning for peace and no more war, a yearning which was to shape the policies of all parties in the inglorious years between 1918 and 1939.

Chapter One

The Great War 1914-1918

1. Introduction: A Summary

It was thought in August 1914 that the First World War would be over by Christmas. The War Office believed that the domestic munitions industry would be able to supply whatever was necessary to secure victory. They flooded the existing arms manufacturers with orders only to find that the manufacturers were unable or unwilling, because they too expected a short war, to invest capital in order to expand production. By the end of the year 1914 orders for ten million shells had been placed but less than half a million had been produced. Many men were volunteering for the forces and this created a shortage of skilled workers, but dilution with semi-skilled labour was strongly opposed by the craft unions. The government was forced to intervene in March 1915 to secure an agreement by which the unions accepted dilution for the duration. The supply situation remained unsatisfactory, for trench warfare demanded vast quantities of artillery and shells. Army headquarters attributed the failure of the British offensive in May 1915 to the inadequacy of supplies and the War Office was blamed. In consequence the Ministry of Munitions was created in June; Lloyd George was appointed minister.

It was the intention of this new ministry to engage the entire industrial capacity of the country in the production of materials for war. This policy was exemplified in Enfield where all the important factories and many small workshops found themselves, within weeks, busy on war work. The Ponders End Shell manufactory, originally set up by an arrangement between the War Office and Rees Roturbo, was vastly expanded by means of grants paid by the Ministry of Munitions and production rapidly increased. Six hundred thousand eight-inch shells were produced and purchased by the government at £9 2s 6d each in the first half of the year 1916. The ministry installed new plant at Cosmos for the production of wireless valves; it rapidly expanded the Royal Small Arms Factory at Enfield Lock and the Royal Gunpowder Factory at Waltham Abbey. Thousands of women found employment in Enfield even,from April 1916, at the RSAF where they had never been employed before. Women took over milk rounds, the work of postmen, became tram conductors and did clerical work. It was easy for them to find jobs as machinists ('sewing shirts for soldiers') while Ediswan, Cosmos and the Ponders End Shell Works employed thousands of women and girls.

Under the Munitions of War Act in July 1915, any factory could be declared a 'controlled establishment'. Profits were then controlled and wages could be increased only with government consent; workers could be bound to their place of employment. New factories like the Rolling Mills, just completed at the beginning of the war, were taken over for the duration. Morson Chemicals went over to the manufacture of poisonous gas. The increasing casualty rate in 1917 at last forced the government to give priority to the manpower requirements of the Army. Factories were vigorously combed for men fit for service. The demand for recruits was given still further urgency by what proved to be the final German offensive in 1918.

Early in the war the country experienced a shortage of sugar. Rationing was initially undertaken in a rough and ready way by the trade, which allocated deliveries to retailers based upon their sales before the war. The system took no account of the movement of population into places like Enfield, by now heavily engaged on war work. Enfield also suffered a serious shortage of potatoes at this time. Lloyd George, in December 1916, established the Ministry of Food. The ministry was determined to increase the production of wheat, to this end it aimed to plough up seven and a half million acres of grass in time to enhance the harvest of 1918. Local committees were to determine what land should be ploughed. The decision was too late to greatly increase the harvest of 1917, but favourable weather in the autumn, winter and spring (1917-18) together with the use of tractors, the work of soldiers, prisoners of war, women and even schoolchildren, enabled both the ministry and the Enfield War Agricultural Committee to reach their targets.

It was towards the end of the year 1917 that the country began to suffer real food shortages; there were long queues for butter, margarine, tea, sugar and meat. At the end of December the registration scheme for sugar was extended to all scarce foods. Price regulation and rationing had been introduced in the summer of 1917 and by the end of the war the scheme covered almost all foodstuffs, although bread remained unrationed to the end. Each householder had to register with a retailer who in turn would register with a wholesaler; both would receive allocations in accordance with their number of registered customers. Ration cards were issued in January 1918, ration books in February. These measures, together with the success of the convoy system in protecting shipping ensured better supplies and more equitable distribution.

The account in this chapter of the setting up and growth of the Edmonton Military Hospital shows how the War Office adapted and expanded such facilities as were available in 1914. Here the excellent but under-used wards and operating theatre of a workhouse infirmary were put to good use. The increasing number of wounded men returned to 'Blighty' led, within months, to insistent demands on the Guardians for more beds and more wards. Wartime prosperity had rendered the extensive premises of the Victorian workhouse superfluous. Its buildings were taken over and brightened up to house more thousands of sick and wounded soldiers. When even these new wards were filled and the corridors and balconies were crammed with beds, large houses and mansions (also rendered superfluous by the times) were taken over and fitted out for the convalescents.

This area of north London played an important and honourable part in the Great War. When it was over the men returned from the trenches and slipped quietly back into their roles as husbands, fathers and breadwinners. Every street must have had one man who had lost a leg or an arm, who was to carry his artificial limb without complaint for the next fifty years. Not all the disabled however were given, like Mr Parker in my own street, Pymmes Gardens South, a council house, 'fit for a hero', with an overgrown garden of half an acre and privet hedges seven feet high.

With every passing year the veterans of the First World War 'fade away'. Armistice services which once attracted weeping mothers and sisters to the cenotaph on Chase Green, in these latter days are reduced to formalities. The hospital in Chase Side, put up to commemorate their heroism, has been demolished. Yet those four years have left an indelible impression, indeed few events in history, before or since, are more likely to excite the imagination of the schoolboy, or are better known among the thousands whose cars bring them to Enfield's shopping centres every week.

2. The War Factories

The year 1914 found the Royal Small Arms Factory with a disgruntled work-force, recently changed management and poor prospects. The unions had fought bitterly for four years against the rationalisation of production which had caused skilled men to be replaced by machines and transferred to semi-skilled work on reduced wages. The estimates for the year commencing March 1914 held out no hope of expansion. The government had not been expecting war, yet within two weeks of the outbreak, production was increasing and by 21 August night shifts were being worked in some departments. More hands were taken on though the management would no longer recruit men aged between nineteen and thirty-five. The factory was working a seven-day week by the end of September.

During the early months of the war private industry was allowed to make large profits from government contracts in order to encourage firms to turn over to war production; later, taxation was increased and prices were controlled. Ediswan's was already on full-time working and more staff had to be recruited in the engineering section to meet contracts for work from the Admiralty. The wives of those men who had joined the Army received half the husband's pay. The enlistment of the men caused little disruption at first for their places were taken by girls and, by the beginning of September, two thousand people were employed there. Small firms too hastened to secure government contracts. The Genotin Blouse Factory, in Genotin Road, offered to produce forty dozen soldiers' shirts a month. In an endeavour to prove its patriotism, the manage-ment of the Brimsdown Lamp Works (Cosmos) sent £250 to the Prince of Wales Fund. 'What', asked the *Enfield Gazette* with a sneer, 'will their German share-holders say to this?' George Ludecke the manager at the Cosmos factory was arrested in November. His house had been searched and a rifle and ammuni-tion found; he was fined 40s with costs. Two Germans had been arrested in September at their lodgings in Westmoor Road. When the war broke out they had been working on the construction of a chimney shaft for the new Enfield Cable Works at Brimsdown. The factory had just been completed when war broke out; it was taken over by the government for the duration. Sixteen reservists from the Metallic Tubing Company in South Street had been called to the colours, others had joined the Territorials. Both the workmen and the company contributed to pay the wives 7s 6d a week with an additional 2s 6d for each child. At this factory too they were working a seven-day week by September;

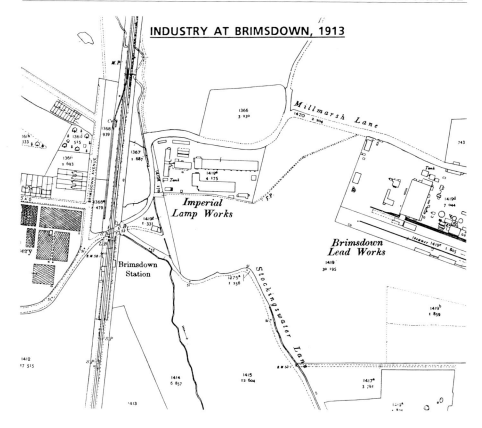

INDUSTRY AT BRIMSDOWN, 1913

it was government controlled for the duration, most of the output being taken by the Admiralty. Flexible metallic tubing was used in charging torpedoes, fuelling submarines, cooling machine guns, and in apparatus for submarine detection.[1]

A number of the men from the Brimsdown White Lead Factory were serving with the forces and the company paid the wives 10s a week with a shilling for each child. Ninety per cent of the firm's production, by October 1915, went to the allied governments. New and greatly enlarged offices were opened and 155 were employed in the works department. T. Morson Chemicals went into war work. The first poison gas made in this country was manufactured there, also the antiseptic field-dressings used by the allied armies. A factory for making lenses was set up in a mansion called Westmoor in Green Street.[2]

The influx of new workers into the district caused difficulties. There was a desperate shortage of houses in Enfield, scarcely any working-class dwellings having been built in the ten years before the war. Great pressure was also placed on an already inadequate tram service. There were four thousand workers at the Royal Small Arms Factory by December 1914 and the journey to work had become a nightmare. The tram company came under increasing criticism. It had no system for turning the cars short of the terminus at Waltham Cross, nor could one car pass another along the route. Long convoys of three to six empty

1.   *Carterhatch Lane looking west from the bridge over the railway. The gate on the right led to the wooden platform on the Cheshunt loop, opened on 2 June 1916 and closed 30 June 1919.*

trams in consequence proceeded blindly on to Waltham Cross while despairing queues built up back down the line. It dawned at last on the Great Eastern Railway Company that here was an opportunity to reopen their Edmonton Cheshunt Line. An auto-train passenger service was launched at the beginning of March 1915. On weekdays, twopenny workmen's returns were issued from Bruce Grove or White Hart Lane on trains arriving at Theobalds Grove by 7am. A new railway station with a wooden platform was subsequently opened, on 2 June 1916, on the north side of the bridge in Carterhatch Lane. Competition from the railway forced the tram company to put its affairs in order, thus public transport was substantially improved, but not for long. A strike broke out in May 1915 and almost all the 170 men at Tramway Avenue came out. Drivers and conductors marched from Holloway, Wood Green and Finchley on the Monday, distributing leaflets setting out their grievances. Nevertheless the Tramway Avenue men relented so far as to agree to carry munition workers to the factories and, that Thursday lunchtime, they marched to Enfield Lock where they held a meeting addressed by Henry Barrass outside the factory. Their demand was for a fifteen per cent increase to meet the rising cost of living. They claimed that they had been working seventy-five hours spread over four and a quarter days for the last eight months, with no more than a shilling a week bonus. Out of the 230 men at the depot before the war, it was said, only one hundred were now left. The men were still out at the end of the month. Women tram conductors had appeared elsewhere in London by 1915, but not hereabouts.

At Ediswan's the volume of work on government contracts grew rapidly. As well as electric light bulbs the firm was now making electrical accessories for the Army and Navy including radio valves, produced for the first time on a large scale. The thermionic valve had been conceived in the Ponders End factory almost by accident. That was in 1904 when Ambrose Fleming, in a moment of inspiration, had realised the potentialities of an apparatus which he had

2.   During the First World War work was continuing on the Great Northern extension to Hertford and in January 1915, excavators were digging the Ponsbourne Tunnel. This photograph shows the further construction of the line in September 1916.

constructed and stored away in a cupboard fifteen years earlier. The increasing tempo of work production in April 1915 required more skilled labour. Advertisements were published offering high wages for toolmakers and automatic machine minders, with overtime and Sunday work. War munitions volunteers were asked to enrol at the public offices in Gentleman's Row in an effort to ensure that all the skilled workmen available were employed on war work.[3]

King George V, with Prince George and Lord Kitchener, visited the Royal Small Arms Factory and the Royal Gunpowder Factory in May 1915. Ladies in the area became concerned about the war effort and Lady Lawrence's committee undertook the provision of refreshments at the RSAF for the night workers, bringing tea into the workshops in the early hours. Tents had to be erected in the factory grounds for the lady caterers. The demand for jobs at the factory was as great as ever; morning after morning crowds of men stood waiting at the gates in the hope of employment. The day shift began at 7am. The Great Eastern now ran threepenny workmen's returns from Liverpool Street but for some reason the train was scheduled to reach Enfield Lock at 6.15am so that the men were forced to hang about for half an hour before starting work.[4]

The Great Northern extension to Hertford had been abandoned in the middle of a field at Cuffley on the completion of the first contract in 1909. Work was now resumed and in July 1915 excavators were engaged on digging the Ponsbourne Tunnel, 2,684 yards in length, just north of Cuffley. It was expected that it would be completed in August. By the end of May 1918 a single track line, as far as Stevenage, was in place and was occasionally used for goods trains. A branch off the GER main line, from Brimsdown station to the Small Arms Factory, was being constructed in October 1915; a start was made in November on the foundations of three bridges along the route. It was even demanded in August 1916 that the GER should run workmen's trains right into the works.[5]

A crisis on the Western Front in 1915 was attributed by Sir John French, Commander of the British Expeditionary Force 1914-15, to a shortage of shells. Consequent criticism in Parliament resulted in the formation of the Coalition Government and the appointment of Lloyd George as Minister of Munitions. A shell factory had been set up at Ponders End early in the year 1915 by the Rees Roturbo Company. The War Office had signed a contract with the firm in December 1914 by which the government was to pay £80,000 (eighty per cent of the capital expenditure) and would also advance £137,000 as working capital. Before the war Rees Roturbo had made electric dynamos and motors, centrifugal pumps and other highly specialised engineering products under patents, but from August 1914 the company turned its resources to war work. H.S.B.Brindley was the London manager and he alone had detailed knowledge of shell manufacture.

The company, early in 1915, secured a factory at Ponders End where mantlepieces had been made, on land which had formerly been used by the Ponders End Cricket Club. Brindley was put in charge. The new Ministry of Munitions advanced the Company £20,000 to be applied to the conversion of existing plant and to the installation of additional plant capable of producing 7,000 forgings a week for six-inch shells. The money was to be paid back out of the profits of production. Within one month the demand for shells on the Western Front had become so insistent that it was ordered that a new forging shop must be erected by 31 March 1916 to produce 12,000 forgings a week. The ministry was to pay eighty per cent of the cost up to £31,000. The new works proved successful and produced a vast and increasing output of shells:

Delivered	8-inch shells	cost each	total
up to 31. 8. 15	11,468	£9 15s	£111,843
31.8 to 31.12.15	37,590	£9 2s 6d	£343,009
31.12.15 to 30. 6.16	65,769	£9 2s 6d	£600,142

By an agreement with the government in March 1915 the unions had undertaken that all disputes should be referred to arbitration. The Munitions of War Act 1915 gave the new ministry power to outlaw strikes and lockouts. Nevertheless there was a demonstration outside the works in June 1915 when the night shift refused to go in because of a dispute over piece-work prices. After discussion the men agreed to begin work but, at eight o'clock, fifty or sixty of them walked out again. The increasing cost of food was responsible for an all-round demand for higher wages at this time. Even the workmen making up the council roads demanded, and were conceded, an extra halfpenny to bring their money up to eighteen pence an hour.[6]

The Edmonton Munitions Company, in July 1915, acquired from Harry Hooper Stockfield his business in Tile Kiln Lane Edmonton, with the plant and machinery. The firm entered into a contract with the government for filling exploders and eighteen-pounder shells. Ninety-six thousand were filled in the first week. Subsequently a contract for 250,000 a week was signed, also for mines and air bombs, and charges for howitzer shells. Advances from the government, it was claimed, were less than the value of the work done and, by June 1918, the firm had an accumulated overdraft of £8,700. A fire in October 1918 destroyed many filling sheds and a large quantity of material. Losses amounted to £17,000, and two Southgate firemen were killed. The factory continued to work for the government after the armistice, breaking down gun-cotton, charges, mines and bombs. A variety of other work was later undertaken, printing certificates for

3.   So serious was the shortage of accommodation for war workers that the YMCA, with a government grant, erected huts near the Royal Small Arms Factory in September 1915 and near the Ponders End Shell Works (shown here) a few months later. Each hut was divided into cubicles which were furnished with a bed and an easy chair. Workers paid 17s 6d a week rent.

discharged soldiers, the manufacture of civilian suits and metal toys. The firm went into liquidation in 1926 still claiming money due to it from the War Office.[7]

The housing shortage became worse as munition workers arrived from all over England. Scarcely a bed was to be had by 1915, let alone a room. To meet the situation the YMCA, with a government grant, erected huts near the Small Arms Factory. Workers paid 17s 6d a week to include laundry. The huts were divided into cubicles each with a bed and an easy chair; bathrooms and a large recreation room were provided. A committee of ladies made itself responsible for home comforts. The first site chosen was a six-acre meadow lying immediately east of the Enfield Lock railway station, part of Welch's farm; it was opened by Mrs Winston Churchill in September 1915. The cubicles were in great demand and by October the kitchens there provided a hundred and twenty dinners and sixty breakfasts and teas every day.

An increase of some one thousand employees was anticipated at the RSAF. There was a shortage of canteen accommodation. The old dining hall, the Sheridan Theatre, had a fully equipped kitchen and the catering was let out to contract. Further dining halls were being put up to be managed by the YMCA, but many of the men preferred to use one or other of the four public houses near the works, the Royal Small Arms Hotel, the Greyhound, the Swan and Pike or the Ordnance Arms. The management was very strict on discipline. One worker in October 1915 was suspended for a month for drunkenness. During this time he was not allowed to apply for work elsewhere because under the Munitions Act (July 1915) a munitions worker leaving employment could not be taken on by another firm within six weeks, unless he produced a leaving certificate. The suspension was therefore equivalent to a fine of £20. He appealed before the Metropolitan Munitions Tribunal, pleading that he had never been cautioned, but his appeal was turned down. That month saw the

4, 5. The Greyhound (above) and the Ordnance Arms, two of the four public houses at Enfield Lock 'nationalised' just before Christmas 1915 (Ordnance Arms from a postcard dated 1909.)

introduction of the 'No Treating Order' by which every drinker had to pay for what he consumed himself. The temperance lobby was still very much alive.

One Saturday night, just before Christmas 1915, the night-shift, coming out for their midnight break, found all the four houses closed by order of the Liquor Control Board. Normally they opened between eleven and twelve o'clock to enable the men to buy a meal or to eat their sandwiches there. A protest meeting was called. Colonel Halse, the deputy superintendent, came down to the works and calmed the situation by granting an extra hour's break to enable those who

6.   *The voluntary ladies who ran the workers' canteen at the Ponders End Shell Factory during the First World War, photographed in February 1916.*

7, 8. King George V on a private visit to Ponders End Shell Factory in February 1917.

lived near enough to go home. Others were given time to get something in the factory dining hall. Many of the men however went home and did not come back that night. On the Sunday, in consequence of the same order, the licensed

9.   Shells for the Western Front
February 1917.

houses were not open until 1 pm and management had again to grant a two-hour break. The new regulation thus resulted in the loss of between eight and nine thousand man-hours. A branch meeting of the Workers Union was convened that evening and a delegation was sent to the Liquor Control Board. After much discussion the houses were allowed to open between eleven and twelve at night but not for the sale of intoxicants.[8]

The situation remained unsatisfactory. J. McGrath, the secretary of the Enfield Lock branch of the Workers Union, told the Central Control Board that his union had no wish that the public houses should be abused by workmen to the detriment of production, but facilities were needed for men leaving off at six o'clock in the morning; the public houses must be open from six to seven. In the evening they should open at 5.30, not 6.30, so that men starting work at six could get a little refreshment. Sunday opening was from one until three but the men left work between twelve and one; McGrath suggested opening from twelve noon until two. The following Wednesday the four public houses were nationalised and the Central Control Board took over the freeholds. A protest came from the Home Counties Public House Trust. Their lessee at the Swan and Pike, they complained, had been catering for hundreds of munition workers every day, providing substantial meals at low prices and the licensee stood to lose a great deal of money. Under state management a new dining room was opened at the Royal Small Arms Tavern by the Duke of Connaught in October 1917. It was capable of providing six hundred meals for both night and day shifts. Some of the locals still refer to the house (now the Rifles) as the 'Canteen'.[9]

10.   Winston Churchill as Minister of Munitions, with Austen Chamberlain, visited the Ponders End Shell Factory in October 1917.

The Ministry of Munitions was established in July 1915. Factories with government contracts were springing up everywhere. The Bycullah Athenaeum was taken over by Klinger's for the manufacture of military clothing and hospital garments. The firm installed a hundred sewing machines and advertised for 'young persons' to sew on buttons at 4d to 5d an hour; 130 girls were working there by September 1915 and there was room for a further hundred. Experienced machinists were paid 5d per hour, handworkers 4d per hour. They began work at 8.30 in the morning and finished in the evening at 7.30, with an hour for lunch and half an hour for tea. The two munitions factories at Waltham Abbey, the Royal Gunpowder Factory and Nobel's Explosives Factory, expanded through the year 1915 and by September shifts were working day and night. There too, cubicle huts had been found necessary, each to hold twenty-two men who paid 17s 6d a week. Nobel's were making cartridges on a large scale, 251,250 were delivered on 20 January 1916, each one was inspected by the government and the bill reduced according to the number rejected. Machinery at the Remington Cartridge factory was adapted to the purposes of the Ministry. The firm, an offshoot of the parent company in Connecticut, had set up in Stockingswater Lane in 1912.[10]

In order to meet the needs of the vast army of workers at the Ponders End Shell Works a large canteen was erected (factory canteens could be written off against wartime taxation) run for the YMCA by fifty voluntary ladies. Lloyd George paid a visit there in February 1916. At this time six-inch, eight-inch and heavy howitzer shells were in production. Women and girls worked the day and night shifts, volunteers served hot meals at 2.30am and eight hundred meals were served daily. The following year (February 1917) George V came on a private visit. There were no demonstrations, no flags, but the streets assumed a 'pre-war' cleanliness, and small knots of people gathered at the gates. Winston

11, 12. Construction of the tramline along Southbury Road was delayed until 20 February 1911 because discussions were continuing about the feasability of linking it to the line in Enfield Town. The link was never made. Two single-deck cars plied the route at first but these were replaced by double-deckers from 3 June 1911, according to C. S. Smeeton, although the Enfield Gazette (26 November 1915) reports the demand for double-deck trams along Southbury Road because of the heavy use by munitions workers. (Postcard of single-deck tram dated 15 October 1914)

Churchill, as Minister of Munitions, visited the factory with Austen Chamberlain in October. The workers were assembled in the central workroom and the band of the Grenadier Guards performed. A hundred cubicles were planned there in December 1915 and a recreation room, also a hundred additional cubicles for RSAF workers. A decision was taken that double-decker trams

13.   *In front of the cottages in Government Row, beyond the railings, was the elevated Lee Navigation. Practically every winter the river flooded over; a permanent watermark, about fifteen inches up the walls, marked the level to which the flood usually rose inside the houses.*

should be run on the Southbury Road route which was heavily used by munitions workers, and the shuttle was extended northward. For their convenience a footbridge over the Lee was erected near the Greyhound to give direct access. Men were being taken on daily, though preference was given to discharged soldiers and men over military age.

Richard Slater described standing as a small boy collecting cigarette cards from the cloth-capped horde of 'lockies' pouring out of the narrow entrance which led through to the 'island bridge' over the back river. His grandfather, as a marker on the rifle range, occupied one of the cottages in Government Row. In front of the cottage, beyond the railings, was the elevated Lee Navigation along which the horse-drawn barges continuously passed. The small back gardens dropped down into the backwaters of the River Lea behind. Practically every winter the river flooded over; a permanent watermark about fifteen inches up the walls, marked the level to which it usually rose inside the house. The whole family, on these occasions, retreated upstairs. Richard Slater's grandfather would stand on the stairs with a walking stick, hooking in the chairs which floated around the living room. Despite these endemic calamities the front doorstep of the house in Government Row was whitewashed every day, when above water-level, and the brass door-knocker, letter-box and door-knob were cleaned and polished with Brasso.

Some of the old buildings near the main entrance of the factory were demolished in February 1917 and new offices were built. All the cubicles in the huts at Ordnance Road were by this time occupied and there was a long waiting list. There was expansion too at Ediswan's where the materials of war were being manufactured on a large scale under government control, from November 1915. Messrs Coley and Wilbraham were building a factory at Brimsdown in November 1916 for the manufacture of chemicals. The Ministry of Munitions installed plant to the value of £3,500 at Cosmos to increase the output of wireless telegraph valves. The plant remained the property of the Ministry, and the firm paid rent.[11]

The great demand for houses pushed up rents. Rent control did not apply to new tenancies, so whenever there was a change of tenancy, rents were put up by sixpence or a shilling a week, but this caused little resentment, for money was plentiful on account of high wages, though only in the war industries. At the RSAF, in April 1915, workers had a rise of twelve per cent on piece-work and 4s a day on day-work, nevertheless in August the men demanded a further ten per cent and a further 4s. The minimum rate at the factory at this time for unskilled work was 27s for a forty-eight hour week, but some were working eighty-two hours. They were paid time and a quarter for the first two hours overtime each day, then time and a half, with double time on Sundays. A letter in *The Times* (22 September 1915) tells of a workman at the RSAF taking £7 10s a week. Labourers, who before the war got 25s, were now drawing £3, skilled mechanics more. These reports of high wages were denied by the unions which claimed that the man earning £7 10s was an isolated example and must have been on piece-work. A single man, who was dismissed in June 1916, in order to make him eligible for the Army, had been earning £4 a week; instead of joining up he went to Erith and got a job in the Vickers Machine Gun Factory at the same wage. Some of the high wages found a way into building societies. The Waltham Abbey Society, by April 1916, had 1,342 members; receipts for the year ending that month amounted to £55,412, £14,000 more than in the previous year. Investments could be made by a monthly subscription of 5s to £5, interest was at five per cent. The high wages were taxable, and by the beginning of the year 1918 a large number of summonses were pending for the non-payment of income tax, mostly against munitions workers who had been earning between £250 and £400 a year. Some of them had, by this time, left munitions and were earning less. Lads leaving school at fourteen were paid 18s a week at the factory which was more than double what they had been paid before the war. They were recruited through an entrance examination in English, measurement and drawing, which they sat at the Ponders End Technical Institute where components for small arms were being made as part of the training. Three thousand boys between fourteen and eighteen were employed in local factories by April 1917. The education committee was no longer so generous in granting exemption to allow boys under fourteen to work, and although 266 exemptions had been granted in 1916, 291 had been refused.[12]

Women were being employed locally as letter-carriers by May 1915; twelve postmen and five indoor staff from the Town post office had joined the forces, and two each from the staffs at Ponders End and Enfield Wash. Women were also taking over milk rounds by the end of that year. 'They can hardly be expected to turn out at five o'clock on a winter's morning', wrote the editor of the *Gazette* (25 November 1915); he suggested a reduction of the rounds. Mrs Churchill opened YMCA huts in September 1915 at Angel Road Edmonton where three thousand women and girls were employed at Eley's. Much of the clerical work for the Metropolitan Water Board was now being done by women clerks earning from £78 to £104 per annum. Such was the demand for labour

14, 15. *Women even took over milk rounds in the First World War, though this was rare for it was very heavy work. The picture shows Mrs Dorothy Payne whose father owned the Oatlands Dairy at Enfield Highway. Subsequently she worked at the RSAF. She married Ernest Payne serving in the Royal Field Artillery.*

that some boys in their teens received what had, before the war, been adult wages. A case was cited in the *Gazette* of a boy who turned down £1 a week and food, saying he could get more. It was feared that standards of behaviour were sadly declining, especially among the young. Older generations were particularly worried about the young people, boys and girls, who travelled from Enfield by twopenny workmen's returns. The trains arrived early and crowds of youngsters were left hanging about promiscuously on Liverpool Street station, until it was time to go to work. The Great Eastern was urged to eradicate the scandal by allowing them to come up on a later train. March 1915 brought another horror story in the *Gazette*. 'What are we coming to?' demanded the editor, disillusioned and disgusted; it had been reported that, about nine o'clock on the previous Monday evening, two girls, only nineteen years of age and thought to be domestic servants, had been seen walking along London Road smoking cigarettes 'as to the manner born'. An elderly gentleman, shocked by this unwonted and unwomanly behaviour, had appealed in vain to a passing policeman.

Female labour was employed for the first time at the RSAF in April 1916 when fifty 'female operatives' were set to work on the machines in the 'big room'. A building was to be erected in Government Row as accommodation for the girls. Between five and six hundred were employed there by August, mostly on machine work in the various shops. They were provided with blue overalls and caps. A dining hall for the women was being built. It was thought to be the intention of the authorities to employ 1,500 females at Enfield Lock and a thousand at the Royal Gunpowder Factory. Girls under sixteen (unskilled) were paid 3d an hour, going up ½d for each year to 4½d at the age of eighteen. Female

16, 17. Women were employed at the RSAF from April 1916.

examiners were paid up to 7½d an hour 'first class', and female skilled tool sharpeners up to 8d. It was planned to train women on more difficult operations like barrel boring and setting, paying them a special day rate while under instruction.[13]

The Metropolitan Munitions Tribunal, in August 1916, protested strongly against single men sheltering in the factories while family men had been discharged and called up. The call-up of a man with a large family might cause real hardship. 'To Mum's dismay', wrote Sid Robinson in his autobiography, 'Dad was called up into the Army sooner than expected and she found herself … with less money than ever'. (He had been employed in the nurseries). 'In retrospect I do not know how we survived from 1917 to 1919, but the seven of us did …. Mum considered herself lucky if she could earn a shilling or two by sitting up late trimming with scissors a long length of lace on a reel, for the Enfield Embroidery Company. It was slave labour ….'

W. D. Cornish, the chief military representative on the Tribunal, in October 1916, referred to the great number of anonymous letters which he was receiving; during the past week there had been sixteen naming alleged shirkers. Men who had not registered at the time of the national registration were difficult to trace. Discharged soldiers were now calling at Ponders End Labour Exchange looking in vain for work in munitions. Allegations were made that some eligible men were paying money in order to retain their jobs. Labour leaders were in the forefront of the campaign for recruitment, though sometimes they flavoured their arguments with a small pinch of class antagonism to please the masses. Thus Will Thorne, addressing a local meeting of Gas Workers and General Labourers in March 1916, criticised young unmarried men still working in munitions '… particularly middle-class'. Orders went out in December 1916 to de-badge all the unskilled and semi-skilled workers under forty-one. Following the de-badging 516 men were released from the Royal Gunpowder Factory and 395 from the Royal Small Arms Factory.

The call for more men to replace heavy casualties at the front became even more insistent from the beginning of the year 1918. In January the RGF and the RSAF were called upon to release a thousand fit young men whose places would be taken by women. Brindley arranged with the military authorities to release a thousand from the Shell Works. He sent in a list but over the ensuing months few were called up (perhaps shells were wanted even more than soldiers) and, while this benefited production, it was considered unfair. The Shell Factory in March 1918 still employed 771 skilled and semi-skilled men of classes A to C3, liable to military service. All the single men under twenty-six however had been discharged. By the end of November 1918, 983 women were employed at the Royal Small Arms Factory, ten per cent of the workforce; at the Royal Gunpowder Factory they now employed 1,145 (twenty-seven per cent).

Elizabeth Macey, aged twenty, died in the Edmonton Infirmary in May 1917 from jaundice caused by TNT poisoning; her mother was in the infirmary with the same illness. The manager (probably at the Edmonton Munitions Factory) said that many women and girls had been suspended by the doctor from working on TNT but some would contrive to continue. The coroner declared that Elizabeth 'had lost her life in the country's cause'. Ediswan's advertised in December 1916 offering good wages for fifty young girls on war work in the dry cell shop. Many married women with children were working. Enfield council even contemplated the establishment of a creche where parents would pay sixpence a day, but it would have had to be subsidised by the government and no subsidy was offered. The local medical officer of health lamented the decline in the birth rate caused by many mothers working in munitions.[14]

May 1917 saw labour troubles among engineering workers spreading into the Lea Valley. Six hundred downed tools at the RSAF and four hundred came out from two other unnamed factories in Enfield. The strike was denounced by J.

McGrath, secretary of the RSAF Workers Union branch, but the engineers had returned to work by the end of the month. Floods caused a stoppage in January 1918 when the area around the RSAF became a vast lake; the road outside the Greyhound was under two and half feet of water. Work was suspended at dinner-time on the Saturday and carts turned up to carry the workers to dry ground.

The German forces were advancing on the Western Front. Easter 1918 was a stay-at-home holiday, there were no hot cross buns on Good Friday, no Easter eggs, and no respite for the munitions workers. The machine-gun department at the RSAF was especially busy; production of three thousand machine-guns a week had been reached. The Shell Factory worked day and night over the holidays. Brindley subsequently received a telegram from Winston Churchill congratulating the Ponders End shell workers on their Easter production; the weekly output of shells had nearly doubled. This was all the more appreciated by the government in view of the strike of fifteen hundred shell workers at Newport in Monmouthshire. Sporadic strikes continued. In September the railway workers on the Great Eastern came out and the trams became even more overcrowded, but the munitions workers still got to their factories. Rumours of peace circulated in October. A notice was posted up at the RSAF that, in order to save coal, the factory would close from lunch-time Saturday until Monday morning.[15]

The war ended in November and the workers at the RSAF were given three days holiday with pay. Enfield had had 12,300 people working on arms and munitions. Henry F. Bowles warned that peace might bring widespread poverty, and he proposed that the war factories be turned over to peacetime needs. Within one week of the armistice, notice was issued that the RSAF would return to a forty-eight hour week, Mondays to Fridays. Many workers, including all those over retirement age, had received two weeks' notice. 'Bert', wrote Doris Shuttlewood of Beaconsfield Road, 'worked at the RSAF during the war and lost his job in the staff reductions after 1918. He became a window cleaner and earned just enough to keep his family going; he carried his ladders on a wooden hand-cart which he pushed from road to road'. Edison Swan Electric Company that year announced profits of £130,000 and the company purchased ten acres adjoining their Ponders End works. There was a proposal that the Shell Factory be converted for the manufacture of railway rolling stock. Winston Churchill paid a visit there, declaring that he had a warm spot in his heart for Ponders End, because of the work that his wife had done over the last three years in the neighbourhood. Hundreds of women munitions workers were paid off. Many more jobs were in jeopardy; skilled men now refused to instruct the semi-skilled. The YMCA had dozens of huts available for disposal.[16]

The Ponders End Shell Works finally closed on 28 March 1919, many of the buildings were subsequently demolished and all hands were discharged. A few weeks earlier hopes had been entertained that the site would be taken by the Straker Motor Company, but since then the firm had opened a new factory in Angel Road Edmonton. During the war some six or seven thousand workers had been employed at the Shell Works but the number had rapidly diminished following the armistice. H.C.R. Brindley died in March 1920, only one year after severing his connection with the gigantic arsenal at Ponders End. It had been his creation; he had been a man of commanding personality and a master of detail.[17]

The future of the Royal Gunpowder Factory was in doubt, production there had increased tenfold from 1914 to 1918 and the number employed had grown from nine hundred to five thousand. There had not been one stoppage or breakdown throughout the whole war. The factory had been in existence since 1561 and it had been a national factory since 1787; it was recognised that it had been of the greatest service to this country. In addition to cordite, gunpowder and fusepowder were made there. Before the war it had a maximum capacity of sixty-four tons of cordite a week, but by the end of the war, after large extensions, it could produce 250 tons. The plant recently installed was efficient but the layout was cramped and this increased the danger from explosions. Gretna, the other major cordite works, had much more space. There seemed to be no valid reason to retain both Gretna and Waltham Abbey, and a commission recommended the retention of Gretna. Nevertheless the Waltham Abbey factory survived and in August 1921 the Gretna Cordite Factory was offered for sale.[18]

The Royal Small Arms Factory too was threatened with closure. The Army Council refused to support the recommendation of the minister that a nucleus of staff should be retained there; the minister felt that it would be uneconomic to have weapons repaired by contractors. He pointed out that the men at the Birmingham Small Arms, who had been employed on rifles and machine-guns, had already been discharged and the machinery, gauges and tools were being removed to Enfield. The opinion of the minister was finally accepted. Nevertheless, one year after the armistice, the RSAF stood almost idle. Of the 1,245 machines in the Large Room only fifteen were being used, only eleven out of 574 in the Sight Room, in the Machine-Gun Shop three out of 373, in the Barrel Shop four out of 552, in the Bayonet Department thirty-nine out of 259 and in the Screws Department twenty out of three hundred, although these automatic screw machines were among the best that could be found in Great Britain. Altogether only 161 out of 3,467 machines were operating at the RSAF.[19]

3. Agriculture and the War

Agriculture in Enfield comprised market gardens which included glasshouses, also fruit farms and dairy farms; much of it was labour-intensive. The loss of men to the forces and to the munitions factories dealt a heavy blow to the farmers. There were urgent calls in the spring of 1916 for women to work on the land. The education committee was urged to release older girls from school so that they could take care of the homes while their mothers worked. It was proposed that boys should be released to work in agriculture, provided that proper wages were paid. Crèches might be set up. A women's agricultural committee was established; it made a house-to-house canvass in June 1916 in a campaign to enlist women. The hay harvest was bountiful, roots promised well, fruit looked likely to be abundant, but the farmers had no labour. There were fewer cows kept in Enfield by May 1916; many owners had reduced their herds because of the increased cost of fodder and the shortage of labour. The average cost of milk in Enfield was 4½d a quart to the retailer, who made but little profit selling it at 5d. By the end of June the price had risen to 6d a quart. A ploughman in Enfield could now earn £2 a week as against 24s before the war. The Women's Social and Political Union (formerly militant suffragettes) campaigned with enthusiasm, organising a women's war procession with a tableau 'Women on the Land'. Six-week scholarships were offered for women to learn milking. Some market gardeners provided special suits for their women workers, Rochford's ladies were particularly elegant in pale blue. Convalescent soldiers were offered 3s 6d a day to work on the farms, finding their own board. Many foreign growers purchased market gardens in the Lea Valley and were engaging foreign labour, mainly Scandinavian, to grow cucumbers and tomatoes; this gave them an advantage, for the English growers, 'as patriots', hesitated to follow their example. Female labour had been tried in the greenhouses but temperatures of up to 120 degrees were too much for women, so men said. The Lea Valley Nurserymen's Association asked the Tribunals to grant exemption to one foreman for every four acres of glass.[20]

Unrestricted warfare by the German U-boats began in February 1917; more than a thousand Allied ships were lost over the first three months of the campaign. There was a shortage of wheat, and flour was adulterated with rice, maize, barley or oatmeal. The government was concerned that bread supplies would not last until autumn. To ensure the maximum harvest in the year 1918 the Middlesex Agricultural Committee, in June 1917, urged that more land should be converted to arable. Every farmer with grassland was to be canvassed, the Board of Agriculture promised labour and machinery to help in ploughing. Some local farmers asserted that arable farming on London clay could never be successful, but others cited the success of William Gundry at North Lodge Farm where the land had been well drained and properly manured. H. W. Middleton a local dairyman, thought the crux of the matter was labour and there was a grave shortage of that. Middlesex, he declared, was good dairying country and to keep up a plentiful supply of milk was the utmost you could expect. Nevertheless the Agricultural Committee continued to press for conversion to arable. Much of the ploughing which had been accomplished in the spring of 1917 had been done by soldiers from the Mill Hill barracks and by the employment of six or seven hundred prisoners of war. That autumn (1917) the Enfield War Agricultural Committee, which had been set up in May 1917, secured a number of the latest type of motor tractors; one working at Maxwell's farm at Enfield Highway proved capable of breaking up ten acres a day. James Neilson, a most well informed estate agent, stated that arrangements were being made to break up more land in Enfield, Southgate and Edmonton. In November the committee requested the school management committee to sanction the release of fifty-four boys for three or four weeks, to help in harvesting the potato crop on Mr Bath's farm, (Bury Farm) but approval was given for only twenty-five boys over thirteen, to work eight hours a day, stipulating that if the weather was unfavourable they must attend school. Children from one council school spent a weekend going systematically over the fields clearing the green crops of caterpillars. The following year the County Agricultural Committee secured a horse-drawn machine, which could be hired at moderate terms, for spraying potatoes. A meeting of Enfield farmers was called at the Public Offices in November 1917. Only sixty-nine acres of grassland had been offered for conversion to arable and then only upon condition that the government did the work. The farmers complained that the tractors had been delayed and now the ground was too wet, also that the military had taken all their skilled ploughmen, practically the last ploughman in Southgate had now been called up. A real shortage of food threatened; seventy Allied merchant ships were sunk during November that year. Conversion to arable had to be speeded up, pressure was applied and eleven hundred acres were broken up in Enfield by May 1918; a further 680 acres would be converted by the autumn. The farmers continued to complain about the prices fixed for milk and hay, and of the scarcity of labour. They pointed out that over two hundred acres in Enfield were still held by the golf clubs, and were largely unproductive. The Bush Hill Park and Crews Hill courses were indeed used to graze sheep but not the Enfield golf course, moreover the clubs employed men who might otherwise have worked on the farms. A new military order in June 1918 withdrew exemption from agricultural workers, thus making the situation on the farms and market gardens even worse. By this time however the convoy system had ensured an adequate importation of grain from the United States and Canada.[21]

4. Edmonton Military Hospital

Wartime prosperity brought about a reduction of the number of paupers in the Edmonton Union workhouse at Silver Street, Edmonton, and the Board of Guardians saw this as an opportunity to off-load some of their costs. They approached the War Office in September 1914 to offer 150 beds in their new and under-used infirmary for the treatment of wounded soldiers. Edmonton Union had an excellent operating theatre and one of the finest surgical units in the United Kingdom; it would be capable of receiving fifty casualties at a day's notice. Eastern Command was impressed and offered 6s a day for each patient. An assistant matron was appointed at £65 a year with a £10 bonus, six sisters at £50 per year plus bonus, and six staff nurses at £40 with bonus. Thirty

18.   *Beds in the Edmonton Union workhouse infirmary (now the North Middlesex Hospital) were offered to the War Office in September 1914 for the treatment of wounded soldiers at 6s a day per patient. The infirmary became the Edmonton Military Hospital.*

19.   *The first of many convoys of wounded soldiers arrived in Edmonton on a Friday evening in*
May 1915. Some forty thousand were to pass through by the end of the First World War.

housemaids were taken on and twenty women to scrub the floors (among them
was my grandmother). Voluntary doctors were to be called in as needed.[22]

The first convoy of 139 wounded soldiers, including ninety-eight stretcher
cases, arrived in Edmonton at 6.15p.m. on Friday evening 14 May 1915. The
men had left Boulogne that morning for Dover, from where they had travelled
in a Great Western Railway hospital train. A large crowd awaited them at
Edmonton Green. Flowering plants were hurriedly brought from Barrowfield
nurseries, someone produced a Union Jack, and the words 'Welcome to Our
Heroes' were chalked up on the wall. It was a long train stretching right across
the level-crossing. The ladies of the VAD rushed around distributing packets of
Woodbines and loose cigarettes. British Red Cross ambulances stood by and a
large number of private motor cars. At the Military Hospital eight medical
officers, a team of nurses, and volunteers from the Edmonton Boy Scouts made
ready for the arrival. It was the first of many such convoys and they had much
to learn, nevertheless by nine o'clock the men were safe at last in bed, though
two or three had died after arrival. Many local men were among the wounded.[23]

A second convoy of eighty-seven badly wounded men arrived at eleven thirty
on the following Sunday morning. Lt Colonel Mort and his staff were required
to work day and night in the operating theatre. The Military Hospital received
another 130 wounded at the beginning of June; the train carried fifty-four
stretcher cases and some who had been gassed. It pulled in at one o'clock in the
morning, but the crowd, which had waited patiently throughout the evening to
welcome the wounded, had dispersed disappointed. Three hundred and sixty
men had so far been received at Edmonton and there had been only three
deaths. Two weeks later the number admitted had risen to five hundred, and
one hundred had been discharged. More soldiers had come in by the end of

20, 21. The first of 139 wounded men arrived at Lower Edmonton low-level station on Friday evening 14 May 1915. A large crowd waited there, flowering plants were brought from Barrowfield nurseries, someone produced a Union Jack and 'Welcome to Our Heroes' was chalked up on the wall.

August, including Australians and New Zealanders, and the military were demanding a further three hundred beds. The Guardians anxiously considered the extensions being forced upon them, in the light of the interests of the Board and its ratepayers, for they were much concerned in case any proposed new buildings should prove superfluous after the war, probably fearing that there

22.   Edmonton Military Hospital, Mary East Ward. The boys were well looked after and well fed; meat pies and fried fish were the favourites. The Board of Guardians kept a large stock of pigs at Chase Farm from which pork sausages were produced for the Tommies.

might not be enough paupers to fill the beds. They took it for granted that their function was to look after paupers; for this reason it had worried them that half the people who had come into the infirmary before 1914 were anything but poor and needy. The Guardians therefore cautiously decided that it would be safer and cheaper to build huts. Tenders were invited for two temporary blocks to hold four hundred men. Work went ahead in October 1915, but the proposed accommodation proved inadequate even before it had been begun; there were eight hundred wounded soldiers in the hospital by late September and the situation had become critical. The military authorities, in November that year, took over the remainder of the buildings of the Edmonton Union Poor Law Infirmary. A number of pauper patients had to be removed to the Enfield workhouse, to Stepney and to other institutions. Nevertheless the hospital was so crowded by December 1915 that the military found it necessary to limit to sixty square feet the area allotted to each casualty.[24]

Space now had to be sought outside the hospital for minor cases and convalescence. Roseneath in Vicars Moor Lane, Winchmore Hill had been taken over early in the war; it had been provided and equipped as a voluntary hospital by a local resident. Nine casualties had been received by December 1914; the number of beds was increased from forty to fifty in October 1915 by which time two hundred patients had passed through. Grovelands at Winchmore Hill was being prepared for the reception of sixty wounded soldiers. The intake of casualties at Edmonton multiplied; there were now 110 staff nurses and sisters, and sixty voluntary nurses. The call went out for more volunteers. Four thousand troops had been treated there by the end of the year 1915. Meals were constantly varied; the Guardians kept a large stock of pigs at Chase Farm and at Chase Side Enfield from which pork sausages were made for the Tommies. Meat pies and fried fish were both very popular. The dining hall was also used for film shows and concerts. Pianos and billiard tables had been donated.

The intensity of the conflict on the Somme was brought home to the people of north London by the arrival of more heavy convoys of wounded men in July 1916. It had been expected that the hospital would have to accommodate 1,100 to 1,200 men, with a further 800 to 900 in the auxiliary institutions, but now the number in the main hospital had increased to 1,600 and some of the wounded had to be placed in the corridors. The unfortunate Guardians faced a demand for a further six hundred beds. The Union infirmary having already been commandeered, the remainder of the workhouse buildings were requisitioned; all the paupers would have to leave. The Board of Guardians was forced to do what logic should have persuaded it to undertake years before the war, that is to pay adequate outdoor relief to enable the indigent sick and the old to live among their own neighbours and relations within their own parishes.[25]

The parsimony of the Guardians achieved headlines in *John Bull* at this time, concerning the case of a soldier rendered insane by the stress of war and consigned in that condition to the care of the Board. The allowance to his wife from the Army ceased automatically when he was demobilised and she had to go into service. 'Then', said *John Bull*, 'those grasping Guardians discovered that £3 6s was due to the soldier for back pay and they conceived a plan to seize it for his maintenance. Discovering where his wife was employed, they sent an official to her with a document for her signature, assigning the money to them. We are glad to say that she refused to sign...we hope that she will, by holding out, prevent their claws from grabbing the money due to her afflicted husband'. The casual ward was also closed in September 1916. There still remained two hundred inmates in the poor law infirmary at Chase Side, Enfield.[26]

Further accommodation was found for the wounded at St Mark's Institute in Bush Hill Park, where the building was fitted out with thirty beds. Two further wards were opened there in March 1917 to accommodate fifteen or twenty more beds, and an operating theatre was installed. Seventy wounded soldiers were being cared for there by May and it was thought that the Institute might have to find room for at least another hundred in view of the coming push on the Western Front. Elm House in Gentleman's Row was placed rent-free at the disposal of the military, with a gift of £300 for alterations and decorations. The house, equipped with forty beds, opened in June 1916; it was considered feasible to provide another forty beds in a hut in the garden.[27]

Queen Mary visited the Edmonton Military Hospital on 14 August 1916. A hundred and one convoys, some carrying as many as three hundred wounded soldiers, had been received there since it had opened. From Edmonton Green the ambulances of the Motor Volunteer Corps had carried them to Silver Street. Repeated practice had perfected the transfer, scarcely any delay now occurred at either the station or the hospital; it took an average of only fifty minutes from train to bed. Relatives of dangerously ill patients were invited to visit and if necessary were assisted with their fares and given lodging allowance; 450 walking wounded had been provided with their fare to visit home. One hundred and sixty-three performances had been put on over the past year in the large hall in the grounds; many artistes came down from the London theatres and there was a variety of film shows. The Edmonton Military Hospital had 2,934 patients by August 1917, including 1,446 in auxiliary hospitals, making it one of the largest hospital units in the United Kingdom. Most of its twenty-nine auxiliary

23.   St Mark's Institute, opened in 1907 by Princess Louise, was used as an annexe to the
Edmonton Military Hospital in the First World War. Seventy wounded soldiers were being cared for
there in May 1917.

24.   A number of houses in the area were used as annexes to the Edmonton Military Hospital. This
picture shows Elm House in Gentleman's Row, equipped with forty beds.

25. *Elm House, Gentleman's Row; the war in France must have seemed a million miles away.*

hospitals were, by this time, equipped with operating theatres and X-ray units; 15,100 patients were received in the twelve months ending 30 June 1917, and there had been only 104 deaths.[28]

Much of the voluntary war effort in Enfield centred on the War Hospital Supply Depot in Sydney Road, set up in October 1916 in the former Gas Company offices. It was the sort of venture where everyone could help. The Gas Company charged no rent for the premises and the District Council charged no rates. Singer's provided the sewing machines free. Week by week large consignments of all sorts of comforts and necessities were dispatched to various hospitals. The Royal Mail Steam Packet Company, for instance, provided worn-out towels and grey blankets too full of holes to be used. These were laid together and covered with patchwork (cretonne) covers to make Bath chair wraps, two of which had the distinction of being pictured in the *Daily Mirror*. Bandages were made, operation shirts, swabs, bed-tables, bed-rests, trays, crutches, leg-rests, lockers and jigsaw puzzles. Old linen was transmuted into handkerchiefs and pillow slips, slippers were made from odds and ends, pyjamas, dressing gowns and bed jackets were supplied. The organisation had three hundred helpers enrolled by August 1917.[29]

The German offensive early in the year 1918 brought more heavy drafts, some as large as seven hundred wounded men, to Silver Street straight from the trenches. The hospital accommodation was put under further strain. Every bed was occupied at Elm House and in St Mark's Institute. But that year saw the end of the war. The great Military Hospital did not close in November for the wards remained full of wounded men. Slowly they were dispersed, some repaired and returned to their families, some to linger on for years having lost their youth and health, some shunted off into nursing homes to die quietly in remote seaside resorts. By July 1919 all Army cases were out and the place was being cleaned and

26.   *The nurses at Elm House. Percy Leggatt (left) and Dudley Leggatt (right), allowed the War Office the house rent free and provided £300 for necessary alterations. In the centre of the second row sits Dr Howard Distin of Holtwhites House.*

painted ready to begin a new life. In September 1920 these buildings, which had once housed the paupers of the Edmonton Union infirmary, where thousands of maimed, wounded and sick soldiers had been cared for throughout the war, became, with the sanction of the Ministry of Health, the North Middlesex

27.   A party of wounded soldiers from St Bartholomew's Hospital was entertained at the Enfield
Golf Club Clubhouse on 11 April 1915.

28.   *Under the shadow of Dr Uvedale's great cedar, the war wounded gather for an entertainment*

in what was left of the 'Palace' garden.

29. A hundred convoys of wounded soldiers had arrived at the Edmonton Military Hospital by
August 1916. From Edmonton Green the ambulances of the Motor Volunteer Corps had carried them
to Silver Street; it took an average of fifty minutes between train and bed. The ambulance illustrated
is a two-wheeled trailer carrying two stretchers and towed by a motor car.

Hospital. Mr Metivier, the chairman, spoke hopefully of the future. The Board
of Guardians, he said, wanted people to know that what was good enough for
forty thousand wounded soldiers was good enough for anybody. The North
Middlesex Hospital would do away with the stigma of pauperism. He put the
case for its use as a public health hospital where the only test was the need for
treatment. He looked forward to the demise of the Guardians. He called for
wider use of the new maternity ward (opened 1918) which had an efficient staff
and was a training school for midwives. Nevertheless not all the Guardians
concurred with these liberal views. The hospital remained encumbered by the
continued administration of their Board and even after the abolition of the
Board of Guardians in 1930, the smell of pauperism lingered on.[30]

5. The Home Front

The threat of war agitated the country towards the end of July 1914. Apprehension in Enfield was intensified by the presence of troops, both at Enfield Lock
and at Waltham Abbey. A contingent of the Somerset Regiment arrived on a
Wednesday night at a quarter past eleven; they were quartered in the old
schoolroom at the Ordnance Factory. On the following day a strong body of
police was drafted into the neighbourhood. Lodgings were being sought for the
men, which suggested that a long stay was intended. Many naval reservists left
Enfield Town. Crowds gathered around the post office to watch the posting up

30.   Men of the Army Ordnance Corps were quartered in the parish hall in Ordnance Road in 1915.

of notices. A hundred reservists assembled near the fountain between eleven and twelve in the morning, the National Anthem was sung and cheering broke out. Horses and motor vehicles were registered in case of need and a number of draught horses were handed over to the authorities. People struggled to buy up every scrap of food, many shops were emptied and had to close. Credit was no longer given.[31]

Troops were on the move everywhere. Thousands of soldiers were seen on the Cambridge line travelling down to London with their guns, horses and baggage. On the last Friday of the month 1300 men of the Royal Field Artillery were camped on Fish's field on the west side of Baker Street (the present site of the council houses), some were billeted in Lancaster and Kynaston Roads where practically every house was full. Said the *Gazette* with pride (28 August 1914) 'The men had no reason to complain of the hospitality'. There were soldiers billeted in George Spicer School, their guns and wagons parked in the recreation ground; Colonel Bowles entertained twelve of the officers at Forty Hall. Billeting was good for business; bakers, butchers and grocers did well. The blacksmith near the Hop Poles was called out of bed in the early hours one Sunday morning to re-shoe a horse as a battery of artillery passed down Lancaster Road. Men of the Hertfordshire Yeomanry were billeted in the former National school in London Road (opposite the present site of Woolworths), their horses were stabled in the old brewery yard (Saville's Brewery). Men of the 2nd Hertfordshire Field Artillery stayed over Saturday night at the Bell, Enfield Highway and officers and men were billeted in local houses. The open space next to the pub was taken over as a gun park.[32]

The call to serve became loud and insistent. Colonel Bowles sought men for the Civic Guard and offered to teach them the rudiments of drill and the use of

31.   Men of the Hertfordshire yeomanry, early in the war, were billeted in the former National School opposite the present site of Woolworth's in London Road; their horses were stabled in the brewery yard (Saville's Brewery). This photograph was taken before the road was widened for trams in 1908.

a rifle; a total of 250 men had registered at the headquarters in London Road by 10 October 1914. The unit became the 'D' (Enfield) company of the Middlesex Volunteer Regiment, for the protection of the area in case of emergency. The unit was provided with grey uniforms and maintained throughout the war, attending regimental camps in Hertfordshire and Essex each summer.

Many men offered their services as special constables. Tradesmen, farmers and gentlemen had to part with their horses, though a fair price was paid. Enfield Rifle Club provided a hundred musketry instructors for the government, the Northmet allowed the use of a miniature rifle range at Millmarsh Lane at 2d for ten shots. Union Jacks were in great demand. A recruiting parade was held through Enfield early one evening in September 1914 led by the band of the National Reserve. Civic Guards and special constables marched from Ponders End by way of Bush Hill Park to the Drill Hall on Windmill Hill. Not everyone was carried away by this wave of enthusiasm. At one recruiting meeting in Edmonton Town Hall the Reverend D.Millen, making an impassioned appeal for more men, was asked, 'Why don't you go yourself?' His reply is not recorded. Enfield Football Club had lost several of its best players through transfers to the forces.[33]

It was rumoured early in September that fifty thousand Belgian and French refugees would soon be in England. Two weeks later, on a Saturday night, three hundred, mostly women and children, arrived by train at Lower Edmonton low-level station in the pouring rain. Flags were hung out and a huge crowd cheered as they left in buses for the Strand Union, the former workhouse in Silver Street which later became Klinger's. On the Wednesday 250 more arrived by bus from

32.   *The former Great Northern Railway terminus on Windmill Hill. From here the local lads of the seventh battalion Middlesex Regiment took the train to go to war.*

Tilbury docks. They continued to come until there were 705 housed at Silver Street. Some remained throughout the war and it was not until May 1918 that the Strand Union workhouse was cleared of Belgians. Enfield had a lesser problem in this respect, but by March 1915 the community sheltered 209 refugees; fifty men, eighty-eight women and seventy-one children. They were cared for by various churches, some were given shelter in the manse at Christ Church Chase Side, some in private homes at a cost of about £60 a week. The Enfield War Refugees Committee held its final reunion at the Enfield County School hall in January 1919.[34]

German spies and saboteurs were sought with excessive enthusiasm. Thus when two men were seen emptying a barrel of powder on the bank of the New River near the Town Park, a hostile crowd gathered, the police were called and the men were arrested. They were marched to the police station, followed by an angry booing and hooting mob, but they turned out to be members of the Enfield Silver Prize Band preparing for an evening concert in the park where certain martial music was to be played. The powder was to provide an appropriate spectacular effect.[35]

The departure of Enfield's local Territorial battalion created great excitement and enthusiasm as the men came marching in from Hornsey. Crowds gathered along London Road and through the Town, people ran into the shops to buy ginger beer and fruit to give to the lads. Sweethearts and wives walked alongside their men, 'perhaps' said the *Gazette*, approaching nearer to the grim truth than it could possibly have foreseen. 'never to see their loved ones again'. The battalion marched through the Town and up Windmill Hill and halted at the former Great Northern Railway terminus (now demolished), where eight hundred men of the seventh battalion Middlesex Regiment, under Colonel

33. *Private Joseph Rye who left Forty Hill School in 1910. He went from job to job until he enlisted, under age, in the Middlesex Regiment. He served in France and survived the war.*

King, were to board the trains. A half-hour delay was expected, rifles were stacked, refreshment taken, tears were shed and wiped dry. Then the bugle sounded, the first party formed up and boarded, and the train slowly moved off leaving half the men to await a second train. A dismal drizzle which had been falling for some time, now became a downpour. There was thunder and lightning, the forecourt became a sea of umbrellas, men tried to find shelter by the station, the early euphoria faded, reality looked as melancholy as the weather and the rain poured down. The second train at last drew in, hurried farewells were taken, the train departed and the umbrellas slowly dispersed. The seventh were sent in the first instance to guard installations on the Medway; from there they proceeded to Gibraltar, returning home in February 1915. They had only a month to prepare before they embarked for the Western Front. Few were to survive the war. The battalion landed at Le Havre on 13 March and joined the 23rd brigade of the eighth division at La Gorgue just as the battle of Neuve Chapelle was drawing to a close. It remained with the eighth throughout the year 1915 and fought at Aubers Ridge on 9 May, before joining the 167th brigade of the fifty-sixth division, moving up to the line at Hebuterne on 16 May. The battalion took part in the attack on the Gommecourt salient, on the extreme left flank of the battle of the Somme. It was withdrawn from the line on 20 August and moved down the Somme valley, and was again in action in front of Combles on 9 September in the battle of Ginchy. On the fifteenth of that month the seventh Middlesex made two desperate assaults on Bouleaux Wood; they were beaten back with heavy losses. This was a fatal day for the seventh Middlesex and a sad one for the people of north London, for it saw the annihilation of the original battalion of local Territorials which had been mobilised two years before. The battalion had lost forty officers and 782 other ranks killed and wounded, besides 153 invalided out. New drafts took the place of those who had gone. The battalion which left the Somme and returned to Flanders was made up of new recruits. At home, men were being recruited for a third battalion 7th Middlesex. Volunteers between nineteen and thirty-eight years old were exhorted to come forward; pay was 21s for a single man, 30s 11d for a married man.

Thousands of Middlesex men went out, not in organised units but to replace those who had fallen. It wasn't the pay that attracted them, not even the glamour; life was tolerable at home and work not hard to find. Joseph Rye was one such. He left Forty Hill school at the age of fourteen in 1910, and got a job with Chandler a local milkman. He did the rounds on a two-wheeled cart delivering milk which he ladled from an urn in pints and half pints into his customers' jugs. The pay was 3d an hour. He left after having to assist unwillingly as midwife at the delivery of a dead calf, and went to work at Ediswan's. Here he also left after a short time, apparently he couldn't stand the women. He then found employment with William Washington, a plumber and gasfitter in Turkey Street, painting the railings along the footpath from Turkey Street to Maidens Bridge at 4d an hour.

The following year he was engaged as a gardeners' boy by Colonel Tisdal of the Royal Small Arms Factory, at his house in the Officers Quarters, Ordnance Road. The lad looked after the grass tennis courts, cleaned the Colonel's uniform and his boots, as well as the cutlery, served in the house and substituted as caddie when the Colonel played golf. The Colonel was an Irishman and very generous; he once gave the boy half a sovereign and was annoyed with him for presuming that it was a mistake. The officers held tennis and bridge parties and General French would often be among the guests. When the Colonel retired in 1913, the lad found work in the Co-op shop at Ordnance Road, making deliveries on a tricycle, he even graduated to serving over the counter. He quitted the Co-op two months after the outbreak of war and tried to get into the Royal Horse Artillery, but was unsuccessful on account of his chest measurement. He therefore took a job on the machines at the RSAF starting at around £2 a week. After another abortive attempt to sign on in the Army, he was surprised to be accepted at the Tottenham Recruiting Office as a private in the Middlesex Regiment and did his initial training on the Tottenham Hotspur football ground.

The recruits, after a few months' training, found their numbers dwindling as men were taken to replace casualties in the battalions in France. At last came the fateful day for Joseph Rye, two weeks embarkation leave, then Folkestone and the boat for Calais. His party journeyed slowly up to Ypres by train, cadging boiling water from the driver at every stop, to brew tea. Once arrived they were dispersed to the various battalions. Joseph Rye ended up in the 12th Middlesex as a Lewis gunner, occasionally also using Vickers machine-guns. He was wounded in the arm at Baupaume and was eventually brought back to a VAD hospital at Saffron Walden. After recovery, and despite much further campaigning, Joseph Rye survived the war and returned to marry and to dwell the rest of his days in his native Enfield.[36]

The outbreak of war had disturbed but little the tranquil flow of life for those left at home. The Electricity Supply Company, in November 1913, opened new offices and a showroom at number 5 Church Street. The Tottenham and District Gas Company, not to be outdone, hurried to complete by May the following year their fine new showroom and offices on the corner of the Market Place. Charles Freeman, the enterprising baker, advertised in March 1915, his new spacious and well-fitted tea-room close to the Great Eastern railway station and to the tram terminus. The rival firm of R. J.Pritchard, a well-known confectioner, set up a model bakery where hot luncheons and dainty teas were served. As winter approached in 1914 people found that the street lighting was virtually non-existent, and even the shop illumination was much reduced. Shops now closed a little earlier — eight o'clock Mondays to Fridays, nine on Saturday.

'In these days of subdued street lighting', urged the *Gazette* (5 March 1915) 'regard should be paid to minimising the dangers of the roads. One possibility of peril is the driving of cattle in the streets at night-time. If beasts must be driven on the highway at night it will need a lantern with a motor horn to give audible notice of their whereabouts'. The rumble of the guns across the Channel remained obviously inaudible in Enfield.

There was a shortage of milk all over London. Much of it was now sent to Army camps, while condensed milk manufacturers consumed large quantities. By the end of the year 1915 margarine was replacing butter on many middle-class tables. Enfield Football Club decided in December 1914 to cancel all their remaining fixtures for the season as did Chase Park FC, their co-tenants at Cherry Orchard Lane.[37]

The recruiting campaign intensified, more than a thousand Enfield men were serving by January 1915. A series of open-air meetings was held during the last week in April; on Tuesday evening at Bush Hill Park, on Wednesday outside the Hop Poles where a thousand people assembled (though only fourteen enlisted) and in the Town on Friday where the meeting was enlivened by the regimental band from Mill Hill, and twenty volunteers signed up in the George. Five or six hundred assembled at the corner of Derby Road at Ponders End on the Saturday night, but altogether the effort produced only 150 recruits in Enfield. In Edmonton two thousand people gathered at the Green and less than fifty were recruited. A cadet corps was formed at the Grammar School.[38]

Intense hostility against Germans followed the sinking of the Lusitania in May. Four thousand people gathered at Seven Sisters Road to vent their hatred, watched by police and 'specials'; a barrage of stones was flung at the windows of Mr Weiffenback; whose name sounded German. There was no intervention by the law until a stone hit a policeman; a youth was arrested. Mr Berger's baker's shop in Braemer Road was also attacked. About eleven o'clock the mob moved down Seven Sisters Road and smashed the windows of the Hygienic Bakery at the corner of Westerfield Road. It was owned by Mr Groessel who had a son serving Britain at the front. Most of the stone-throwers were youths between sixteen and nineteen. There was also trouble at Wood Green High Road, St Anne's Road, Philip Lane and Myddleton Road. Tom Lewis, a very active member of the local history society, recalled seeing an attack on the shop of a German pork butcher in Upper Fore Street, Edmonton. An incident at

34. *The recruiting campaign intensified in 1915, half a million volunteers were urgently demanded. This recruiting office in a shop formerly belonging to the picture dealer Donald Risley, lay on the west side of Hertford Road north of the police station. Displayed are the portraits of dead local heroes; the posters urge the need for more.*

Bush Hill Park is related by Sid Robinson in his autobiography, *Sid's Family Robinson*.

'Mum usually cut my hair', he writes, 'but when she was absent in Bury, Dad sent me just across the road from our house in Seventh Avenue to Rhumbke's, the barber, with a note saying that my hair should be cropped short. When I got back home about two hours later, with no hair left except an inch of fringe in the front, I told the family that I was not going to the barber's any more because boys had to wait until there were no more grown-ups in the shop, even if they came in after us. A few days later, I was pleased to see the barber's shop windows smashed. At dinner time I asked Dad why, and he told me that there had been a lot of rioting after the Lusitania was sunk, and that Rhumbke was a German. He said that people were fairly worked up. Rhumbke must have cleared out, because Hooper took over the shop as a newsagent. Even Mr Yelloly, the boot and shoe repairer at Forty Hill, was rumoured to be a German and was suspected of signalling to zeppelins, although any name less Teutonic than his would be hard to find.'[39]

Drunkenness diminished during the war for three reasons: the higher taxation on alcoholic drinks, the shorter opening hours of the public houses, and the 'No Treating' Order of 1915. The Order led to a striking diminution in the number of prosecutions for drunkenness. According to the Metropolitan Police returns, in 1914, before the restrictions, the weekly average was 1,287, but in 1915, after the restriction, it was 784. The Order continued to be enforced. The barmaid at the Bush Hill Park Hotel was fined 40s in June 1917 for serving James Moore with two bitters, price 10d under the watchful eye of a plain-clothed policeman; the two customers were fined 10s each. Prosecutions for drunkenness were to fall still further, and there were only 263 in the week ending 27 May 1917.[40]

Week after week the local paper printed photographs of young Enfield men killed in France. Mr and Mrs Chappell of Eastfield Road were told of the death of their son Charles who fell at St Eloi. Only a few weeks earlier they had received news of the death of their adopted son William Aylott of the Royal Fusiliers, killed by a rifle shot while repairing a wire entanglement; another son George lay wounded in hospital. Such casualties could not but bring about some realization of the seriousness of the war, and there was certainly a decline in ostentatious patriotism among the boys in khaki. This was noticed with displeasure by an indignant correspondent in the *Gazette* (4 June 1915). 'What evoked some comment by spectators in the park' he wrote 'was that while children could be seen in an attitude of loyalty (during the playing of the National Anthem) there were some young fellows in khaki who were too tired to rise from the ground, much less stand to attention'. His patriotic pomposity drew no rebuke. 'Patriotism in the trenches', wrote Robert Graves, (*Goodbye to All That*) 'was too remote a sentiment, and at once rejected as fit only for civilians'.

Posters calling for recruits had been displayed throughout the district, many were now hanging torn and tattered. A patriotic whist drive was held at the Bush Hill Park Conservative Club. At the end of October 1915, on the completion of the national register, notices were issued to all men of military age except starred men, those whose work was so important to industry that they could not be spared, inviting them to undertake military service. At the close of the year 1915, in order to divert insistent demands for conscription, Lord Derby drew up a scheme under which men of military age were invited to attest their willingness to serve when called upon. Few at first came forward to attest but, on the last weekend, the recruiting office (no. 1 London Road) found itself besieged. A long queue of would-be attesters awaited the opening of the doors on the Saturday morning. So great was the crush later that day that two queues had to be formed, one in London Road, the other at the rear of the building, from where it stretched into Cecil Road. Attestation went on all day and hundreds of men were still waiting for a medical in the cold biting wind at two o'clock in the morning. The men were admitted ten at a time and three doctors worked without respite; those found unfit were granted exemption certificates. The attestation had to be resumed on the Sunday when large numbers came over from the Royal Small Arms and other factories in the Lea Valley. Even after the attestations were completed, medicals had to be continued over the following three days. Those who had attested were promised an armlet. Some young single men chose immediate enlistment.[41]

The first Military Service Act in January 1916, ended voluntary recruitment and imposed conscription on unmarried men. Tribunals were set up at the Highway and in the Town; they were kept busy over the ensuing months investigating men who claimed exemption from call-up. A hairdresser with a widowed mother and a sister to support had his call-up suspended for two months. A conscientious objector, who worked at the RSAF earning £3 a week, and who claimed that he 'belonged to the Lord Jesus Christ', was refused exemption. A greengrocer, who had declined to work at the Ponders End Shell Factory for conscientious reasons, now agreed to serve in the RAMC. A fifth year medical student was granted an eighteen month extension to complete his studies. An evangelical preacher who conducted services at the Whitewebbs chapel, at Ponders End chapel and at Edmonton, and who claimed to suffer palpitations of the heart, but declined to join the RAMC, had his application turned down. More special constables were needed in eastern Enfield but only men above military age were to be recruited. Single men were finding it difficult to obtain exemption. In June an application was refused from a printing firm on behalf of the twenty-seven-year-old foreman of their rotary printing department. At the same time the military representative on the Tribunal appealed against the exemption of a nineteen-year-old carman employed at the RSAF to cart the rifles to the Great Eastern Railway Station. The applications of one conscientious objector who did not go to church, and one who was a Seventh Day Adventist, were denied. The local press provided embarrassing publicity to all those applying for exemption, which must have deterred many. Protests multiplied concerning eligible single men still employed at the RSAF, the RGF and other munitions works. It was declared to be a scandal that the Tribunal should send away married men with families while single men remained at home. Among the hard cases quoted in one week in August were four married men between thirty-five and forty, one of whom had seven children; all four had been discharged from munitions works. These men declined to appeal on other grounds and joined the Army. A forty-year-old man with nine children, two of whom were themselves serving in the Army, was discharged from the Shell Factory. Long lists of local men dead, wounded or missing, continued to appear every week in the *Gazette*.[42]

Soon after the outbreak of the war an aerodrome and a naval air station was established on the marshes south of Lea Valley Road, partly in Enfield and partly in Chingford. A forty-two acre airfield at Westpole Farm, part of Trent Park, was used by 39 squadron, part of 49 wing. Between the wars it became a private landing-field used by Sir Philip Sassoon of Trent Park. An anti-aircraft station was established on the Ridgeway and a searchlight station in Hadley Road. During the year 1916 a tramcar in Enfield was fitted with a searchlight; it was

35.   On the night of Saturday 3 September 1916, a German airship dropped bombs at the junction of Southbury Road and Ponders End High Street and was shot down in flames over Cuffley. Thousands of souvenir hunters, some shown in the picture, rose early on the Sunday morning and set out for the scene of the crash by bicycle, car and train.

normally positioned outside the tram terminus in Southbury Road. The danger from air raids throughout the first two years of war did not appear to the authorities to be so pressing as to warrant emergency measures. 'It is simply monstrous', wrote one indignant correspondent (*Gazette* 11 February 1916) 'that during the recent raid on the Midlands the lighting in Enfield was practically normal and the trams were proceeding with their customary noise, loud enough to drown even the Zeppelin engines'. From March 1916 house lighting had to be shaded by blinds or curtains. It was announced in June that, for the benefit of cinemagoers, slides would be exhibited on the screen to warn of air raids. One Saturday night (2/3 September 1915) saw the first enemy airship over Enfield. Bombs fell on the Stud Farm at Clay Hill causing a fire in which three horses were killed and some cottages were damaged. High explosive bombs fell at Ponders End and Enfield Highway, at Forty Hill and at Turkey Street. When the anti-aircraft guns opened up the engines of the airship were switched off, but its great bulk was picked out over northern Enfield by the searchlights. A minute later the sharp rattle of a machine-gun was heard and flames burst forth from the hull. It came down on fire in a large field adjoining the Plough at Cuffley. The flames lit up the sky, people in Baker Street, Chase Side and the Town spilled out of their houses to see the sight, shouting and dancing in triumph. Orders were telegraphed to Enfield police station to send all available specials immediately to Cuffley. Many constables had been dismissed only ten minutes earlier, whistles were vigorously blown to recall them and motor cars were commandeered to take them to the scene of the crash. On the Sunday morning thousands of sightseers poured through and out of Enfield on bicycles and in cars; the trains to Cuffley were packed. One enterprising

36.   *One Saturday morning a 'V' shaped formation of German Taubes appeared over the top of the old Co-op building in Ordnance Road. Mothers rushed their children into shops and stood behind plate glass windows for protection.*

Cuffley householder charged 2d to allow access to the site of the disaster through his back garden. So many souvenir hunters swarmed over the village that their return home caused chaos. Cuffley station was besieged and in the end the staff had to stop the issue of further tickets. Carriers and owners of brakes made a fortune. A month later, on the night 1/2 October, came another air raid warning. Despite the order to take shelter, curiosity outweighed prudence and people stayed out to watch. The airship dropped bombs at Cheshunt but as soon as it was caught in the searchlights the anti-aircraft guns opened up, fire broke out aboard and it descended slowly in flames towards Potters Bar.[43]

Enfield's most frightening air raid occurred on 7 July 1917. German aeroplanes were sighted on the Saturday morning, about ten o'clock, approaching, according to one witness, 'in a circular formation like a flock of crows', at between four and five thousand feet. British fighters went up to intercept them. Despite warnings by police to take shelter, excited knots of spectators gathered in the streets. The only death was that of Mrs Edith Halse, killed by a piece of shrapnel from our anti-aircraft guns on the front lawn of the officers' quarters in Ordnance Road. Several munitions workers who disregarded advice to take cover were also struck by shrapnel. Bombs fell in the vicinity of the sewage farm (Cuckoo Hall Lane), an anti-aircraft shell caused considerable damage to the cemetery boardroom at Enfield Highway, and the cookery department of a local elementary school was hit. A man named Dench who was serving at a coffee stall was struck in the thumb by shrapnel, and a boy was hit in the foot; it had to be amputated. Several pieces of shrapnel went through the windows of a local picture palace, probably the Premier. Richard Slater as a small boy had reason to remember the occasion. 'My sister and I', he said 'were walking along

DR RIDGE

37.   During the First World War Dr R. L. Ridge, a very well-known local doctor, later president of the Enfield Liberal Party, put seven buglers from the Boys Brigade at the disposal of the police, to sound the all clear. (Gazette 6 June 1925)

Ordnance Road on Saturday morning when the air-raid warning was given and in the sky over the old Co-op building came a small 'V' shaped formation of German Taubes or Gothas. Thinking we were about to be bombed into oblivion my mother rushed us into a baker's shop opposite the Co-op where we stood behind the counter up against the wall. What good this would have done had a bomb dropped I never knew. All I was concerned about was the wonder of being behind a shop counter and gazing at the tempting array of cakes in front of me. The planes passed over and we emerged into the street, my sister and I clutching a fritter each which my mother had felt obliged to buy as recompense for sanctuary. I felt a few more air-raids wouldn't be out of place if I got a fritter each time'. Nevertheless Enfield Council expressed its profound indignation at the failure of our aerial defences and a mass meeting at Ediswan's protested against the failure to give adequate warning of the approach of enemy aircraft; the management promised an observation post on the highest point at the works and bomb-proof shelters protected by sandbags. Arrangements were made that in future, upon receipt of a 'take cover' notice, two sound rockets would be fired from the police station Enfield Town at an interval of fifteen seconds. Dr R. L. Ridge put seven buglers from the Boys Brigade at the disposal of the police to sound the all clear.[44]

Home Office regulations now required shops to close by 7pm Monday to Thursday, 8pm Friday and 9pm Saturday. There was a serious shortage of potatoes following the poor harvest of 1916. In Percival Road a long queue formed outside a greengrocer's shop, a large panel of glass in the shop door was broken by the pressure from behind. At a greengrocer's in Lancaster Road the police had to be called to keep order. Shops in eastern Enfield rationed customers to their regular requirement. When news circulated that a truck-load

38.   *There was a serious shortage of potatoes following a poor harvest in 1916. In Percival Road a long queue struggled to get into Ive's greengrocer's shop (the eighth one along) and the glass in the shop door was broken by the pushing.*

of potatoes had been delivered at Mr Turrell's at Enfield Wash, his shop was besieged by hundreds of people with baskets and bags. Mr Turrell continued serving until the shop closed at seven o'clock and a new queue formed the following morning. Four policemen were called to control the crowd at Mr Lane's shop at 35 Silver Street after he had received a large consignment of potatoes. 'I queued for potatoes', wrote Sid Robinson 'sometimes having to make do with swedes or turnips which I disliked. Mum gave us boiled rice but I had difficulty eating it without milk or sugar. Once I was sent to Mrs Curson's, the corn chandler, to buy some chicken maize which mum boiled … but it was a failure, we hated it. Ivy (Sid's sister) could eat dog biscuits, but I could not'. The Reverend W. Colville, the minister at St Paul's Presbyterian church, died when he ate cooked rhubarb leaves after trying out a recipe in a women's weekly journal. The shortage gave rise to a demand for more allotments. Before the war eighty-four acres in Enfield had been assigned for this purpose. Enfield War Agricultural Committee found vacant land available in Oak Avenue, Drapers Road, Holtwhites Hill, Cedar Park Road, Browning Road, Armfield Road, Cecil Road, London Road and Wellington Road, sixty-five acres in all. The Council staked out 838 plots, for which there were 789 applicants. By November 1917 twelve hundred new plots had been set out and let, but more were needed and Binstead's field in Holly Walk was acquired early in the year 1918.[45]

There was also a shortage of sugar in the summer of 1917. Supplies amounted to only half what had been available in 1915, but shopkeepers risked resentment when they attempted to restrict sales to regular customers. Seventy Allied merchant ships were sunk during the month of November 1917. The shortage of food supplies in the area gave rise to grave dissatisfaction among the munitions workers, and there was a protest meeting at the RSAF. Major Newman, the member for Enfield, demanded, in the House of Commons, to know whether the Minister was aware that there was a feeling that the working-class and residential areas on the outskirts of London were not getting their proper share of rationed necessities like tea, sugar and butter. 'Has full regard been taken of the vastly increased population of munition workers?' he demanded. The Enfield Wash and Ponders End Traders Association claimed that the population in their area had increased by fifteen thousand since the beginning of the war. The sugar registration scheme came into operation in mid-December, forms were to be handed in to grocers who would issue a sugar ticket for each form. This was the Enfield Food Committee's first experience in rationing. There were lengthening queues outside the provision shops and complaints that preferential treatment was being given to regular customers. Many soldiers' wives had to work long hours in factories and then had to stand in queues half the evening. The children then often took their places and stood shivering from 6.30 until 10 p.m. Geoffrey Gillam (*Enfield at War 1914-18*) quotes a letter from a young girl to her father serving in France: 'Ruby and I stood in a queue yesterday waiting for marg and lard', she writes, 'but they sold out before it was out turn. Mum has got to stand in a queue ever such a lot of times to get things for us …'. A protest meeting was called at Chesterfield School to demand compulsory rationing, like that already adopted in Birmingham. You never saw the rich waiting in queues', declared David Weston a former RSAF worker, subsequently chairman of the UDC. The situation was becoming desperate. In Edmonton a van carrying margarine was pursued by a crowd of three hundred people until it stopped outside a multiple shop in Fore Street. The crowd then rushed the doors, the police had to be called and the van was driven away under police escort. Another large crowd gathered outside a multiple store on Edmonton Green on the report that margarine had been delivered. The manager, not perceiving the danger, or perhaps revelling in his new-found power, came out and announced that none would be sold until the following day. The women were not in the mood to go home empty-handed, they rushed the doors, knocking over and trampling the unfortunate manager underfoot; he had to be rescued by the police who then remained to guard the shop.[46] On another occasion it became known that a large consignment of margarine had been delivered at the Maypole Stores in Church Street, Enfield. Hundreds of men, women and children gathered outside the premises, desperate to secure a share. They swarmed into the shop, so many that the assistants were unable to cope. The police were called and closed the doors but it was a long time before the crowds dispersed.

Sid Robinson in his autobiography writes of the Maypole dairy: 'I would be told to run a mile or so to the shop and join the queue', he says. 'If I was successful Mum would be pleased, too often however the iron gates at the entrance to the shop would be closed before my turn came'. To make matters worse coal became almost unobtainable through the dreadful winter of 1917. 'Dad', says Sid Robinson, 'tried to burn anthracite from the nursery boiler stokeholds on the kitchen range, but it was no good. Fred and I would trundle our old box on pram wheels to Cowell's the coal merchant in Fourth Avenue, in the hope that he would be able to shovel a bit from the floor boards of his front room, on which, in ordinary times, there was a small mountain of it … now I was frozen both at home and in school.'

Early in the year 1918 the food situation had reached a crisis, and there were widespread complaints of unequal distribution. On one occasion the Food Office (in the Central Library, Cecil Road) was besieged by an angry crowd and emergency supplies of meat and margarine had to be distributed to retailers. Action followed, and in February a hundred volunteers were called in to write-up and send out 110,000 food cards; it was all done in three weeks. A comprehensive national rationing scheme was introduced in July covering meat, butter, margarine, sugar and lard. Fifty-five thousand ration books were distributed. Jam was added to the list in October. These books remained current until September 1919 when a new ration card was issued. The Enfield Food Committee was not dissolved until June 1920. With the introduction of rationing and success at last against the U-boats, the situation slowly ameliorated through 1918.[47] In an effort to improve the distribution of coal the Coal Distribution Order required householders and other users to put in requisitions for 1918, stating the amount of coal they had in stock. Requisitions were not required for amounts of 2cwt and less. Delivery of larger quantities of coal would in future not be permitted without the consent of the Coal Overseer.[48]

The dreadful influenza epidemic hit the area in October. Its effects were particularly felt in eastern Enfield where some factories were in difficulty because so many work-people were ill. 147 children were absent in Bush Hill Park School, 120 at Forty Hill, all the Edmonton schools were closed. At Chase Farm 242 children and eight staff had the flu although not one child died. Many of the police were sick and a large proportion of the *Gazette* staff. All hospital visiting had to be cancelled. In the week ending 12 October there were thirty-nine deaths. There was a shortage of nurses at the Edmonton Military Hospital. The epidemic was dying down by the middle of November and was gone by the beginning of December. There had been 136 deaths in Enfield.[49]

Rumours of the armistice spread about nine o'clock on 11 November; people came out onto the streets where they stood in groups, talking. At eleven came the firing of guns which announced to the nation that the Great War was over. Workers downed tools and cheered, shops and schools closed, church bells rang, vendors of flags and bunting were quickly on the streets which were decorated for celebrations. 'A party of wounded soldiers', said the *Gazette*, 'came struggling along singing "After the War", a song known only to the troops in France.' Translated into everyday English this would probably have been:

'When this … war is over
Oh how happy I will be'

Not everyone could celebrate. In the *Gazette* three photographs were printed of the latest dead, Gunner Tom Sturgeon of Sixth Avenue, Private J. Tharby who had once worked for Fairhead's, and Private William Coombes of Uckfield Road.[50]

Notes to Chapter One

1   *Enfield Gazette* 4 S, 11 S 1914
2   *ibid* 26 My 1916
3   *ibid* 18 D 1914, 26 My 1916, 9 Ap 1915
4   *ibid* 11 Je 1915
5   *ibid* 15 Jl 1915, 31 My 1918
6   MUN4. 5303

7   *Gazette* 19 F 1926
8   *ibid* 10 D, 17 D 1915
9   *ibid* 14 Ja 1916, 19 Oct 1917
10 *ibid* 24 S 1926
11 *ibid* 19,26 N 1915, 5 My 1916, 5F 1917, C.S. Smeeton *Metropolitan Electric Tramways* V 1 1984 p.155
12 *Gazette* 6 Au 1915, 30 Je, 7 Ap 1916, 22 Mr 1918
13 *ibid* 7 Ja, 21Jl 1916, MUN4. 3896
14 *Gazette* 22 Mr 1918, 17 Mr 1916, 11 My 1917
15 *ibid*, 31 Ja 1919, 21 Ap, 18 Oct 1918
16 *ibid* 10 Ja 1919
17 *ibid* 28 Mr 1919, 2 Ap 1920
18 MUN 4. 5334, *Gazette* 2 S 1921
19 MUN 4. 6699
20 *Gazette* 19 My, 23 Je 1916
21 *ibid* 15 Je, 3 Au, 27 Jl, 28 S, 9 N, 30 N, 7 D 1917
22 *ibid* 4 S 1914
23 *ibid* 21 My 1915
24 *Enfield Weekly Herald* 4 Je 1915, 11 Au 1916
25 *Gazette* 21 Jl 1916
26 *ibid* 28 Jl, 29 S 1916, 27 Jl, 1917
27 *ibid* 21 Jl 1916
28 *ibid* 24 Au 1917
29 *ibid* 31 Au 1917
30 *ibid* 10 S, 1 Oct 1920
31 *ibid* 31 Jl 1914
32 *ibid* 7 Au, 14 Au, 21 Au, 1914
33 *ibid* 5 Ap 1929, 11 S 1914
34 *ibid* 18 S 1914, Enfield 362.92 (1893) 1919
35 *Gazette* 11 S 1914
36 *ibid* 7 Au 1914, 21 Au 1925
37 *ibid* 14 My 1915, 18 N 1914, 23 Jl 1915
38 *ibid* 15 Ja 1915
39 *Enfield Herald* 14 My 1915, Richard Slater
40 *Gazette* 15 Je 1917
41 *ibid* 4 Je, 29 Oct, 31 D 1915
42 *ibid* 10 Mr, 23 Je, 30 Je, 25 Au, 29 S, 8 S 1916
43 *ibid* 16 Je 1916, 21 My 1920, 16 Oct 1916, information Alan Jacques
44 *ibid* 13 Jl, 26 Oct 1917
45 *ibid* 27 Oct 1916, 16 Mr, 6 Ap, 11 My, 9 N 1917, 19 Ap 1918
46 *ibid* 7 D 1917, 2 Jl 1920, 25 Ja 1918
47 *ibid* 1 F 1918, 2 Jl 1920
48 *ibid* 7 D 1917
49 *ibid* 20 D, 25 Oct, 22 N 1918, 19 Ja 1919, Enfield MOH report 1918
50 *Gazette* 15 N 1918

Chapter Two
Industry Between the Wars

1. Introduction

Britain, emerging victorious from the Great War in 1918, found its Empire intact but all its traditional industries in decline. Between the wars production of cloth fell by sixty per cent, coal output by sixty million tons, shipyards were building less than half the ships they had been building in 1913. The consequences of this recession were at their worst in mining areas like South Wales and in shipbuilding towns like Jarrow. The problem of unemployment was thus unevenly distributed. It fell on areas where pottery was manufactured, upon cotton operatives, workers in iron and steel, shipbuilders and ship-repairers. Areas like Enfield, where new industries were developed close to their consumers, escaped the worst of the pain. England had become two nations.

It was as a result of these new industries that Britain in 1939 'looked a great deal more like a twentieth century economy than she had done in 1920' (E. J. Hobsbawn, *Industry and Empire*). Factories now sought sites with access to roads rather than railways or canals. The building of the A10 (Cambridge Road) and the A406 (North Circular) created new sites for industry. With hindsight more should have been created, but housing was unfortunately allowed to occupy many of the frontages. The years between the wars saw a great many take-overs and amalgamations which concentrated industrial resources to enable the use of higher technology. Ediswan's for instance took over parts of both British Thompson Houston and Metro Vickers; by 1931 Edwardson's was the only large factory in Enfield remaining in family ownership. Although firms which concentrated on exports suffered in the slump, other industries, catering for the home market, benefited by the low cost of raw materials.

The electrical industries, so dominant in Enfield, flourished in consequence of the expansion of electricity supply following the establishment of the National Grid. They prospered still more with the boom in house building in the Thirties. The number of electricity consumers increased from 750,000 in 1920 to nine million in 1938. The output of electrical goods nationally almost doubled between 1924 and 1935, as did the supply of electricity. The number of workers in the electrical industries trebled in the years between the wars. There was an overall improvement in the standard of living of both the working and the middle classes, at least among those with jobs, and the range of electrical goods displayed to tempt them, at moderate prices, widened. Show houses on new estates, a Sunday afternoon outing for upwardly mobile families, were fitted with electric cookers and fires, had points for electric irons and vacuum cleaners and of course almost every home had a wireless.

Retailing now aimed to cater for the needs of the poorest people; Woolworth's met a demand for cheap domestic articles (nothing over sixpence), the Fifty Shilling Tailor could dress a worker in a Sunday suit for the price stated, markets like the one on Edmonton Green prospered on the sale of cheap fruit and vegetables. Boots provided low price cosmetics and patent medicines, the Co-op did well on its 'divi'. The cost of living was falling, one pound in 1933 bought as much as 24s had done in 1924. The output per head of British industry grew faster between 1924 and 1937 than it had grown at the height of the Victorian economic expansion. That growth was achieved thanks to the new industries like the wireless and electrical industries.

2. Transport

The proposal to build the Cambridge Road and the North Circular Road came not as the solution to a serious traffic problem, but from the need to provide work for the unemployed. The plans had been formulated as early as 1912. The Ministry of Transport offered fifty per cent of the cost, but only as a loan, so that the total expense would ultimately have to be borne by the county rate. 'A wide, well constructed road through what was mostly agricultural land', said the *Gazette* (6 December 1920) 'would enhance the value of property along the route.'[1]

The work was to be done by the urban district councils on behalf of the County Council. The Cambridge Road was begun early in March 1921, working southward from the Cheshunt boundary as far as Turkey Street; it was constructed twenty-four feet wide with a path on one side and flanked by ditches. Twenty-five men were taken on at first, but the number rose to sixty-eight in Enfield by the beginning of May at which time five hundred feet of road neared completion in Tottenham; footpaths were being made there and side ditches cut. From the Tottenham boundary to Silver Street Edmonton, the top soil had been taken off, and immediately north of Silver Street men were filling in the gravel quarry near Hedge Lane to carry the road on towards Church Street Edmonton. From Church Street as far as the Great Eastern railway line to Enfield Town, notices to take possession had been served on the owners of land. A large portion of the Stuart Low nursery at Bush Hill Park was compulsorily purchased in September; the ground contained 22,000 fruit trees which were offered for sale.[2]

The depression of 1921-2 increased unemployment. At the same time government cuts restricted public expenditure and work virtually ceased on the Cambridge Road; foundations which had been laid were abandoned for more than a year and became a mass of weeds. Construction was resumed in May 1922 and a concrete road surface was put down in Edmonton between Silver Street and Bury Street, kerbing was completed between Silver Street and Church Street and preparations were made to build a bridge over the railway at Bush Hill Park. It was promised that, in October, forty or fifty more men would be taken on. McAlpine at that time secured the contract to continue the road north from the Hertfordshire boundary.[3]

The work was completed through Enfield by February 1924, except for the bridge over the railway which was then in course of construction. The road was

39. Surfacing work on the new Cambridge arterial road was resumed between Silver Street and Bury Street in May 1922.

40. The Cambridge Road through Enfield was completed by February 1924. This illustration shows the junction with Silver Street in Edmonton, probably about 1928.

41.   Southbury Road looking east across the Cambridge Road towards Enfield Highway. The chimneys of the brickworks can be seen in the distance, the Cambridge Road is not yet completed, 1923 or 1924.

42.   The tram terminus in Southbury Road, about 1930.

opened for traffic in September 1924, but no traffic came. The great stretch of empty roadway became a playground for children on roller-skates. The County Council was disconcerted. 'Some means must be devised', said the chairman, 'to induce the motorist to use it'. Traffic had increased enough by November 1932 to warrant the installation of automatic traffic signals at the junction with Southbury Road and in August 1937 a second carriageway was begun from Lordship Lane in Tottenham as far as the North Circular Road. The North Circular Road through Edmonton and Southgate was completed in 1924 as far east as the railway bridge in Angel Road. The great viaduct across the marshes was opened in November 1927; by that time the County had spent seven million pounds on arterial roads. Another Enfield scheme, approved by the Ministry of Transport in June 1922, was the widening of Bullsmoor Lane to sixty feet from the railway bridge to Bulls Cross, at a cost of £79,000.[4]

The congestion on the railways in the inter-war years, and the high freight charges, encouraged road hauliers, Meeson Bros set up at Bush Hill Park and Jackson's at Palace Gardens.[5]

Notice was published in May 1922 of the closure for improvement of the Lee Navigation above Enfield Lock. The lock and the bridge by the Royal Small Arms Factory were to be reconstructed, as were Waltham lock and bridge and other locks and bridges as far north as Ware. The waterway was to be deepened. Hitherto no barge of more than seventy tons had been able to reach Ware but with the reconstruction the river would be navigable by Thames barges of up to

43. The announcement of improvement work on the Lee Navigation north from Enfield lock in May 1922 drew hundreds of unemployed into the area in search of work. The photograph shows the rebuilding of Waltham lock.

a hundred tons; this was expected to reduce costs. The news of the work on the Lee brought renewed hope to the 2,400 registered unemployed in Enfield, for there had been talk of 1,250 jobs. 'Went down', wrote one man, 'to apply for one of the 1,250 jobs on the Lee Navigation and found a thousand to fifteen hundred unemployed men there. After waiting for hours we were told no men would be taken on that morning'. There had been reports in the evening papers that large numbers would be engaged and as a result hundreds of men invaded the district from as far away as Cambridge. Almost all were disappointed. The work was finished by June 1923 at a cost of £100,000. The Stort Navigation from Field's Weir at Rye House, as far as Bishops Stortford, had also been reconstructed. [6]

3. Industry and Unemployment in the Twenties

While the government arms factories in Enfield closed or drastically reduced their production immediately after the war, private industry expanded. Ediswan's, in January 1919, reported profits in the previous year amounting to £130,000 and the company purchased ten acres adjoining the Ponders End Works. Gas Company men could again be seen laying pipes for street lamps. At the same time large numbers of women and girls were being discharged from war work. They were reluctant to go back into domestic service, although many positions were advertised in the local press; a cook general might be offered anything between £30 and £50 a year with board, a general servant or a parlourmaid between £35 and £40; most servants were expected to live in. A Miss Bartlett who held an agency in Church Street, had interviewed four hundred girls but only

fourteen wanted to work as servants. Most of them expressed the view that by doing so they would be lowering themselves. Those who had left shopwork for factories were scarcely less reluctant to return. Yet large numbers of former women war workers found themselves unable to find work and in March 1920 the Ministry of Labour opened a centre in the district to train them in tailoring, dressmaking, cookery and the laundry trade.[7]

The recovery of local industry continued through the year 1919. Ruberoid expanded and a large factory for Spicer and Sons was erected at Brimsdown; staff, transferred from Tottenham, moved in at the end of December. The works employed four hundred and there was plenty of room for expansion on the site. A new steel and concrete single-storey extension at Ediswan's in Duck Lees Lane was planned, it would be the first of its type in Enfield. Four thousand seven hundred workers were employed there in February 1920. Expansion proceeded, and it was predicted that a further thousand would eventually be taken on. A girls' musical society and an orchestra had been set up, also a provident society contributions to which, through 1919, amounted to £1,566. Concrete Manufacturers secured seventeen acres immediately west of Brimsdown station, abutting on Green Street. The firm, encouraged by the shortage of bricks, proposed to produce concrete blocks for building; a railway siding was built there. The company, by 1924, had provided materials for houses all over the country, including one in Sarnsfield Road, one at Brimsdown, a garage at Palmers Green, and a number of local nursery chimneys. Cosmos Lamp factory was enlarged as were the Enfield Edison Cable, the Brimsdown Lead factory and the London Foundry Company works. Edwardson's Glue Company replaced its temporary wooden buildings with permanent premises in brick; railway sidings were taken into each of these works. Jaeger's, a woollen goods manufacturer, purchased a large house called Westmoor at the eastern end of Green Street in December 1919. Lenses had been made there during the war for the government, formerly it had been occupied for many years by a Mr L. Gray. The firm proposed to use the house as a factory. It was known by 1925 as Westmoor Ltd, employing high class tailors (all men) and a number of machinists. The house (demolished 1929) stood in nine acres, and tennis courts and croquet lawns were provided for the staff. The General Iron Company was building a foundry which was almost completed by June 1920. The greater part of the Granville estate at Ponders End was staked out for factory sites.[8]

Enfield was becoming a centre for the new and expanding electrical goods industry. Messrs Hayward, a manufacturer of pavement lights, put up a factory in Lincoln Road, Bush Hill Park. It produced lights, steel gates, sashes and fireproof doors. New workshops and a porcelain foundry were added to the Vulcan factory in Southbury Road (east of the Kingsway). The spread of electricity supply lines created an increased demand for porcelain; it was said that Ediswan's could deliver a million electric light roses if they could obtain the porcelain fittings. A film factory was built at Crews Hill. Graham Bros had extended the workshops behind their showrooms in Church Street. The Birkbeck Laundry, erected in Trinity Street in 1908, was doubled in size, five motor vehicles were employed on collection and delivery.[9]

1919 was a year of inflation; prices rose twice as fast as they had done in the worst years of the war. Trade unions struggled to keep wages in line with prices. Industrial rebuilding was marred by a series of disputes, local and national, over the years 1919-1921. A strike by bakers in August 1919 caused a shortage of bread. Men came out at the Golden Crust Company in Lincoln Road and fifty pickets were mounted throughout the week, yet the firm still managed to produce four thousand loaves a day against its normal output of six thousand. The moulders were on strike at Edison Accumulators, the firm threatened that it would have to close, an order to supply two electric dust-carts for Enfield UDC could not be met. At this time there was a police strike at Edmonton and Tottenham. The men were demanding the right to join the National Union of Police and Prison Officers; thirteen officers at Edmonton and fifty-one at Tottenham were dismissed. The strike gave rise to some disorder; a mob of two thousand gathered in Fore Street and threw handfuls of gravel at the station windows. Many cleared off when the thirty night-duty men marched out, but knots of people hung about until after midnight. There were more serious disturbances at Wood Green High Road on Bank Holiday Sunday night; fences and brickwork were torn down and hurled at the police, several of whom were injured. Two youths were sentenced to two months hard labour.[10]

A national railway strike occurred in September 1919; Enfield Chase and Gordon Hill stations were closed, there were pickets at Enfield Town. Many Enfield residents volunteered for transport and other strike duties; Lady Meux of Theobalds Park offered herself (and was accepted) as a ticket collector at Liverpool Street Station. The strike gave rise to a serious shortage of coal, some merchants had hardly a sack to send out. It was the poor who suffered; as one correspondent complained in the *Gazette*, a few months earlier coal was being delivered to the big houses around the Ridgeway in such huge quantities that the middle-class residents were unable to accommodate it in their cellars and it had to be shot outside. Difficulties in the nursery industry, caused by a shortage of anthracite, became so serious by March 1920 that local MPs brought the situation to the attention of Parliament; the industry employed six or seven thousand hands locally, it was said, and consumed 300,000 tons of anthracite each year, this meant a weekly delivery of about four hundred truck loads. There was only two weeks supply in hand; a crisis had been avoided so far only because of unseasonably warm weather.[11]

There was a strike at Edison Cables (no connection with Edison and Swan) in April, some five hundred hands were employed there. It began among members of the Electrical Trade Union, others remained at work at first but subsequently they joined the electricians, making a total of 440 on strike; sixty remained stubbornly at work. On the Friday evening two or three hundred strikers carrying a banner and headed by cornet players marched to the works at Brimsdown. When the strike breakers came out at five o'clock they were met by a barrage of eggs and stones and the police had to be called to escort them from the factory. The strikers followed and at the level-crossing in Green Street two arrests were made. Further down Green Street, near the White Horse, the way was blocked by a cordon of strikers who fought with the police in an attempt to release the prisoners. The engineering trade at this time was badly hit by the protracted strike of moulders. A coal strike was threatened in August 1920; fortunately it was avoided, for coal stocks had hardly recovered from the effects of the rail strike and Enfield continued to face a serious shortage. None of the coal merchants had more than one week's supply, nor had the factories any large stocks. Ediswan's came to an agreement with the shop stewards on shortened hours.[12]

The miners' strike began in earnest in October 1920 and threatened to turn

45.   *Edward Ernest Leggatt of Gentleman's Row* (Gazette *5 June 1925*).

into a general strike as the Triple Alliance (an agreement for common action set up in 1915 between the miners, railwaymen and the transport workers' unions) seemed set to bring out the railwaymen and the transport workers. An Emergency Powers Act was passed. Troops were posted at the Royal Small Arms Factory and barbed wire entanglements were put up around the perimeter. Reservists, called up by the government, were leaving from all the Enfield stations. The middle classes flocked to the Drill Hall in Old Park Avenue to enrol in defence units. Major Leggatt supplied blankets and mattresses for the volunteers sleeping there; he opened Elm House in Gentleman's Row to enable them to get a bath. The atmosphere was reminiscent of August 1914, but there was no foreign enemy. Men trained in the Town Park; recruitment into the Metropolitan Special Constabulary was opened. The National Union of Railwaymen called mass meetings at Tottenham, Edmonton, Enfield and Waltham Cross, where calls were made to support the miners. The National Union of Horticultural Workers threatened a lightning strike in the Lea Valley. The Council surveyor, at the end of April, reported that household coal in the hands of Enfield retailers was down to a mere thirty-two tons. Recalling the time, Doris Shuttlewood of Beaconsfield Road Enfield Wash described how Grandad had to go to collect the coal in a small hand-cart from the sidings at Enfield Lock station. There was short-time working in many factories, the lamp department at Ediswan's closed because of a shortage of gas. Little work had been done, since the commencement of the miners' strike, at the London Foundry works in Brimsdown; a hundred men had been discharged there, also 120 at the Cortecine factory. Short-time was being worked at the Metallic Tubing Company, at the Cable Works, at Brimsdown Lead factory, at Eley Bros Explosives in Waltham Abbey, at Ruberoid, and at Spicer's. Nearly a thousand street lamps were out of use, football trains had to be cancelled.[13]

The postwar boom broke abruptly in the winter of 1920-21. Twenty-five hundred men were registered at the Ponders End labour exchange in April that year. When their unemployment insurance ran out, which was after twenty-six weeks, they became a charge on the Board of Guardians which by this time was spending £6,000 a week on unemployment relief. It cost the Enfield ratepayers an additional £8,730 in the half-year ending that April. The ratepayers moreover found themselves burdened by increased county, police and education rates. Relief payments for a man and his wife then stood at 5s each in money and

46.   The miners' strike which began in October 1920 threatened to turn into a general strike. An Emergency Powers Act was passed. The middle classes flocked to the Drill Hall in Old Park Avenue to enrol in defence units. Major Leggatt supplied blankets and mattresses for the volunteers sleeping there. The atmosphere was reminiscent of August 1914 but there was no foreign enemy. Two of the Leggatt brothers are shown leading the parade with Henry Ernest Grout, front rank nearest the camera.

4s each in kind, with 1s in money and 4s in kind for the first child, and 1s in money and 3s in kind for each other child. Relief in kind was distributed in the form of tickets which could be exchanged for goods in the shops. The *Gazette* complained that most of these food tickets were used in the Co-op in order to get the dividend; the editor urged that this dividend money ought to be handed back to the Guardians. The politicians sought to relieve unemployment by schemes of public works, paid for through the local rates. One such scheme, devised by the Labour-controlled Enfield Council, was the installation of surface water drains, but the work was held up because no one was prepared to advance the money. It was now proposed to provide work, with assistance from the government, by the construction of new roads. Thus the Great Cambridge Road and the North Circular came to be built.[14]

Enfield Urban District Council made accommodation available at the Highway branch library as a headquarters for the organisation of the unemployed. Voluntary efforts by the Enfield Unemployed Relief Fund continued, but house to house collectors found that householders could no longer contribute so generously because of rising rents and rates. Local tradesmen provided meat, potatoes, bread and groceries at practically wholesale prices. The Guardians, by the beginning of July 1921, were relieving 1,600 able-bodied men, with 5,200 dependents, at a cost of £1,600 a week, also 3,500 sick, lame, old or widowed, at a cost of £1,400. Many of these must have been the aged parents of those who had lost their jobs and who were unable any longer to support them. Some large firms in the area were so badly hit by the slump, it was said, that should rates increase further, industry would be forced to move out; it was reported that one large firm had recently left Edmonton for a less highly rated parish. Four thousand unemployed men marched with banners to the workhouse in Bridport Road in September, headed by a brass band. A large body of foot and mounted police was posted in the roadway outside the boardroom, but the demonstration remained orderly in spite of the refusal of the Guardians to receive any deputation.[15]

The dispute in the coal industry was settled in August 1921, but there came no indication that trade was looking up. Two thousand five hundred men were still registered unemployed at the Ponders End labour exchange, including eight hundred ex-servicemen, also one thousand women and five hundred boys and girls. The situation seemed unlikely to improve. The nursery trade was nearing the end of the season and discharges were inevitable; work on the arterial road was making little progress because of the disinclination of the local authorities to incur more expense. Even domestic service was no longer short of labour and mistresses refused to take girls without experience. A crowd of unemployed men gathered outside T.Ridgewell's brushmaking factory in Acacia Road in December, they demanded to know why his men were working overtime when so many were unemployed. Ridgewell offered to give work to any man who was a brushmaker; he defended himself by saying that he employed only trade union labour. The following week the unemployed occupied Ediswan's in a protest about overtime. There was no violence. The demonstration set out from Edmonton, many joined it at Ponders End and more near the factory; a police escort accompanied the march. Factory staff managed to lock the gates but the demonstrators clambered over the walls and took over the workshops. A hundred police were called, but after the management promised that overtime would cease at Christmas, the unemployed formed up again and

47.   Following a post-war boom, depression set in in 1921, and 2,500 were registered unemployed at Ponders End labour exchange. Ediswan's was occupied by out-of-work men in a protest about overtime. Staff managed to lock the gates but the demonstrators clambered over the walls and occupied the workshops.

marched off singing the '*Red Flag*'. Five hundred unemployed attended the Guardians' meeting when they discussed extra Christmas relief. A deputation was received this time and the Guardians granted a single payment of 2s 6d for each adult and 1s 6d for each child at a cost of £1,400. Eighty thousand were said to be unemployed in the area of the Edmonton Union by January 1922. The Guardians, in many cases, were now supplementing unemployment benefit; they paid 18s a week for a man and wife, up to 9s rent, the first child 5s and all other children 4s. Thus for a man, wife and two children they paid 36s. From this had to be deducted the man's unemployment benefit of 15s, his wife's at 5s and 1s each for the children, which made 22s. The net grant from the Guardians was therefore 14s. Enfield Council now approached the Board with a scheme which would ensure that men worked for what they got in relief. They should work 31½ hours and receive in all 39s 6d (i.e. 1s 3d an hour) made up of 22s unemployment relief (as above) and 17s 6d earned. Since before the scheme they had been getting 36s, this to some may have looked like 3s 6d for 31½ hours. The basic wage for a council labourer at this time was 30s, plus 22s bonus, out of which he paid 2s 6d superannuation, leaving him with 49s 6d.[16]

A year after the armistice the Royal Small Arms Factory stood almost idle. From June 1919 power was taken from the Northmet at Brimsdown although the generating plant at the factory was not closed down. Examinations were still held for apprenticeships in the government factories. There were 163 candidates in 1920 for forty-three places and ten were secured by students from the Ponders End Trade School. The following year 238 candidates sat the examination although only eighteen apprentices were required for both Enfield and

48. *The Royal Small Arms Factory fire brigade with wives and families in a charabanc outside the fire station at Ponders End. In the back row in a bowler hat is Mr Slater who was the marker on the rifle range. To his right is his son who worked in the factory during the First World War, to his left is the fire chief who lived in Government Row, and in the front in a trilby hat sits Mr Wilson, the local swimming champion, and his wife.*

Woolwich; five of the successful candidates came from the Ponders End Trade School. A government scheme in January 1921 to absorb more of the unemployed by a reduction of hours, which would have meant that workers would lose one week in six, was strongly opposed by the unions in the factory. Railway wagon repair work was introduced at the RSAF in 1921; at first it was done in the open but subsequently a large building was adapted and railway lines were laid. A slackness in that work however threatened its continuance by August, and soon afterwards it was stopped. Some 230 men, mostly taken on since January 1921, were discharged.[17]

The depression worsened in 1922 and cuts in public expenditure were ordered. The RSAF church, after sixty years was closed by the Army Council as an economy measure in January that year and the grant of £200 a year was withdrawn. The church moved away from the factory to the former parish hall in Ordnance Road. Another economy measure taken at this time was the removal of tea-making facilities from the workshops; these had been installed during the war. Mr Carnegie, recently appointed superintendent there, was replaced by Mr Roberts who was also to be in charge of the Royal Gunpowder Factory. Several of the foremen who were about sixty years of age were given notice. Foremen ranked as civil servants and as such received pensions. The Geddes axe was beginning to take its toll locally as well as nationally. Management was determined not to allow trade unions to interfere with the exercise of management functions; it emphasized this in a memorandum and the unions called a protest meeting during the dinner hour.[18]

The estimates in April 1922 provided more bad news for the workers. Personnel at the RSAF was to be reduced by six hundred to 1,350, at the rate of thirty-five a week. The pre-war strength had been 1,800. Yet there came a glimmer of hope in July with the announcement that the Army Council was considering a reduction in the weight of the regulation rifle from 8lb 10ozs to 6lb. Enfield Lock was now the only government rifle factory in the country. It was determined, in September, that the personnel there should number 1,214, already 585 men had fallen victim to government economies. A huge sale of plant and machinery was announced in October. Wages had decreased, labourers employed at the factory were paid £2 4s 6d, which compared badly even with a council labourer of £2 13s 6d.[19] They were given a 3s increase in March 1924, but this still left their wages below the poverty line. A union meeting at the assembly rooms in Ordnance Road demanded a further 10s, but it was not granted and the labourers continued to be paid considerably less than council road sweepers who by now got 51s a week. Despite this, the next pay award in June gave 6s a week to the skilled workers, but gave nothing to the labourers. The continual discharges caused real hardship, for even skilled men found it difficult to save money against such a contingency. Men leaving at sixty to sixty-five received only a small gratuity. The struggle to secure superannuation had been going on for fifty-four years.[20] Most of the discharged men would have to wait two or three years to get their old age pension (10s a week) and during that time they would have to pay the full insurance contribution; it meant that they would be forced to apply to the Guardians for assistance.

The efficiency of the works was the subject of an article in the *Daily Express* in March 1926. It was alleged that the factory was twenty-five years behind the times and was using machinery installed at the time of the Indian Mutiny. A hundred more men were sacked in March 1927, mostly unskilled; there were by this time

49. For many years a flourishing market, on both Saturdays and weekdays, was held at Enfield Lock. Many lockies would have their wives and families meet them at the gates at mid-day on Saturdays to get their shopping off the stalls and carts; pigs' trotters and cowheel were common favourites. The market fell into disuse at the time of the First World War and part of this Market Place was enclosed with the factory when the position of the entrance gates was changed in 1919. Some of the old buildings shown here were demolished in 1917.

50. It was customary for dinners to be collected from workers' homes in square dinner baskets, the lids secured by a skewer. They were brought to the Market Place for distribution, and the contents eaten either in the factory dining room, or perhaps in one of the pubs with a pint. Jack Burchell used two carts for this work, and there were others like Mr Oakley who had a shop in Church Street.

fourteen hundred employed. The works had kept going since the war on repair work, but this was now exhausted. The factory waited upon the adoption of a new service rifle.[21]

The Royal Gunpowder Factory was already fifty per cent below its 1914 strength, yet it was announced in April 1922 that half the employees were to be discharged at the rate of fifteen a week, to leave only 230. Those most experienced in the manufacture of cordite would be retained, thus they would include very few ex-servicemen. There was a mass protest meeting at Waltham Cross attended by representatives of the unions, the local councils and the Board of Guardians, but the country had a ten year supply of explosives. Members of the Geddes committee recommended scrapping the Royal Gunpowder Factory. The great munitions factory at Gretna, which had cost £9m to build during the war, was closed, and in January 1924 it was sold off. The Waltham Abbey factory remained at a standstill. Nearby, Nobel's Cartridge Factory at Waltham Abbey closed early in the year 1925; work was transferred to Birmingham.[22]

Some two thousand were employed at Ediswan's by November 1921 and for a time the number of girls there slowly increased. The engineering shop remained in a sad way, the foundry and turret shop had closed down. Such recovery as had occurred did not last. There were heavy discharges of labour just before Christmas 1921 because of a slackness of trade in electric lamps. In May 1922 the firm put forward a plan to reduce wages and a number of girls, resisting, were locked out. The unions were attempting to organise in the factory but with girls on short-time, the moment was unpropitious. Schemes to relieve unemployment by public works gave rise to heavy rates, up to 21s 4d in the pound. The sum demanded from Ediswan's in rates amounted to £8,000 a year; the firm alleged that this was the reason why it had been forced to close some of the shops. A sad casualty of the cut-backs was the factory fire brigade, for it had a high reputation. The loss must have occasioned considerable regret when, at the end of November 1922 there occurred a disastrous fire at the works. The Enfield and District Manufacturers Association was established in February 1922, its chairman was T. D. Morson, Managing Director of Thomas Morson and Sons, a chemical manufacturer. The association represented a rateable value of £30,000 which was expected soon to reach £55,000, thus it had to be deeply concerned about local government expenditure. It claimed that high rates were deterring new industry from coming to Enfield. Mr Morson's views were plain; 'A feature of our national finance', he said, 'is the abnormal growth of expenditure on social services, insurance, education and pensions ... The amount absorbed in 1922', he went on, 'was nearly six times that of 1913 ... the nation is indulging in a sort of Rake's Progress ...'. In other quarters Enfield Urban District Council was criticised for lagging behind neighbouring districts in the promotion of public works. There were still two thousand unemployed in Enfield in 1923.[23]

Industry in Enfield began to expand again and unemployment to decline by 1924. Edwardson's, a large manufacturer of flexible glue for bookbinding, diversified into soap making, 'Edwardson's Easy Washer'. Their spacious works close to Brimsdown railway station covered three acres between the railway and the navigation. The decision to diversify had been taken in order to survive the slump. Messrs Reeves, at the Greyhound Works in Lincoln Road, were producing materials for artists and draughtsmen by early 1924, six delivery vans were kept busy. Some of the luxury trades were again expanding. The Enfield

51. Industry remained depressed and unemployment high in October 1922. 'Bring all your troubles to Fishpool', the advertisement urges, 'he will see that you get what you want'. You can judge Fishpool's prices against the wages of labourers at the RSAF who earned £2 4s 6d a week.

Embroidery Co., at Charles Street Bush Hill Park, had originated in a small shop in Percival Road. It was taken over about 1902 by Alex Jamieson and Co. Work was done to order from high-class emporiums like Maple's, Shoolbread's and Hampton's; much was exported to Australia, the Cape and South America. The

52.   *George Reynolds Wright, the miller, died in 1914. He had come to Enfield fifty years earlier as manager for George Dilley and was taken into partnership.*

fingers of many a working-class mother and wife, in one or other of the neighbouring cottages east of the railway line, were kept busy far into the night trimming reels of lace to earn an extra half a crown (Sid Robinson, *Sid's Family Robinson*). The firm had broken into what had been, until recently, a Swiss monopoly in the embroidery of curtains. Another small firm successful in the export trade was Salmon and Webster, makers of cricket bats and tennis rackets, housed in the former Conservative Club in Hertford Road (opposite the end of Ordnance Road). Their products, almost entirely handmade, were exported to Australia, India and China. The Selig racket works in Canonbury Road prospered on the middle-class enthusiasm for tennis.[24]

The firm T. Morson, chemical manufacturer, had been established in 1821; it had come to Ponders End in 1901 to set up the Summerfield Works adjoining the railway. A large laboratory was established there in 1924. That same year Yager's Charlotte Cabinet Works took over the site which had formerly been occupied by the Ponders End Shell Works. The construction of the King George V Reservoir had necessitated the abandonment of the use of water power at Wright's Mill in 1909, and it became the first commercial undertaking to use power supplied by the Northmet. George Reynolds Wright died in 1914. He had come to Enfield fifty years earlier as the manager for George Dilley Young and had subsequently been taken into partnership. Six electric motors were working there by 1924, yet the old mill remained proud of its traditional methods. Seven pairs of stones four foot six in diameter produced the 'Imperial Wholemeal Flour', much eulogised by medical writers. Grain was brought either by road or by barge coming up from London in one day's journey. A roller mill which produced white flour had operated from 1892, at first powered by steam but later by electricity. A biscuit factory was set up in Enfield Highway in 1926. At Brimsdown, Booth and Fox were engaged in the manufacture of quilts, mattresses and stuffed furnishings, importing down from China via the British treaty ports. Also at Brimsdown was the Enfield Stone Company, making paving,

53. *Booth and Fox, Brimsdown in the Twenties.*

kerbstones, building stone and objects for garden decoration.[25]

The electrical industry in 1922 was in chaos, voltages varied throughout the country, there were 23 different types of power plug, yet the potential for growth was apparent and Enfield became a centre for the growing electrical industry. The enormous factory of the Enfield Cable Works had just been completed at the outbreak of the war, and throughout the war years it had been taken over for government work. It was in business for itself for the first time in the year 1919 when it produced 164 tons of cable; in 1923 it produced 933 tons. The works covered six and a half acres and some eight hundred men and girls were employed there; a night-shift had been working for some time. At the beginning of the year 1924 the company acquired the derelict premises, on twenty acres, formerly used for the manufacture of steel by the London Foundry Company. Plant was purchased from Krupps of Austria and the works were converted, as Enfield Rolling Mills, into one of the most up-to-date rolling mills in the country. Fifty staff were recruited, mostly local labour. Copper rod, until then, had been imported from the USA, but the firm now proposed to manufacture its own from ingots. Output was in the form of electrolytic copper rod, strip and wire, used exclusively in the electrical industry. The copper ingots, mainly American, were received in barge loads of fifty to a hundred tons. It took ten hours from London Docks to Brimsdown where the cargoes were transferred to rail trucks. Gross profits for the year ending 30 June 1924 amounted to £72,972, as against £43,646 in the previous year. £19,000 had been made in the purchase and sale of the assets of the former London Foundry Company. Profits for the year 1924/5 amounted to £89,447, and the following year to £106,927.[26]

The recent great advances in the use of electrical equipment resulted in the evolution of many specialised trades. J. and A. Hart, established in the Queensway in October 1923, specialised in the insulation of copper wire of all gauges from .0004 inches upward.[27]

54. *Enfield Cable Works had just been completed at the outbreak of the First World War. The building was immediately taken over for government work, the firm was not in business for itself until 1919.*

55. *United Flexible Metallic Tubing factory. Its products were used in gas and electrical installation, railways, furnaces and in hundreds of other ways throughout the world. The consignment here being dispatched was going to the Medical Department in the East African Protectorate. The factory was totally demolished in 1991.*

The United Flexible Metallic Tubing in South Street, originally set up to meet the needs of an expanding gas industry, was now the biggest metallic tubing works in the country. Many of its products were still used in gas installation, but were also used in electrical installations, by the railways for brake pipes and steam heating pipes, in furnace work, for spraying, for rock drills and in motor cars. The workshops and offices of Edison and Swan covered twenty-three acres

56.   *Girls on piece-work at Ediswan's putting the filaments into the lamps. The girl in the middle of the row is Grace Watson.*

by 1924 and two thousand were employed there. Spacious workshops were devoted to the production of wireless valves, the assembly of wireless sets, earphones and accumulators. Much government work was being done. The annual profit for the year ending 31 December 1928 amounted to £76,991, as against

57. *Ediswan's was becoming prosperous by the late Twenties making wireless valves, wireless sets, accumulators and doing a great deal of work for the government.*

£59,508 in the previous year. Towards the end of the year 1928 the firm was involved in merger negotiations with Metropolitan Vickers, British Thomson-Houston and Ferguson Pailin, to create the giant AEI.[28]

The power station had last been extended in 1921. Coal storage bunkers were built in 1925 to hold eight weeks supply. Coal had been delivered by rail, road and barge, but transport on the Lee Navigation was no longer considered reliable. During the previous winter floods had held up delivery for three weeks and lorries had to be used to bring the coal from Brimsdown station. The coal was pulverised and sucked in through a vacuum pipe at the rate of fifty tons an hour. Most of the water for cooling was obtained from two artesian wells. Output was increasing rapidly, 1923 saw a twenty per cent increase over 1922, and 1924 a twenty-three per cent increase over 1923. Capital expenditure in 1924 amounted to £358,000. Mains were being laid to Elstree and Boreham Wood, and at Potters Bar and Totteridge. The Northmet advertised electric vacuum cleaners in October 1923. By the beginning of the year 1925 the electricity show-house at 178 Village Road had been visited by 3,800 people. Later that year the company was able to offer a substantial reduction of price, ten per cent on lighting, and twenty-five per cent on heating. The load had doubled in the four years up to March 1926.[29]

That year the company purchased from Trinity College Cambridge, forty acres which lay alongside their works at Brimsdown and work was begun on the building of a modern power station. It would be capable of producing 50,000 kilowatts, more than double the existing capacity. The new station, known as Brimsdown B, cost £800,000, and consumed two thousand tons of coal a week. There was room to install three further 25,000 kilowatt turbo alternators when the need arose. Five hundred staff were engaged in preparation for the opening in the summer of 1928. Members of the Central Electricity Board visited Brimsdown in November that year. Northmet by this time had 45,000 direct

58.   *Brimsdown B was opened in 1928, the cooling towers were built in 1930.*

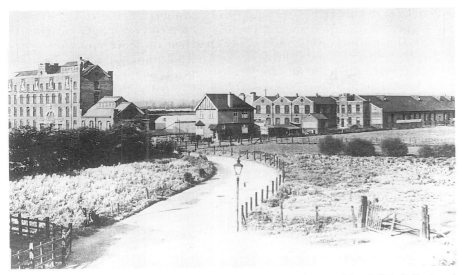

59.   Cosmos, extreme left, was established in 1908 for the manufacture of electric light bulbs; it took over the premises of a former varnish factory.

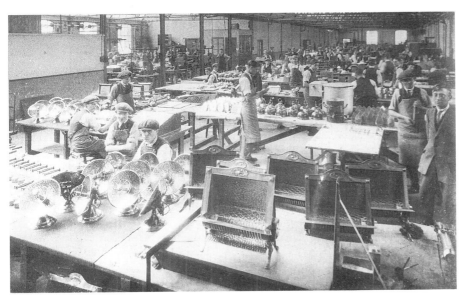

60.   In the years following the First World War Cosmos expanded into the production of electric fires, kettles, urns and irons.

consumers and 1,100 employees. There were complaints from local residents about smoke and dirt. A large area between the new site and the railway line lay empty and ideal for the erection of more factories. Steps were being taken in the summer of 1927 towards a unified power supply system to cover south-east

61.   Wootton and Co. works outing in a Meeson coach, 1925.

England. The Electricity Commissioners ordered the Northmet and the London Electricity Supply Company to supply electricity in bulk to each other; for this their mains had to be connected.[30]

Cosmos, established in 1908 for the manufacture of electric light bulbs, had diversified since the war to manufacture, in 1924, electrical heating and cooking apparatus, electric irons, kettles, shaving pots, glue pots and urns. British Sangamo, just over the railway line in Duck Lees Lane, had begun work in 1920; more than two hundred electric meters a day were produced there by 1924. New factories were being built on the Queensway in Ponders End. The Rogat Tool and Stamping Company took premises there to manufacture press tools, moulds, embossing dies and stampings. The tools to produce fire-bars for Belling's electric fires were made there, also the tools to make imitation bars of Fry's chocolate used in shop window displays. Hart Bros Electrical Manufacturing Company had opened in the Queensway by August 1927. At Ponders End High Street, behind the Technical Institute, Messrs Wootton's factory produced electrical woodwork, meter boards, sunk switches, and the walnut frames used by MK Electric at Edmonton. The business was set up in 1919 from men formerly employed as a team at Ediswan's under Charlie Wootton. It became an independent company and by 1924 had forty employees. Belling's moved from Edmonton to open the Bridge Works in Southbury Road, taking over ten acres formerly used as a brickfield. The new factory provided 23,400 square feet of floor space, but this soon proved insufficient and in 1926 a four-bay extension was built with four hundred square feet in each bay, also a canteen was provided and three hundred extra staff were taken on. The Foundation Company, in September 1927, built a large factory on a cauliflower field at Brimsdown for the manufacture of electrical goods.[31]

The Vulcan Electrical and Mechanical Company in Southbury Road produced dynamos, electric motors, wireless equipment and vacuum pumps, as well as doing some general engineering. They had gone into business on the site in 1915 and the works had been extended in 1921. A motor produced there, equipped with a pump for air conditioning in railway carriages, was in use on the railways in southern India. The firm proposed to build a casting foundry for malleable iron, the first of its kind in the London area; previously castings had to be procured from Birmingham. The company was short of skilled labour and this was attributed to the housing shortage in Enfield.

The wireless industry was beginning its great expansion. Belling Lee, begun at the Queensway in 1922, produced a new four-valve mains radio set in 1925 which sold retail at about £40. Most of the production there was based upon the firm's own patents. Eighty staff were employed. Also at the Queensway was the Electric Cord Company and the Newall Engineering Company which had moved there from Walthamstow in 1929; this firm made gauges. What the *Gazette* described as 'a splendid range of modern factories' had been erected in Lincoln Road by October 1925, it included Mears Cabinet Works where a whole department was devoted to the manufacture of plywood. Some new small electrical factories were set up in the Town and at Ponders End in 1926. A high proportion of local school leavers now found employment in Enfield factories, particularly in electric lamp and instrument making. Mr Morson, in March 1926, attributed much of the industrial expansion to good housekeeping by the local authority. 'Moderate rates mean more factories in the Lea Valley', he explained, 'and genuine employment instead of rate-aided grants for relief work. Six years ago manufacturers were frightened away by high rates, but they now regard the Lea Valley with a favourable eye.'[32]

The breakdown of negotiations to end a dispute in the coal industry led in May 1926, to the General Strike. The government proclaimed a state of emergency and a national appeal was issued. Volunteers were required, not for strike-breaking it was claimed, but in the interests of the community. Five hundred had enrolled in Enfield on the first Tuesday morning of the strike; they were needed to serve as train drivers, conductors, guards, tube train drivers and lorry drivers. Recruitment of special constables proceeded at the police stations. The railway stations in Enfield were closed, little knots of strikers gathered at street corners. The Admiral buses were still running and were packed, a large number of private cars took people to the City. Several charabancs were lined up in the Town, but some left half empty. Other people cycled to work, some even walked. There was a well-attended Labour Party meeting around the fountain in the Town. Councillor Bill Preye of Edmonton addressed a meeting at Green Street to try to persuade Redburn's men to come out, but they refused. The situation for the Admiral service became difficult, however, when four or five hundred strikers posted themselves outside the Queens Head in Green Lanes (their garage was at Willow Walk, West Green Road) and threatened to turn the vehicles over. The drivers were intimidated and decided to run the buses into the garage. No trams were running nor General Omnibuses, but the private buses, including Redburn's, Lewington's and BB (Biss Bros) operated at first. They were forced to stop on the Tuesday evening by hostile demonstrations.[33]

The Royal Small Arms Factory continued to work until the Wednesday when eight hundred came out. A detachment of soldiers arrived to guard the

62.   Lewington's business was run by Lewington's Cycles at 579 Hertford Road. The initials stand for George, Wilfred and Leslie, the three brothers Lewington. Their bus was red and white and was made by Thorneycroft.

premises. Members of the engineering union were called out at the power station and pickets were posted at the gates. The AEU men came out at Ediswan's, and a few came out at Cosmos.

Four trams which left Tramway Avenue depot on the Wednesday afternoon, driven by officials, were met with jeers from the strikers and were held up for a time in Hertford Road; eventually they got away carrying policemen fore and aft. They went as far as Finsbury Park and one had its windows smashed near Manor House, few passengers rode on them. The Admiral service and Redburn's resumed work on the Friday with police escorts, but were later withdrawn after an attack on the Admiral premises in West Green Road. At ten o'clock on 12 May BBC 2LO announced the end of the General Strike. There were the odd repercussions locally, like Philip Ashley who was fined £5 (or twenty-eight days) for breaking two windows of a Redburn's bus in Hertford Road. The return to work was rapid and no one was penalised for striking. Reaction to the strike among the middle class in non-industrial suburbs like Southgate and Winchmore Hill had been far more partisan than in Enfield. At Southgate 715 special constables had signed up during the crisis, and four hundred had been on duty every twenty-four hours, probably anticipating a revolution.[34]

The miners continued their strike alone; there was a fuel shortage in Enfield. Certain coal merchants were accused of profiteering on stock which had been held in the railway yards since before the strike began. What had been purchased at the pit head for 22s a ton was now being sold to poor people at 3s 4d a cwt. Enfield collections raised £1,000 to relieve the suffering of the wives and children of the miners. Power cuts due to the coal shortage caused difficulties in some local factories in the autumn, the power station was finding it difficult to get foreign (German) coal and stocks were diminishing. Firms were asked to close at 4.30 a.m., Monday to Friday and not to work on Saturdays. Steelwork for building the new power station was held up because of the strike. Members of the Lea Valley Growers Association considered changing to oil because of the high price of coal and coke. E. E. Gayler at St Margaret's nursery in Crews Hill was the first to install an oil-burning furnace. He was driven to experiment during the coal strike by the loss of hundreds of pounds worth of plants; he had even lit bonfires in the greenhouses in an endeavour to save them.[35]

The number of persons unemployed in Enfield was increasing again in the autumn of 1927. During the last week in September there were 367 men in receipt of relief and unemployment insurance benefit, and 1,016 married men were receiving full relief from the Guardians because their unemployment insurance benefit was exhausted. This was a decided increase on the previous month and a much greater increase was likely over the winter. Enfield UDC spent £21,219 in the last six months of 1927 on relief works, such as the construction of children's lakes in Durants Park.[36] The situation was far worse in Tottenham and in Edmonton.

The Ministry of Health inspector accused the Guardians of extravagance; he was of the opinion that they ought to be able to effect economies in out-door relief. In the first week in April 1925 the average amount spent on each case was 14s 2d, in April 1926 it had risen to 20s 3d, in the first week in September 1927 it was 23s 1d. Meanwhile, administrative costs per head had increased by sixty-five per cent, yet the cost of living over these seventeen months had fallen. Eleven per cent of the able-bodied men receiving relief in January 1927 had been receiving relief for four years or more. The inspector cited an instance where family income and relief totalled £6 8s a week for six persons. Mr Edwardson, who was a member of the Board of Guardians, quoted a further instance: a strong and healthy young man had married while on relief and in the following four years he had four children, all at the expense of the ratepayers. Each week £1,000 was paid in out-door relief in Enfield. With that money, said the inspector, it should have been possible to find work for five hundred men. Whenever the labour exchange turned down applicants because they were not genuinely seeking work, they merely went to the Guardians who gave them what the Ministry had refused. One Guardian defended this alleged generosity; 'What does the Ministry suggest for people with four children or more on relief? The Ministry says; "You must starve them into work". You shake your head Mr Inspector … did you not say you must reduce relief?' He went on to point out that, from 28 January 1928, every man over sixty-five would have to come off the labour exchange and must live on a pension of 10s. Inevitably, they would have to come to the Guardians and the burden of out-relief would be 30s to 35s a week for each pensioner.[37]

The Guardians came under further criticism from the Ministry of Health for giving more relief in money than in kind, but they defended their policy. It cost an extra 5s to give 10s worth of relief in kind and many of the recipients sold the food tickets for ready money at less than their face value. The poor could certainly get better value for cash than the shopkeepers would give them on food tickets. One Guardian demanded to know whether the Ministry regarded

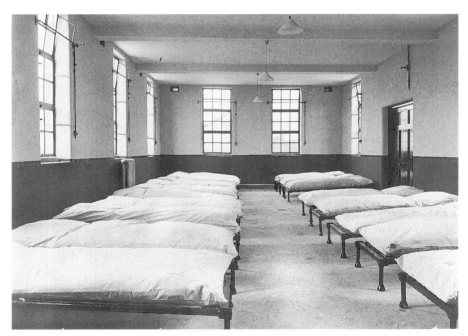

63.   *The casual ward at the Edmonton Union. 'Tramps' complained the* Enfield Gazette *in 1928, 'are flocking to Edmonton', apparently to enjoy the new feather beds, spring mattresses and shower baths. Among them must have been many men from the distressed areas looking for work.*

64. *The last meeting of the Board of Guardians, 1930, at the Edmonton Union workhouse, Silver Street Edmonton.*

food tickets as a form of deterrent. The Guardians were attacked by the *Gazette* for the new casual wards which they had built. 'Tramps are flocking to Edmonton from near and far', the paper alleged, apparently to enjoy the new

65.   *During the prolonged miners' strike of 1926 Enfield adopted two poverty-stricken mining villages, Abergwynfi and Blaengwynfi. A relief lorry being prepared outside the Baptist church in Cecil Road.*

'feather beds, spring mattresses and shower baths'. Among these must have been many men coming from depressed areas in search of work. Parishes in the Edmonton Union, which bore the cost of extreme poverty in Edmonton and Tottenham, stood to benefit when the poor rate was equalised over the whole county after 1929. All the functions of the Board of Guardians were transferred in March 1930, by the Local Government Act of 1929 and the Poor Law Act 1930, to Middlesex County Council.[38]

67.   *Nearly all the factories in the Queensway were taken by 1929, mostly by firms engaged in the wireless and electrical industries. Photographs 1992.*

The depression was less enduring and less severe in Enfield than it was in many other places. Enfield was an area of high technology in which the electrical industries predominated. 'Many of our manufacturers', said Mr Morson, 'continued an important export trade'. Conditions were in no way comparable to South Wales, where Enfield adopted two mining villages, Abergwynfi and Blaengwynfi, with a combined population of five thousand. Almost all the men in these villages were unemployed as the Christmas of 1928 approached. One house, visited by Enfield charity organisers, was bare except for a bed, mattress and coverlet. There was no bed clothing, no floor-cloth, no chairs, nor any other furniture. The *Enfield Gazette* at this time displayed advertisements showing enticing toys for children; doll's prams 7s 6d to £4 10s, a milk-float in wood for 9s 6d, a General omnibus at 14s 6d, fairy cycles 36s 6d to 65s, and for mum perhaps, a cosy ladies dressing gown 4s 11d (in silk from 29s 11d). For dad a gramophone, the 'table grand' with three records would cost £2 2s, a consul model anything from £7 19s 6d, a four valve portable wireless could be had for £27 10s. Wages, apart from those of the miners, remained stable over the three years 1926-29 while the cost of living fell by fifteen points.[39]

Industry was relieved of two-thirds of its contribution to local rates by the budget of April 1928; that relief was increased to seventy-five per cent under the Local Government Act of 1929. Now future expansion locally looked likely to be hampered only by a lack of skilled labour, for there remained a serious shortage of working-class houses, and skilled men in search of work had little hope of finding homes to rent in Enfield. Indeed many of the workmen employed in Enfield factories travelled from London. There was a strike at Yager's in 1929. Three hundred men came out when the firm decided to introduce Saturday morning working without extending the hours or paying overtime; this would mean fares six days a week and no extra pay.[40]

The Acme Show Card Company planned to build a factory at Brimsdown in September 1929 to employ some two hundred and fifty hands. The firm wanted to bring its own skilled labour and applied to the Council for twenty or thirty houses on the new Brimsdown estate. They offered to purchase them for £25 down and the rest by instalments, but the Council refused, insisting upon their three-year residential qualification. Nevertheless the firm went ahead and put up a modern factory in Green Street.[41]

Late in the year 1928 industry began to take advantage of the area opened up by the Cambridge arterial road. The first to do so was British Sangamo, makers of electric meters, which moved there from Ponders End. The firm, which had large factories in other parts of the world, took nine acres; the new site would include a sports field. Nearly all the factories in the Queensway, built to let, were taken by 1929. Industry remained concentrated south of Southbury Road, but new factories were being attracted further north where areas were designated for industry between the King George reservoir and the railway, and between the Cambridge Road and the Hertford Road.[42]

4. Industry and Depression in the Thirties

A world-wide slump was triggered off by the Wall Street crash of October 1929. The year 1930 was one of lamentable depression, there was heavy loss of wages at the RSAF. The best that could be said at Enfield Cables was that 1930 was no worse than 1929. The firm had had some successes. The laying of cables in Sydney Harbour had been completed on time, the company had been awarded

INDUSTRY AT BRIMSDOWN, 1936

A This was originally the site of the Brimsdown Lead Works, subsequently
   the London Foundry Co. The Rolling Mills were set up in 1924.

B The original building was formerly a varnish factory.

Many of the factories are served by railway sidings.

a special contract in north-west England to install the grid system for the Central
Electricity Board, also the contract for cable to connect power stations and sub-
stations in the east Midlands. The profits for the year ending 31 December 1930
were £160,775 as against £129,775 for the previous year. Cosmos had now
become part of Associated Electrical Industries; the factory concentrated on the
manufacture of Mazda wireless valves.[43]

   The number of unemployed in the Enfield Unemployment Exchange Area
(which also included Waltham Cross, Waltham Abbey and Cheshunt) continued to increase through the year 1930-31, among men by eight per cent, among
women by a hundred and twenty-five per cent. There were, in August 1931,
plans to build a second carriageway on both the Cambridge Road and the North
Circular Road, as an unemployment relief scheme. Unemployment benefit was
cut by the new National Government that autumn and its duration was reduced,
leaving it finally at twenty-six weeks. After this period the unemployed had to

apply to the local Public Assistance Committee (from 1934 to the Unemployment Assistance Board) where relief was paid subject to a means test. The National Unemployed Workers Union held a march early in December from Nags Head Road to Edmonton Green and thence to the Union Workhouse. The Amalgamated Society of Woodworkers called a strike of its members working on the council housing estate at Suffolks. Unemployment continued to rise; most of the unemployed who found work, found it for themselves and not through the labour exchanges, where the staff now spent more time paying out benefit than in placing men in employment. The County had been forced to spend £350,000 on outdoor relief over the year 1931/2 as against £250,000 in the previous twelve months.[44]

Yet steady expansion was maintained in the local electrical industry. Belling Lee were making satisfactory progress at the Queensway; theirs was the only factory in England specialising in the manufacture of terminals for wireless work. The firm took a new two and a quarter acre site on the Cambridge Road and building began there in February 1932. It would have 22,000 square feet of floor space, more than double the size of the Queensway factory, and it would employ six hundred workers. They proposed a research department and a workshop for the manufacture of tools. The factory architect was Donald Hamilton, who also designed the Tudor Room in Gentleman's Row and was working on houses in Glebe Avenue and Windmill Hill. The radio factory with its white stuccoed front was ready by June 1932. Belling Lee had been set up by C. R. Belling and E. M. Lee only ten years earlier. Until 1924 it had made radios but it was found that the production of components was more remunerative. The new works covered only one-third of the Cambridge Road site, for the time being the remainder could be used as a sports club ground, with swimming, netball and cricket sections.[45]

There was another strike in February 1931 at Yager's Charlotte Cabinet Works in Wharf Road. Four hundred men and women came out because the ten

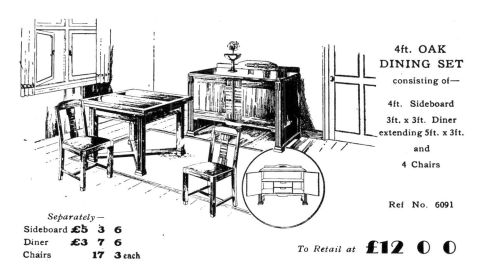

4ft. OAK
DINING SET
consisting of—

4ft. Sideboard
3ft. x 3ft. Diner
extending 5ft. x 3ft.
and
4 Chairs

Ref No. 6091

Separately —
Sideboard £5 3 6
Diner   £3 7 6
Chairs   17 3 each

To Retail at £12 0 0

68. Furniture produced at Yager's, 1934.

minute tea break, mornings and afternoons, had been withdrawn. The firm advertised for replacement labour, offering 'union rates and over …, constant employment guaranteed'.[46]

At the Royal Small Arms Factory there were grievances among the work-force, piece-work was being abolished and it was claimed that 160 skilled men and 340 unskilled men would lose 13s to 20s a week. Numbers at the factory had been reduced to little more than a thousand. A seven per cent wage cut was imposed on skilled workers in September 1931 and labourers found their wages reduced from 49s to 46s a week. A total of eight hundred men were affected. London General Omnibus Company busmen also suffered cuts in their wages, yet at this time a substantial increase in the salaries of local government officers was recommended by chief officers and adopted by the Urban District Council. Local government salaries in Enfield were said to be thirty-three per cent higher than the average for England and Wales. The total cost of Council salaries in 1914 had been £4,780. In 1922 it was £13,530, in 1931 it was £15,997, yet the cost of living in 1931 was lower than it had been in 1922. The rise in local government salaries was not in line with the trend of middle-class pay in general. In October, the bazaar at St Stephen's Church, in a very middle-class area, was postponed 'because of potential and actual reductions in incomes caused by the disturbing position of national finance'. Many of the unskilled and semi-skilled workers at the RSAF were members of the Transport and General Workers Union, formerly the Workers Union. The engineers belonged to the Amalgamated Engineering Union which summoned a meeting to oppose the wage cuts, but by November 1931 seven or eight hundred men were faced with another cut in wages. Men now found themselves discharged at the age of sixty-one. A hundred and fifty semi-skilled men were sacked in 1932. A deputation from the RSAF and the powder mills, led by J. McGrath went to the War Office in February 1933, once again to demand the restoration of pension rights which had been abolished as long ago as 1870; to fill the gap the trade unions ran pension schemes of their own. Another deputation went to see Duff Cooper (Financial Secretary at the War Office 1931-4) to ask for a 10s increase, but their claim was rejected. Exclusive of a war bonus (12s) the rates for a forty-seven hour week in April 1933 were: mechanics 49s 6d, machinists 36s 6d and labourers 34s. They were certainly not better paid than other local factory workers. J. M. McGrath retired from the factory after forty years service in July 1933. He was a native of Birmingham, of Irish parentage, and he had come to Enfield before the turn of the century when, he said, 'there was neither house nor light between Ordnance Road and Waltham Cross'. In 1903 he became the secretary of the Factory Union of Small Arms Workers which was amalgamated in 1915 with the Workers Union. The Workers Union, in 1928, became part of the Transport & General Workers' Union. McGrath remained local secretary until April 1938. The War Office, up to 1909, had refused to recognise the union, wages at that time had been 7s to 10s for a fifty-four hour week. The unions had fought throughout for the restoration of their long lost pension rights. It was not until early in the year 1939, with the threat of war again hanging over the country, that an arrangement was reached for a pension scheme to be administered by a private insurance company.[47]

The boom which began in private house building in the early Thirties proved a great stimulus to the electrical industry in the area. Ediswan's had recently incorporated the wiring supply department of British Thompson Houston, also

69.   *Gigantic concrete cooling towers 168 feet high were erected at the Brimsdown power station in 1930; they were said to be the first of their kind in England.*

the commercial lighting business of Metro Vickers, in consequence the Ponders End factory was equipped with the latest machinery. The firm purchased a new fleet of vans in December 1932, 'This' said the managing director, 'is an indication of our optimism'. British electrical manufacturers were making a big push to capture the whole of the domestic market in electrical appliances and radio. There had been a vast increase since the war in signs and advertisements using coloured electrical light bulbs, many of them produced at Ediswan's. The firm was making an all-electric wireless receiver called the Pentogram.[48]

Gigantic concrete cooling towers 168 feet high were erected at the power station in 1930, they were said to be the first of their kind in England. There had been many wooden cooling towers but these were the first made round (or oval) and constructed of concrete; they were built in the shape of milk churns. The company had previously drawn water from the Lea, under contract, to cool the condensers, but now it had been forced to find water elsewhere. At the beginning of the year 1932, the Northmet sought power in Parliament to raise a further £1.5m. The company continued to grow; in 1919 its business had covered 326 square miles, by 1934 it covered 660 square miles; in 1919 it had produced 53 million units, by 1934, 352 million. By the end of the year 1934 there were 254,735 consumers. The role of the company in the life of north London was brought home to the public when a fire occurred at the power station in September 1935; trams and tubes came to a halt, factories shut, and homes and cinemas were plunged into darkness.[49]

By the beginning of 1932 there was growing optimism over the prospects for industry in Enfield; rumour asserted that many foreign firms were moving into north London. Enfield by this time had at least fifteen factories employing overall more than two thousand people in the radio industry, which continued to expand despite the depression. British Sangamo employed three hundred at their works on the Cambridge Road where they made five hundred electric meters a day and all the parts were produced in England. Bakelite was the material of the moment; invented in Germany, it had been used in America since 1925. It was now being processed in Enfield at the Bell Moulding Company in the Queensway. So widespread was the use of bakelite parts that several local factories had set up special departments to meet their own requirements.[50]

Another firm which prospered despite the depression was Edwardson's Enfield Soap Works. A new thirty-foot boiler was installed there in November 1931 as part of an expansion. It was to be used for the manufacture of 'Diamond' soap flakes. Edwardson's was the only large local factory which remained a one-man undertaking; it was owned and managed by E. W. Edwardson, chairman of the Urban District Council and chairman of the Enfield Manufacturers Association. Morson's was now the largest manufacturer of potassium iodide in the country. A new factory was built in 1931 at Brimsdown for the Acme Show Card Company. The Tottenham and District Gas Company reported a rapid and continuous increase in business. There was a strong feeling of optimism. Dr Raymond Unwin, the town planning specialist, was invited to survey the Lea Valley. He proposed that the ten miles from Walthamstow to Waltham Cross should be converted into a model industrial area with model factories and workshops, recreation grounds, walks and parks, of over six hundred and fifty acres.[51]

Unemployment nevertheless persisted and was still rising; it reached a peak of nearly three million in January 1933. Even in Enfield, 3,825 were registered at the unemployment exchange in March 1932, which was a rise of 757 over the previous year, a thousand of them were no longer in receipt of benefit, having been unemployed more than 156 days. Practically every night the numbers arriving at the casual ward, and these included many men from the depressed areas looking for work, exceeded the accommodation available there. An unemployed Enfield man from Grove Road West got six months for poaching in the home plantation in Theobalds Park (owned by James Warren JP) although he claimed that he was only after rabbits; the man had a wife and six children under fourteen. Several hundred hunger marchers passed through eastern Enfield in October 1932 in a protest against the means test; they were

HARLIE BROS. NEW FACTORY

ON THE CAMBRIDGE ARTERIAL ROAD

70. Despite the depression Harlie Bros built this fine factory on the Cambridge Road, opened in 1932, to manufacture equipment for the 'talkies', gramophone motors and pick-ups, loudspeakers and microphones. The architect was Donald Hamilton. (Gazette 8 July 1932)

joined by a contingent from Edmonton. The numbers of unemployed locally however, from 1933 began slowly to decline; according to figures from the Enfield Emergency Employment Council, in June 1933 there were 1,633 men out of work. Local industry was expanding rapidly, 138 factories had been built in the eight years up to 1932 at a cost of £500,000 and forty-two more were in the course of erection in the summer of 1932 including Harlie Bros new factory covering twenty thousand square feet on the Cambridge Road. The firm had moved there from Edmonton; it made electric gramophone motors, loudspeakers and microphones. Industry was moving south from Yorkshire and Lancashire. A huge scrap-yard in Old Road near the Roebuck, stacked high with the remains of dismantled factories like Nobel's and the Brimsdown Lead Works, was evidence of the changing nature of local industry.[52]

The year 1933 had been a difficult one at the Rolling Mills but, although the company had faced vicious competition, more orders came in during the second half of the year and trading profits rose. There was an industrial dispute in May 1934 among the men transferred from Scotland, who claimed that a verbal assurance given to them about wages and the cost of rail fares had not been kept. A number of these men had been dismissed and the firm, although willing to recognise their union, was unwilling to reinstate those discharged. A settlement was arrived at in June. The dismissed Scottish workmen were to return to their previous employment with compensation, and the company offered to pay their fares and removal expenses. Enfield Cables, by the beginning of the year 1933, could claim to be 'in the forefront of the industry', its plant 'right up to date' and designed for the production of the highest class electric cables, wire and strips. The firm was busier than it had been for years. By 1935 it had almost reached the level of prosperity it had enjoyed before the

slump in 1929. Its shares at the beginning of the year stood at 82s; at the end of
the year they had reached 130s. The year 1936 surpassed all previous years in
production and in the number employed at the firm, machinery was being
constantly replaced and an up-to-date rubber plant would be completed by
September 1937. The expansion went on throughout the year 1938 when the
trading profit amounted to £94,000, which compared well with £76,000 in 1937,
£9,000 in 1936 and £6,000 in 1935. A rod rolling mill which had closed in
September 1937 was reopened; £80,000 had been spent on further stocks of
copper and £70,000 on increasing refinery capacity. Production costs had been
brought down.[53]

Permission was given by the Ministry in March 1934 to build twelve new single
storey factories in South Street, thus reversing a previous decision of the Urban
District Council. Four modern factories were being offered on the Brimsdown
factory estate in 1934, each measuring sixty feet by a hundred and twenty-six, to
be let or sold by the Northmet Company ready for occupation. One of the few
remaining industrial sites on the Cambridge Road was sold in December 1934
to Sidney S. Bird and Son precision engineers, makers of radio instruments. It
was the third nationally known radio firm to have acquired a site in the vicinity
within three years. The building was nearing completion in June 1935, looking
very modern in black faience with rustless steel bands and balustrading. Also on
the Cambridge Road, British Sangamo had developed so rapidly that the works
had to be extended time and time again. The opening of a major extension at
the beginning of August 1935 was marked by a celebration in which the deputy
sales manager played the part of the mayor of Spike Island. (The area in Duck
Lees Lane, over the railway line, which had been the site of their first factory in
1920). The firm was a pioneer in the manufacture of meters and time switches. It
introduced the three-coin electric meter, to take a penny, sixpence or a shilling.[54]

Five hundred girls had been taken on at Cosmos in the second half of the year
1934. The factory had recently been extended. It was the home of the Mazda
valve and was one of the largest valve manufacturing centres in the country. The
firm was having so much difficulty finding skilled labour that a training centre
had been established. Fifteen hundred people were employed in the works and
eight hundred sat down to dinner in the staff canteen. There was a social and
sports club with nine hundred members. A second carriageway was opened in
July 1934 on the Cambridge Road stretching north as far as Silver Street Edmonton, also on the North Circular between Edmonton and Palmers Green.[55]

There was an overall shortage of skilled labour in Enfield in 1935. An appeal
was made in September for householders willing to board and lodge lads
between fourteen and eighteen coming from depressed areas who wanted to
take jobs locally. The Ministry of Labour paid their travel costs and helped with
the rent of lodgings. Twenty-seven lads from South Wales found work here in
the electrical industry. A number of unemployed men from Hartlepool were
invited to the RSAF in October 1935 for an interview and a month's trial, but
most of them were rejected on medical grounds. The management then refused
to provide railway warrants to get them back home, but fortunately the AEU
supplied the money.[56]

The shortage of labour in Enfield had become worse by 1936. Belling Lee had
vacancies for skilled men on radio and aircraft work, the minimum wage was £3
10s for a 40-hour week in summer, and a 47 to 54-hour week (including
overtime) in winter, with paid holidays after one year. Boys were offered training

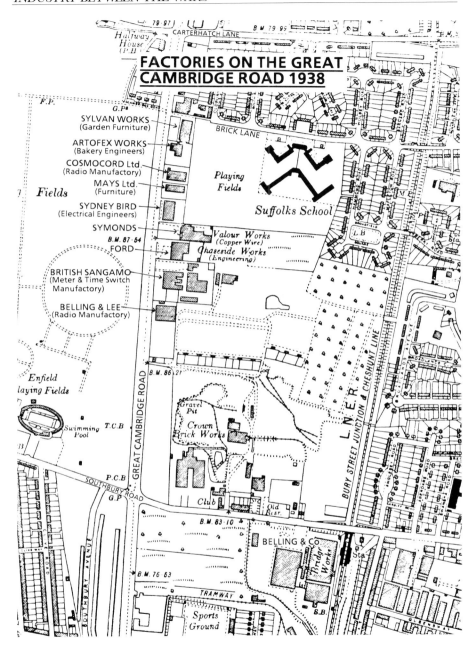

FACTORIES ON THE GREAT CAMBRIDGE ROAD 1938

SYLVAN WORKS
(Garden Furniture)

ARTOFEX WORKS
(Bakery Engineers)

COSMOCORD Ltd.
(Radio Manufactory)

MAYS Ltd.
(Furniture)

SYDNEY BIRD
(Electrical Engineers)

SYMONDS

FORD

BRITISH SANGAMO
(Meter & Time Switch
Manufactory)

BELLING & LEE
(Radio Manufactory)

and were paid 16s at the age of fourteen, rising to 27s at the age of eighteen and 54s at twenty-one. Girls were paid 25s at the age of eighteen and 31s at the age of twenty-one. A canteen was provided. Freeder's Paper Mills in Millmarsh Lane advertised for labour in November 1936 to meet vast orders for Christmas and

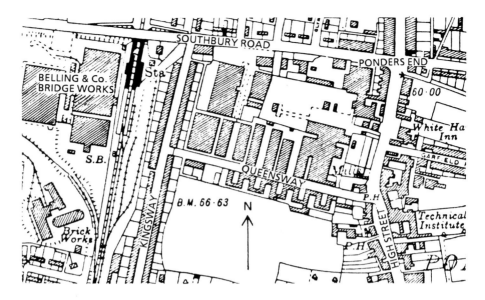

Electrical Factories in the Queensway, 1938

North side   South side

Kaye, E and E, wire manfrs.   British Electrical Resistance Co.
Rogat Tool and Stamping Co.   Electrical Products Ltd.
Knyveton electric cable manfrs.   Stadium Ltd. bakelite moulders
A E F accumulator makers   Haynes radio manfrs.
C W S radio cabinet factory   Standard Fuse Co.

Southbury Station opened in 1891 as Churchbury Station.
There was no passenger service between 1909 and 1960,
when the station re-opened as Southbury.

Coronation decorations. There were vacancies for fifty to a hundred men on day
and night shifts, also for girls on the day shifts. The firm paid Board of Trade
rates plus twenty-five per cent for overtime and fifty per cent for Saturday work.
Chamberlain and Willows announced a shortage of arterial road industrial sites
in the area. The Council took its duties in zoning industry seriously and the
application of Tricity Cookers in Parsonage Lane to extend was turned down;
nevertheless this little factory survived until the early Sixties. There was a strong
demand for single-storey factory premises and although the prices had risen,
such buildings were eagerly purchased. A shortage of land scheduled for
industrial purposes in Enfield was becoming apparent by January 1937 and
extensions had been made to fifty-two others. Commercial Structures Ltd
sought permission to build seven factories on the south-east corner of the
Cambridge Road junction with Lincoln Road, but they were in dispute with the

*71. Industry expanded rapidly
in the Brimsdown area in the
twelve months up to April 1937.
Industrial smells ruined the lives
of those who lived on nearby
estates.* (Gazette *26 March 1937*)

BRIMSDOWN'S EASTER EGG

County Council which wanted to limit to one, the number of access points onto
the Cambridge Road.[57]

Belling and Co. celebrated a twenty-fifth anniversary in December 1937. The
firm had commenced business in a garage (which still stands) at the back of the
Hop Poles in Lancaster Road, in 1912. Charles Belling had formerly worked for
Crompton and Co. Later he joined Ediswan's as superintendent of three
departments, then resolved to start up business for himself, making electric
fires. His capital amounted to only £450, but he employed a fitter and a boy, who
had to make their own benches and stools on which they fitted up a few vices,
drills and other small assembling appliances. Charles Belling devised and
patented the first successful electric firebar by winding a resistance wire on the
face of a strip of fire-clay. He also patented an electric geyser. The first Belling
electric fire was marketed in 1912, although at that time only about two per cent
of homes were connected to the mains. Belling's first catalogue was printed by
Bennett and Starling on Windmill Hill and orders began to come in fast. The
following year the firm moved to Derby Road Edmonton and during the First
World War it did a great deal of work for the Admiralty. The Derby Road factory
was gutted by fire in 1921 and for some time the company used the former shell
works at the end of South Street. A ten-acre site in Southbury Road was
purchased in 1924 and a new factory was built. At first it comprised only six bays,
but by 1937 forty bays had been erected and it employed between seven
hundred and fifty and a thousand workers. It was among the largest factories in
the country devoted exclusively to the manufacture of electric heating and
cooking appliances. At the Royal Small Arms Factory the Lewis gun was being
replaced by a Czechoslovakian designed weapon known as the Brende; the War
Office had reached an agreement to use the Czech patent. The Brende gun
(subsequently the Bren) was said to have greater portability than the Lewis and
it would cost less. It was further asserted by one of our forward-looking army
commanders that it would be 'suitable for the cavalry'. Leslie Hore-Belisha, the
War Minister, visited the factory in January 1939 to see the manufacture of Bren
gun parts, the weapon by this time was in full production. War was on the

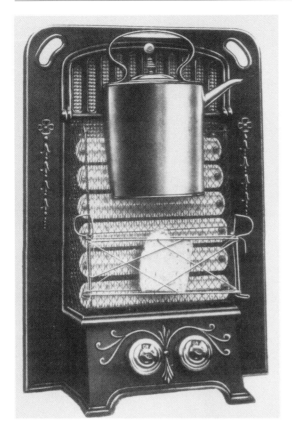

72.   The 3kW 'Standard' was the first Belling electric fire to go into production. The frame, built high and wide enough to cover up a normal fireplace, was made for Charles Belling by Mr Oxspring of Ponders End who had formerly been a pattern maker at Ediswan's. The firebars were manufactured in Burslem. This design remained in production until 1927. Tea and toast apparently in preparation.

73.   The Derby Road Works Edmonton, 1913.

horizon, and concrete dug-outs had been constructed on the open space at the rear of the factory. The Bren was being produced in thousands using up-to-date plant; the Enfield factory was the main producer in this country. Two years earlier only nine hundred men had been employed at the RSAF, by 1938 there were 3,400 workers and full production had been reached. For many years the unions at the factory had sought a pension scheme, now at last terms were agreed for pensions to be taken over by a private insurance company.[58]

5. Brickworks

Brickmaking remained at a standstill after the First World War. At one time the trade had employed many hundreds of men in Enfield. 'For the last two years', said the *Gazette* (15 February 1918) 'hardly any bricks have been made... now the brick-kilns are deserted'. Valuable plant had been lying idle for ten years at the London Brick Company premises in Southbury Road. The company was bankrupt. The receiver offered to allow the works to open provided the profits were used to pay the debts, but work was not resumed. There was such a desperate shortage of bricks in the area in 1919 that bricks from the recently demolished Fir Tree House in Silver Street sold for £34.[59]

The brick trade had many problems. There was labour trouble. The workers had agreed a hundred per cent pay rise but they now demanded a hundred and fifty per cent and they had some justification, for the percentage offered was on pre-war wages, and prices had risen by a hundred and fifty per cent. The industry was impeded by the poor state of the railways; coal was difficult to get, sand had to be brought from beyond Southend, and the chalk from Kent.

The manufacture of London yellow stock bricks, of which most of the houses in Enfield had been built before the war, was a seasonal trade. Preparation was done in the autumn and winter, the making in the spring and summer. The main producing season was from Easter until the end of October, after this the weather became too cold and damp to dry the bricks outside, for they had to be dried before they were burnt. Only a few skilled men were employed throughout the whole year, the remainder were stood down at the end of each season. Brickmaking was a relatively well-paid job, though employees had to work hard for long hours at piece-rates to get their money. Some of the men managed to live on what they had saved during the working season, others found winter work elsewhere, as at Ponders End gas works where they needed additional workers every winter. Fletton or Peterborough bricks could be produced throughout the year, being made by machinery and from an entirely different material.

The Ministry of Health in 1919 investigated the supply of bricks for urgently needed housing and reported that ample stocks existed in Enfield. The Ministry was wrong, said the trade, the only bricks in the district were at Mr Dearsley's Crown Brickworks in Southbury Road and these had been standing there for years and were fit only for interior work, or exteriors intended to be roughcast. There was a large quantity of bricks in Edmonton; these had been commandeered by the government during the war but had now been released following the armistice. One prominent brickmaker stated that he knew of no other stock of bricks in north or east London, and no yards were working in that whole area in the summer of 1919.[60]

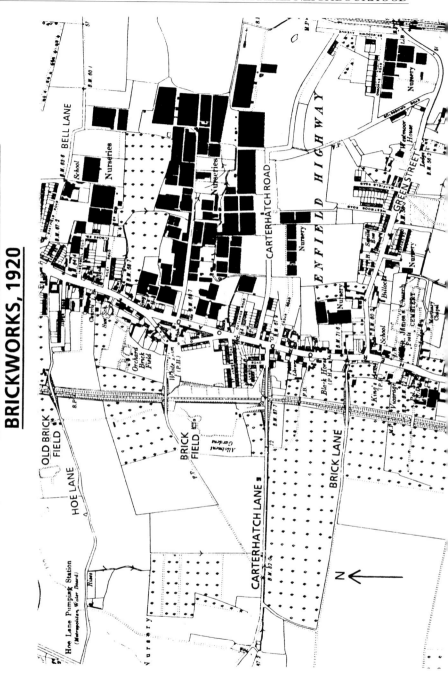

MAP OF THE ORCHARDS, NURSERIES AND BRICKWORKS, 1920

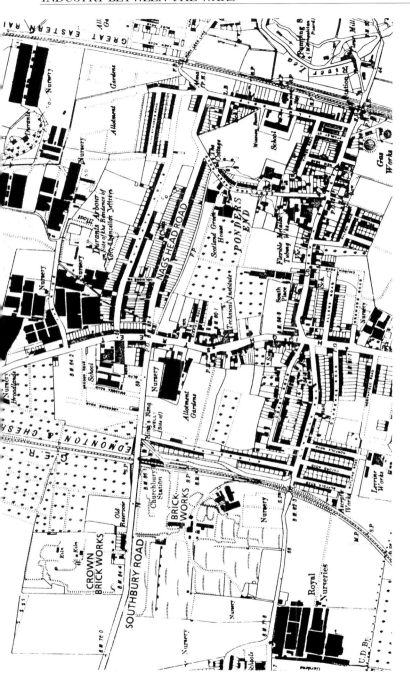

NURSERIES

ORCHARDS

<u>KEY</u>

The local brick industry was operating again by 1924. The Enfield Red Brick Company, part of the London Brick Co., had fields of seventy acres stretching from Churchbury station (now Southbury Road) to Lincoln Road. The firm had a drying plant installed. The *Enfield Gazette* (27 June 1924) described their process in some detail. The top-soil was removed by spade to about eighteen inches. The clay was then dug and heaped to mature for about six weeks. It was then moistened to the right consistency, loaded into tip wagons and passed into a mixer, then into a Monarch Sextuple machine which made six bricks at a time and delivered the moulded bricks on boards. Seventy thousand best quality sand-faced red bricks could now be produced ready for drying, in fifty hours. The drying plant had four huge chambers, fifteen feet by a hundred and thirty feet. Each could accommodate thirty-five thousand bricks and was heated by hot water pipes. The baking was done in a Hoffman kiln, built by J. C. Hill in 1898; he had already been using this type of kiln at Fletton.[61] It was he who introduced all-the-year-round production in Enfield. The Hoffman kiln, located near the railway line, just north of what is now Lincoln Way, was an oval building. Its tall chimney became a landmark across the flat countryside between Ponders End and the Town. The Enfield Red Brick Company continued to produce top quality red bricks until about 1937. The Hoffman kiln was subsequently used as metal smelting works by Platt Metals Ltd.

Firms making bricks by hand could only compete by producing bricks of the highest quality, as Cornish did. Four thousand workers in the brick, tile and pipe industries were registered unemployed in the spring of 1924, despite the fact that there was a serious shortage of bricks and the price was rising. The Crown Brickworks, set up in Southbury Road somewhere about 1898 (it became the Crown Brickworks in 1903), reopened there in July 1924. It was an old brickfield covering twenty-eight acres of which fourteen acres were being worked; output by 1925 was running at five million a year. The firm took over the Lea Valley Brickworks just to the north. The yellow stock bricks in which the firm specialised were of the finest quality and extremely enduring. The work called for hand labour from start to finish. Brick-earth (seventy-five per cent) was mixed with twelve and a half per cent fine ashes from the Council's dust collection, the remainder was chalk paste. The chalk was brought from Ware and it gave the bricks their characteristic yellow colour. The owners, Kirk and Randall, went bankrupt in March 1927. The new owners retained the name Crown Brickworks and by 1929, apart from bricks, they were doing a good trade in breeze slabs and in ballast dug on the ground. By 1930 the firm was so far mechanised that the material for brickmaking was being pumped from the mill in liquid state.[62] The firm continued working at least until 1955. Cornish's too continued after the Second World War, working an area south of the Enfield Crematorium, where they had four beehive type kilns producing about fifty thousand high quality red bricks a week. Many went to the building of the new towns at Harlow and Stevenage. The Cornish family finally handed over to Gabriel's in 1963 and brick production continued there until 1976; after that the firm concentrated on gravel extraction. Brickmakers in Enfield found it difficult to obtain labour in the years after 1945 and were dependent on the skills of a few elderly men. Thus brickmaking finally ceased in Enfield in 1976. Most of this information is taken from the late Sidney M. Beadle's *Bricks and Brickmaking in Enfield, Edmonton and Tottenham*, which he kindly allowed me to consult before publication.

6. Nurseries and Farms

Milk production after the war moved away from the vicinity of London, and although some of Middleton's milk was still produced locally in 1919, it could be produced much more cheaply at places fifty or sixty miles into the country. Milk consumption in Enfield decreased, it was said, by a thousand gallons a week when the price went up in November 1918 to a shilling a quart. Dairy farming nevertheless continued throughout the 1920s. Harry Hobson, of Olive Cottage Farm in Crews Hill, had one of the finest Friesian herds in the county; it was sold in 1928.[63]

T. H. Roest developed a large poultry farm in Turkey Street. Beginning in the early Twenties with a few fowls, he carefully chose the most suitable breeds to prosper in local muddy conditions; Rhode Island Reds, White Wyandottes, Buff Orpingtons and, his first choice, White Leghornes. He began with an eighty-egg incubator and by 1925 he had forty buildings in use, hatching eight hundred chicks at a time. Keeping chickens was a popular pastime among the working-class suburban householders for whom the firm mainly catered That was the reason why all their birds were kept in open wire pens, on earth floors, drained with clinker and covered with six inches of golden sand from Hertford Heath. The firm ran into desperate financial difficulty in 1933 and it led to the suicide of Danny Roest. [64]

A good many pigs were kept in Enfield. It was said that London swill fattened London pork, but Mr Moore who held Olive Cottage Farm in 1926, stocked three hundred pigs and insisted that he used only natural food. Adjacent to Southbury Road, at Bury Farm, Alfred Bath carried on market gardening and fruit growing and had 150 pigs as a sideline, fed upon his surplus produce with the addition of good barley. The pigs were given the run of his orchards and meadows. He sold most of them to local butchers. Chase Farm School kept a hundred pigs and supplied the North Middlesex Hospital. Fruit growers, in the late Twenties, faced new difficulties from gangs of youths from all over north London who came out along the new arterial road to carry out wholesale raids on the orchards.[65]

Following the armistice many local disabled soldiers were trained at Bury Farm in Southbury Road to take smallholdings, but market gardening no longer flourished in Enfield as it had done before the war and they did badly. Alfred Bath JP of Bury Farm, attributed the decline to a steep fall in prices which had been accompanied by no corresponding fall in the cost of production. The withdrawal of the government subsidy at the end of the war had added to farmers' difficulties. Mr Bath had seen certified accounts showing a loss to one grower of £2,574 in 1921, and £1,626 in 1922. Mr Bath felt that the difference between the retail price and the price of produce on leaving the farm was too wide. The year 1923 was a bad one for the glasshouse industry. At Parson's Nursery, where the houses covered nearly twenty acres, three thousand tons of anthracite had to be used through the cold spring. Two large motor lorries left the firm's Carterhatch Road nurseries two or three times a day for Covent Garden. Output each season was four hundred tons of tomatoes and thirty thousand dozen cucumbers, but the company faced strong competition from Holland and the Channel Islands, where wages were only 30s a week. At home the nursery industry was afflicted by unrest over wage rates, the minimum paid was 10d an hour. Workers at two nurseries at Turnford considered strike action, but decided to negotiate. They were seeking 48s for a forty-eight hour week, with overtime at time and a quarter and Sunday work at time and a half.[66]

The industry survived and in 1926 the Lea Valley remained the largest tomato growing district in the country, with a thousand acres devoted to this one crop and an output of 35,000 tons. Only about three varieties were grown, Ailsa Craig was perhaps the favourite. Tomatoes occupied the glasshouses for so many months of the year that it was impossible to grow a second (different) crop. Between 15,000 and 17,000 plants grew in each house, right up to the top of the roof, so that steps had to be used to pick them. All this fruit had to be sold immediately. The great grievance in the industry was that the French and the Dutch crop entered the country duty free, and foreign production costs were lower. Vine growing in the neighbourhood, it was said, had been almost wiped out by foreign competition, though grapes were still being grown by E. Matthews at Durants Arbour in 1929.[67]

There had been no organisation to represent the interests of the growers until 1909. At that time the Lea Valley Growers Association had been set up to fight an attempt by the Edmonton Union to raise the assessments on the nurseries. The matter was contested in the county court at Hertford, which found in favour of the nurserymen. The association had been instrumental in establishing an experimental and research station at Cheshunt in 1914; in June 1925 this was replaced by a more advanced research station at Turners Hill. The association had some two hundred members by 1926. Non-returnable boxes were then being made for the Glasshouse Marketing Association at a large factory in Bullsmoor Lane.[68]

Stuart Low held a hundred acres at Carterhatch Lane where shrubs were grown and the firm still operated its Bush Hill Park nursery where they produced fruit trees, roses and carnations. Many of their carnation varieties were given local names; 'Sir Philip Sassoon', 'Lady Inverforth' and 'Arnos Grove'. The Tollgate nurseries at Bullsmoor Lane had a vast collection of ferns kept in sixty greenhouses. Carter Page had five acres of glasshouses at Hyde Side Edmonton, and sixteen acres at Eversley Park Road, mainly given over to the development of dahlias. Pollard's had nineteen acres at Cheshunt, eight acres at Waltham Cross, and nine acres at Turnford; they grew tomatoes, cucumbers, roses and arum lilies and had formerly grown grapes. George Monro Ltd provided various services to the local greenhouse industry; soil analysis, fertilisers, insecticides, boxes and stores. The LNER, becoming belatedly conscious of increasing competition from road transport, in June 1926 offered to provide additional sidings at Cheshunt and Broxbourne to meet the requirements of the nurserymen.[69]

Foreign competition continued to bear heavily on the industry as the winter approached in 1927. It was thought that many hands would have to be discharged, and since the workers were not covered by unemployment insurance, they would not be able to claim the dole. Under the Rating and Valuation Act 1927, the nurseries were relieved of seventy-five per cent of the poor rate

74 (opposite).   The glasshouse industry, although much diminished, survived in the area into the 1960s. The photographs show (top to bottom) the Carterhatch Nursery at the east end of Carterhatch Road, Smith's nursery on the north side of Turkey Street and Fidler's on the south side of Turkey Street, east of the Cambridge Road.

while the budget of 1928 made provision that agricultural land and buildings should be relieved from the payment of all rates from January 1929. These concessions were most welcome in a time of difficulty.[70]

Market gardening suffered badly in the worst years of the slump, 1929 and 1930. Alderman Bath was unable to dispose of his produce at a profit, either in the London markets or to local retailers; crops sent to market were often returned and thrown away. The glasshouse industry was badly affected by the unemployment in the north, its best customers for tomatoes and cucumbers had been the miners and northern factory workers. By 1931 hundreds of acres in the Lea Valley had gone out of production since the war. Two hundred out-of-work nurserymen responded to an advertisement for one gardener.[71]

An article in *The Times* on the tomato industry spoke of the difficulties caused by the unrestricted import of Dutch produce. One firm had shut down a hundred and twenty-five greenhouses, complaining that they were uneconomic, requiring heating six months in every year and consuming two thousand tons of expensive Welsh anthracite. The prices obtained by English growers had steadily declined. The gross price for 12lb of tomatoes in 1925 had been 6s 4d, by 1930 it had fallen to 5s. Randall of Cheshunt, who had been in business for twenty years, said that things were now more difficult than they had ever been. He had visited Holland to find out how the Dutch could produce so cheaply and he had concluded that the Dutch worked longer hours for lower wages. Fuel there was cheaper, and transport, being by canal, cost less than in this country. Water there was readily available from the canals, whereas here we had to dig wells three hundred feet deep.[72]

Badly needed help was given to the ailing industry by the exemption from rates after April 1929. At this time there were only nine hundred acres of tomatoes under glass in the Lea Valley and seventy-five acres of grapes. Acres of glass lay derelict, rendered useless by foreign imports. Grape growing was being killed by duties imposed in France and America. More relief was given by the Horticultural Products Act, passed in February 1932 which imposed permanent tariffs on the import of cucumbers, tomatoes, chrysanthemums and rose trees, all produced in the Lea Valley. The growers continued to complain, alleging that the duty on tomatoes was insufficient, nevertheless it was anticipated that many of the derelict glasshouses would soon be brought back into use. The Lea Valley at this time grew only tomatoes, cucumbers and chrysanthemums and there was a need to find new crops.[73]

An extension to the Cheshunt Research Station was begun in March 1932. It opened in July, and the Ministry of Agriculture agreed to pay seventy-five per cent of the costs. The imposition of tariffs had enabled growers to experiment; lettuce was proving to be a useful 'catch' crop at those times when the houses were empty. H. O. Larsen, chairman of the Lea Valley Growers Association, put the capital required for glasshouse production at £3,000 an acre, the gross output at £1,800 an acre. H. O. Larsen was a remarkable character, a Dane whose prosperity had grown from small beginnings. He acquired a castle in Denmark and the Beech Hill Park estate at Waltham Abbey and committed suicide in July 1934. Half the glasshouse industry of this country was still in the Lea Valley in 1932 and it remained the most intensively cultivated region in the world. New glasshouses were being built early in 1933, especially at Cheshunt, where lettuce was to be produced to replace imports from southern France. [74] The prosperity engendered by protection however proved short lived and by

August 1934 the market was flooded with Dutch produce sold at prices lower than before the war. Tomato growers faced ruin, workers were being dismissed. The tariffs imposed were now described as laughable.[75]

Notes to Chapter Two

1. *Gazette* 5 N, 17 D 1920, C. W. Radcliffe *Middlesex* 1939 p163
2. *Gazette* 11 F, 6 My, 23 S 1921
3. *ibid* 4 Au, 6 Oct, 5 My 1922
4. *ibid* 8 Au 1924, 5 Mr 1925, 25 N 1927, 16 Je, 4 Au 1922
5. *ibid* 5 Ja 1920
6. *ibid* 21 Jl 1922
7. *ibid* 3 Ja 1919, 12 N 1920, 24 Ja 1919, 26 Mr 1920
8. *ibid* 19 D, 14 N, 28 N 1919, 7 Mr 1924, 19 S 1919, 8 F 1929, 16 Ja 1920
9. *ibid* 27 Au, 21 Ja, 17 S 1920
10. *Tottenham and Edmonton Weekly Herald* 8, 15 Au 1919
11. *Gazette* 17 Oct 1919, 2 Ap 1920, Information Richard Slater
12. 25 Ap, 27 Au, 10 S 1920
13. *ibid* 8, 15, 29 Ap, 13 My 1921
14. *ibid* 21 Ap, 28 Oct 1921, 17 D 1920, 7 Ja, 11 F, 6 My 1921
15. *ibid* 14 Ja, 15 Ap, 1 Jl, 23 S 1921
16. *ibid* 16 D, 23 D 1921, 27 Ja, 28 Jl 1922
17. *ibid* 20 Je 1919, 23 Jl 1920, 21 Ja, 29 Jl, 12 Au 1921
18. *ibid* 13 Ja, 24 Mr, 1922
19. *ibid* 14 Jl, 1 S, 13 Oct 1922, 6 Ap 1923
20. *ibid* 2 My, 6 Je 1924
21. *ibid* 19 Mr 1926, 11 F 1927
22. *ibid* 7 Ap, 9 Je 1922, 11 Ja 1924, 20 F 1925
23. *ibid* 18 N 1921, 19, 26 My, 1 D 1922, 22 Je, 28 S 1923, 6 Mr 1925, 18 Ap 1924
24. *ibid* 18 Ja 1924, 20 Jl 1923, 1 F, 5 Jl 1924, 21 My 1926
25. *ibid* 9 Oct 1925, 20 N 1914, 5 S 1924, 24 F 1928, 1 Mr 1929
26. *ibid* 25 N 1927, 8 Au 1924, 13 Au 1926, mss *History of Enfield Rolling Mills* 1977
27. *Gazette* 16 My 1924
28. *ibid* 6 Je, 1 Au, 8 Au 1924, 13 S 1929
29. *ibid* 10 Ap, 27 F 1925, 12 Oct 1923, 11 S 1925
30. *ibid* 7 Oct 1927, 31 My 1929, 19 Mr 1926, 19 Au, 23 S 1927
31. *ibid* 22 F, 29 F, 21 Mr 1924, 26 Au 1927, 19 D 1924, 2 Jl 1926, 16 S 1927
32. *ibid* 30 Ja, 1 My 1925, 18 Ja 1929, 9 Oct 1925, 22 F 1929, 19 N, 26 Mr 1926
33. *ibid* 7 My 1926
34. *ibid* 14 My, 21My 1926
35. *ibid* 30 Jl, 15 Oct, 3 D, 10 D 1926, 2 D 1927
36. *ibid* 7 Oct, 25 N, 16 D 1927, information Michael Rye
37. *ibid* 30 S 1927
38. *ibid* 6 Ja, 20 Jl 1928, 22 Mr 1929
39. *ibid* 14 D 1928
40. *ibid* 27 Ap 1928, 19 Ap 1929
41. *ibid* 20 S, 11 Oct 1929
42. *ibid* 19 Oct 1928, 2 Au 1929
43. *ibid* 22 Au 1930, 21 Ja, 6 Mr 1931, 18 Jl 1930
44. *ibid* 26 Je, 7 Au, 4 D 1931, 13 My, 20 My, 3 Je 1932
45. *ibid* 31 Ja 1931, 12 F, 3 Je, 17 Je 1932
46. *ibid* 27 F 1931
47. *ibid* 28 Mr 1930, 11 S 1931, 26 F 1932, 18 S, 16 Oct, 25 S, 20 N 1931,5 F, 12 F, 26

F 1932, 24 F, 31 Mr, 7 Ap, 28 Jl 1933, 3 F 1939

48. *ibid* 18 D 1931, 9 D 1932, 2 My, 21 N 1930
49. *ibid* 2 My 1930, 15 Mr, 13 S 1935
50. *ibid* 29 Ja 1932, 13 N, 31 Jl 1931
51. *ibid* 2 Ja, 13 Mr, 22 My 1931
52. *ibid* 18 Mr 1932, 3 Ap 1931, 29 Ja, 28 Oct, 25N 1932, 22 Je 1933, 1 Jl, 8 Jl 1932, 2 Ja 1931, 26 Au 1932
53. *ibid* 2 Mr, 25 My, 8 Je 1934, 20 Ja 1933, 3 Ap 1936, 22 Ja 1937, 9 D 1938
54. *ibid* 11 My, 7 D 1934, 7 Je 1935
55. *ibid* 14 D, 6 Jl 1934
56. *ibid* 24 My, 27 S, 25 Oct 1935
57. *ibid* 2 Oct, 9 Oct, 27 N 1936, 8 Ja, 30 Ap, 4 Je 1937
58. *ibid* 24 D 1937, 2 Au 1935, 3 F 1939
59. *ibid* 28 Mr 1919
60. *ibid* 1 Au 1919
61. *ibid* 27 Je 1924
62. *ibid* 16 My 1924, 13 N 1925, 1 F 1929, 5 D 1930
63. *ibid* 12S 1919, 14 S 1928
64. *ibid* 6 F 1925, 25 Au 1933
65. *ibid* 22 Oct 1926, 14 Au 1925
66. *ibid* 4 My 1923, 1 Je 1923, 7 Mr 1924
67. *ibid* 13 S, 5 Ap 1929
68. *ibid* 27 Au 1926
69. *ibid* 28 Au 1929, 21 Au, 4 S, 16 Oct 1925, 18 Je 1926
70. *ibid* 21 Oct 1927, 27 Ap 1928
71. *ibid* 10 Oct, 5 D 1930
72. *ibid* 21 Au 1931
73. *ibid* 11 D 1931, 12 Au, 12 F, 29 Jl 1932
74. *ibid* 29 Jl 1932, 3 Mr 1933
75. *ibid* 31 Au 1934

Chapter Three

Housing and Politics Between the Wars

1. Introduction

Almost everybody, before the First World War, lived in private rented accommodation. By 1918 there was a desperate housing shortage in Enfield; only 163 additional houses had become available between 1912 and 1919. The high price of building, £1 per foot super, now rendered it uneconomic to build houses to rent to the less well-off. It was widely asserted that houses for the working class could only be provided by local authorities subsidised by central government but even these subsidised rents were too high for those for whom the houses were intended. Many tenants of the early municipal houses built in Enfield could only pay the rent by taking in lodgers. It was 1924 before Enfield Council began to seek economies by building terraced houses on cheaper sites; by this time too, building costs had fallen to 9s 4d per foot super. Lower costs meant lower rents and some of those living in the earlier more expensive council houses sought transfers to the new cheaper dwellings.

Private enterprise in Enfield tentatively resumed house building in 1923, but the houses they built were for sale. The high price of materials continued to discourage building, and house prices remained beyond the reach of people earning £3 to £4 a week. Two factors induced the boom which began in the Thirties. First there had been a growth in well-paid service and administrative jobs which, combined with a falling cost of living and low taxation (5½ per cent of income in 1937), gave the middle class greater purchasing power. Second, building societies, by reducing the rate of interest offered to savers late in the year 1932, were able to reduce mortgage interest to five and a half per cent; it subsequently fell to five per cent and even to four and a half per cent. Societies were by this time prepared to advance up to ninety per cent of the purchase price and repayment periods were extended from fifteen to twenty and even to thirty years. Further means were sought to reduce deposits to no more than five per cent of the building society valuations. Competition kept mortgage interest down throughout the Thirties. Building costs reached their lowest level in 1934.

People seeking new homes tended to move out radially from Tottenham, Edmonton and Wood Green to Enfield, Southgate, Cheshunt and Broxbourne. The new houses could offer electric light and power to people moving from privately rented, gas-lit accommodation. Bathrooms and inside water closets were an irresistible attraction. The upper middle class, no longer able to find

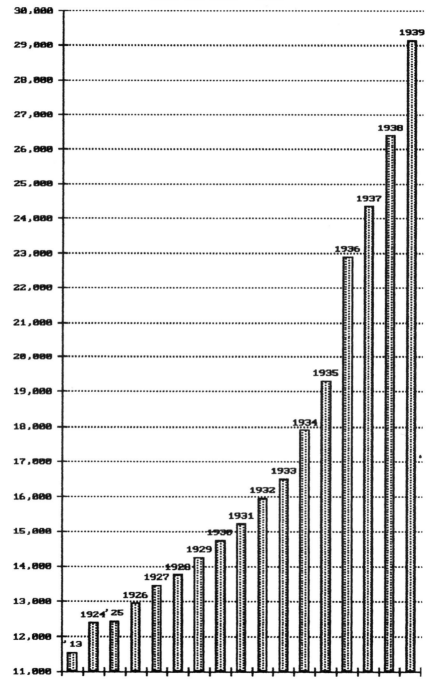

ENFIELD - INHABITED HOUSES
1913 and 1924 - 1939

servants, deserted their pre-war mansions for the modern detached or semi-detached. The semi-detached, built at between ten and twelve to an acre, offered privacy and living space, tree-lined roads and varied elevations, as for instance at Grange Park. The middle or well-paid working class, wishing to move, had little alternative but to buy.

The Piccadilly extension sought to encourage house building by low fares and through fares were issued on tube, bus and train to Enfield, thus passengers were attracted away from the steam trains on the lines to Enfield Town and Enfield Chase. The Piccadilly extension however got off to a slow start, only 500,000 passengers a year travelled from Arnos Grove in 1934 and little house building was begun around Oakwood, the nearest station to Enfield, until 1935. The provision of upper-middle-class housing ultimately reached saturation point and the builders turned their attention to the lower end of the middle-class market, even tempting the well-paid workman to purchase his own home.

Building societies promulgated a 'safe rule'; that total outgoings, including rates, should not exceed twenty-five per cent of income. Repayments could be as low as 9s a week plus rates. Larger firms like John Laing were able to buy land and materials in bulk at low cost and were prepared to accept a modest profit on a large turnover. Moreover they could supply professional, technical and skilled labour from within the organisation, thus eliminating the need to sub-contract. Similar economies could be effected by a group of companies; developer, builder and estate agent working together. In this way Hilbery Chaplin, the estate agent, was able to offer six-roomed houses locally for £390 freehold. The cheaper houses were terraced and some were provided with service roads at the back. Bungalows were often built where land was cheap, as at Theobalds Park Road. Until the mid-Thirties it was the practice for builders to cut down all the trees on newly acquired sites, but in order to attract buyers trees were now left standing, especially on former orchard land or parkland, as at Clydesdale, or on the South Lodge estate.

Building styles remained conservative between the wars. Houses in the manner of the modern movement, like those built in Park Crescent in 1932, were not sufficiently popular to be copied elsewhere in the area and flat roof building was abandoned by 1935. The provision of roads on new estates improved. Throughout the Twenties these had been constructed of granite chips or gravel, and sometimes they were left unmade long after the household-ers had moved in, so that mud in the winter and dust in the summer plagued the residents for years. By the early Thirties concrete roads were being provided. Shops were built on large estates, no longer corner shops, but grouped in small shopping centres like that in Fillebrook Avenue, where there was a fishmonger, grocer (Co-op), fruiterer, ironmonger, chemist, sweets tobacco and papers, and an off-licence. Also occasionally provided were sites for churches and even synagogues.

The expansion of the built-up area in Enfield was circumscribed, after 1930, by the Green Belt, also by the absence of sewerage in the outlying areas. Nevertheless some large agglomerations of housing had already grown up in certain outlying places well served by the railways, like Potters Bar, Cuffley and Hadley Wood. The Green Belt (London and Home Counties) Act was passed in 1938, from that year too, house building was badly hit by the war scare and it came to a complete stop in the spring of 1940.[1]

2. Public Transport in the Twenties

In the years immediately after the war road traffic remained light and public transport poor. Tar surfaces were laid in May 1921 in Church Street, Chase Side, Silver Street and the Ridgeway, but it was rather to provide work for the unemployed than because the level of traffic warranted money spent on improvements. Gangs of out-of-work men were employed breaking up the main road through Ponders End and re-laying patches where the wood blocks were bulging. The General Omnibus Company in October 1919 began running an experimental Sunday service from Finsbury Park to Wormley. Redburn's started a half-hourly omnibus service in April 1923 between Waltham Cross and London, using Straker Squire double-deckers. It was extended to Hertford on Sundays. The National extended their service from Watford Junction via Elstree and Barnet to Enfield Town in March 1923. A. T. Bennett of the Admiral Bus Company introduced his new pneumatic tyred 'saloon' buses on the route from the Holly Bush to Finsbury Park in April 1925. The route went via Chase Side, buses being unable to use Baker Street because of weight restrictions on the New River bridge (near present site of Civic Centre). The war between the General Omnibus Company, the 'pirates' and the trams was beginning to hot up. The buses of five different companies were now racing each other, and the trams, along Ponders End High Street, each striving to be first at the next stop. There were those who protested, there always are, but I rather think the majority of passengers revelled in the fast and frequent service and the low fares.[2]

The Ministry of Transport began to introduce regulation in 1926, forcing the withdrawal of the Enfield to Finsbury Park service; ninety thousand passengers signed a protest. The independent operators commenced a campaign against the restrictions. Colonel Applin the local MP gave his support. He told the Commons that the independent omnibus companies had carried half a million people in Enfield in the previous twelve months and local tradesmen had increased their takings by fourteen per cent. Redburn's bus service, in November 1926, was absorbed into the London General Omnibus Company; employees over forty were rejected as unfit or unsuitable. Admiral at this time started a new bus service from the Angel in Edmonton, via Southbury Road to Arkley; A.T. Bennett, the proprietor took Adelaide House at Forty Hill in January 1927 and built a garage on vacant land adjoining.[3]

The Metropolitan Electric Tramway Company had been doing badly for years. Before the war it had been able to pay a small dividend of two or three per cent, even reaching six per cent in 1912. The company's receipts in 1918 had been £620,000, by 1922 takings had risen to £980,000, but this success had attracted fierce competition from the buses. The Tramway Company had drastically to reduce fares and receipts dropped to £745,000 in 1924 and £658,000 in 1925. The estimated takings for the year 1926 were only £625,000. The company now demanded protection from competition. The Traffic Trust had bought up almost all the independent bus services by April 1928; inevitably fares increased. In June that year the Metropolitan Electric Tram Company made application for a further increase in fares.

The use of private cars was expanding by the late Twenties. A car park was opened on the former site of the 'Palace' in May 1928. A mechanical system for controlling traffic was tried at Cockfosters, it had to be operated by a constable on a control pedestal, as the signal changed a bell was rung.[4]

75.   Redburn's started a half-hourly bus service in April 1923 between Waltham Cross and
London, using Straker Squire double-deckers.

THE "BUS WAR" AT PALMERS GREEN.

WHEN WILL IT REACH ENFIELD?

76. *By 1923 the war at Palmers Green between the General, Admiral and other omnibus companies, to say nothing of the trams, had become so fierce that it gave rise to this cartoon in the* Gazette *(6 July 1923).*

As early as 1923 thousands of people petitioned for the extension of the Underground to Enfield, but the proposal was met with polite evasion. Lord Ashfield, when he dealt with the programme for the extension of the tube network, excluded the Enfield area. In November 1925 the Inquiry into Traffic Facilities in North London was told that any extension of the Piccadilly Line north from Finsbury Park was a 'hopeless proposition financially'. Yet it was rumoured, at the beginning of the year 1927, that the Arnos Grove estate in Southgate, then far remote from public transport, would ultimately be covered by between twenty-five hundred and three thousand houses. Proposals were finally received from the London Electric Rail Company in November 1929 for providing an extension of the tube as far as Cockfosters. The company sought statutory authority. Enfield Urban District Council expressed regret that the line would not have a station near the Town, pointing out that Cockfosters would be of very little use to the people of Enfield. Only seven stations to Cockfosters were contemplated at this time, Enfield West (Oakwood) was an afterthought.[5]

ENFIELD ST. ANDREW'S CHURCH AND MARKET PLACE

77.   *Car ownership was becoming more widespread by 1931, the year this postcard was delivered. The Chase Side Motor Co. had opened large service facilities and showrooms on the Cambridge Road in 1930 and by 1935 a Ford Popular could be purchased for £115.*

78.   *Traffic had become sufficiently heavy by 1928 to warrant this mechanical system of control during road re-surfacing at Cockfosters. It had to be operated by a constable on a pedestal, a bell was rung as the signal changed.*

The Railways Act 1921 amalgamated the railways under four private companies and these survived until nationalisation in 1948; from 1921 until 1948 the local railways formed part of the London and North-Eastern Railways system. The railway extension between Cuffley and Stevenage opened for passenger traffic on 2 June 1924. Some of the trains, which had terminated at Gordon Hill or Cuffley, now went through to Hertford and a service was provided between Hertford and Hitchin via Stevenage. The Enfield Town line, by the end of the year 1927, was carrying only thirty per cent of the passengers which had travelled on it before the war, the carriages were said to be dirty and the trains slow.[6]

3. Houses and Politics in the Twenties

At the time the First World War ended in 1918 almost everybody lived in private rented accommodation. The inter-war years gave rise to two new classes of householder, the council house tenant and the owner-occupier buying his home by means of a mortgage. There was a desperate housing shortage in Enfield after the war, one advertisement in the *Gazette* (21 January 1919) offering a flat to let, elicited eighty responses, yet builders were reluctant to build small dwellings for rent. Seebohm Rowntree was of the opinion that the cost of building was so high that working-class houses could be erected only with a government subsidy; this would, in most cases, mean council housing. Alfred Bowyer, chairman of the housing committee and with many years local experience of housing management, considered that a workman's cottage of six rooms, with a twenty-three feet frontage, would cost £525 to erect, law charges and land would add another £100; with rates, taxes, insurance and management, the rent could not be less than 14s 6d. He suggested that the council should acquire land for housing immediately, before it appreciated in value.

The Representation of the People Act 1918 gave Middlesex seventeen parliamentary seats, Edmonton became a separate constituency and Southgate became part of the Wood Green constituency. The Act established universal adult male suffrage and granted votes to women over thirty in parliamentary elections; about ten thousand names were added to the Enfield register. The franchise in local government elections was confined to ratepayers until 1948. A general election was announced for 14 December 1918. Enfield parliamentary constituency comprised 30,103 voters. Besides Enfield it included South Mimms (352 voters) and Potters Bar (958 voters); 11,500 women in the constituency now had the vote. There were three candidates; Henry Ferryman Bowles supporting the wartime coalition government, W.E. Hill the assistant secretary of the Railway Clerks' Association, Labour, and Janet McEwan the vice-chairman of the Enfield Education Committee, Liberal. Bowles was elected and the figures show the decline locally of the Liberal Party. The Liberal candidate would have been Asquithite, i.e. denied the coupon. The results were:

Colonel H. F. Bowles	8,290
W. E. Hill	6,176
Mrs J. McEwan	1,987

The wartime coalition nationally was returned with a large majority. A few months later the Labour Party won an overwhelming victory in the UDC election, taking all three seats in the Bush Hill Park ward, three out of four in

Ordnance ward, all four in Chase and Bulls Cross ward, only one in Green Street, and none in the Town ward. Enfield's first woman councillor, Edith Newman, was returned for the Labour Party.[7]

The numbers and cost of Council staff now began a seemingly infinite upward spiral; within one year the wages bill was up by £4,800, a rate of 5d in the pound. Considerable dissatisfaction was caused in middle-class Grange Park where those living in the Enfield Urban District were paying higher rates than those living in Southgate. The amount required in Enfield for the year 1920/21 was £241,238. The beginning of the financial year 1921/22 brought more complaints about the 'intolerable burden' of local taxation, also concerning the increased expenditure imposed indirectly upon local ratepayers by the demands of bodies which had no responsibility for levying taxation, merely a licence to spend the money. The Board of Guardians demanded £8,730 more than it had required in the previous half-year, the County £2,474 more, the Metropolitan Police required an increase of £1,264. The cost of elementary education was also up by £1,750. Application was made by the Enfield UDC to the Ministry of Health, at the end of March 1920, to enable it to take over the duties of the parish overseers and the Burial Board. It meant the end in Enfield of the ancient office of vestry clerk; all that would now remain to the vestry would be the appointment of trustees to charities.[8]

The Council was empowered to embark on municipal housing by the Housing and Town Planning Act of 1919, known ever since as the Addison Act after its creator, Dr Addison who, in that year, had become President of the Local Government Board in Lloyd George's government and our first ever Minister of Health. The act broke new ground in providing for a partnership between local authorities and central government in which the former built the houses and then owned and managed them, while central government footed almost the entire bill. Once the ministry had approved the scheme, it then shouldered all financial costs except for the product of a penny rate which was the contribution of the local authority, and it was merely a token one.

Rents of new houses moreover, were not to be fixed by how much they had cost, i.e. an economic rent. Instead, the rents of local working-class houses were to be taken as a guide and these had been controlled since 1915 by act of parliament to prevent wartime rent inflation leading to wage inflation. It is true that some addition was to be made to allow for the superior amenities of the new houses. The local authority was to fix the rents but it had to obtain Ministry of Health agreement to them. Thus began an erosion of the powers of local authorities.

There were 12,283 houses on the rate book in 1919, eighty per cent of which were rated at less than £16. There had been 9,370 houses in 1902, 10,785 by 1905, and in 1912 there had been 12,120. From 1912 to 1919 only 163 additional dwellings had been added to the housing stock in Enfield. Private landlords found the ownership of controlled rented property uneconomic owing to rent controls imposed by the government during the war to assuage the resentment of the labour force over rising prices. They felt, with some reason, that their treatment was unjust. The following gives a good indication of the nature of landlords' complaints.

'Fifty yeas ago I arrived with a bag of tools', said one landlord who was, in March 1920, approaching old age and an uncertain future. 'I got to work at my trade on piece-work, six o'clock in the morning until seven o'clock at night and saved every shilling. With my savings and a big mortgage I became the owner of a block of well-built cottages let at 7s a week. Since that time rates have doubled, income tax is now 6s in the pound and the mortgage interest has gone up. All my cottages are full of lodgers so that many of my tenants are living rent-free and getting three times the wages they were paid pre-war. When the houses get into a filthy condition one tells the other; "Send for the sanitary inspector, he'll make the landlord clean it up". My income has vanished, the government, afraid of Labour, will not allow me to charge a six-pence extra rent and I cannot, having this property, claim old age pension'.[9]

The price of vacant land was very high and building materials were so expensive and scarce that only local authorities, with government subsidies, seemed likely to be able to build working-class houses in the foreseeable future. The Government had relinquished its wartime control of bricks. 'If Enfield must grow', said the *Gazette* (21 March 1919) 'let it grow decently, or the fate which has overtaken Edmonton and Tottenham will be Enfield's fate'. The housing committee of the Labour controlled Council at once selected a number of sites on which it proposed to build houses. Near St George's Church it planned to build forty-eight, near Southbury School fifty-two, near Gordon Hill station thirty-two, near George Spicer School fifty, and on the Ridgeway, south of Hadley Road, sixty-eight, a total of two hundred and fifty houses at an estimated cost of £178,000, an average cost of £712 per house. Whitehall wanted them completed by February 1921. The ministry refused to sanction the plan to build on the Ridgeway. It was an area of large detached residences, they said, and Hugh Trenchard, nearby at Wolverton, sent an irritated protest against this threatened encroachment upon his privacy. The other sites were sanctioned but the ministry proposed building economies; the reduction of room height from 8 feet 6 inches to eight feet and the elimination of dormer windows. The Council refused to accept these alterations but, without assistance from the ministry, it was found impossible to raise the necessary capital; building thus appeared to be indefinitely delayed. Huts were considered, the YMCA certainly had a surplus from wartime but they were priced at £100 each and with the transfer to housing sites and furnishing, the cost would amount to £300. The housing shortage meantime was causing great hardship. It was particularly felt to be a grievance among discharged soldiers who had been promised 'homes fit for heroes'. The Ministry of Health, in January 1920, required that four to five hundred houses should be built in Enfield and the Council purchased from the churchwardens, land at Lavender Hill for £1,250.[10]

Preparations were being made to begin building on the Lavender Hill site by the end of November 1920. Attempts by the London Housing Board to secure a reduction of the height of the downstairs rooms to eight feet had been successfully resisted. Even after the Council had accepted a tender from Allen Fairhead, the Board sent eighty-seven further proposed modifications to the plans, but under pressure from the Ministry of Health these objections were withdrawn. Building started in January 1921 and by the middle of the month the ground was staked out for twenty-eight houses, trenches had been dug for sixteen, while eighteen more were further advanced. Arrangements were going ahead for a stone-laying ceremony by Edith Newman, previously mentioned as the first woman councillor in Enfield. The Tottenham and District Gas Company offered to install gas supply at only £7 a house which, it claimed, was no more than a fraction of the cost. The houses would be semi-detached, no doors

79.   *Enfield Council made its first venture into house building in 1920. Rents were high. 'What is the use of putting up houses for ex-servicemen who will have to pay 21s 6d a week when many are only drawing £1?', it was asked. Council houses in Lavender Gardens in 1992.*

or principal windows would face north, and a central road would be built opening off Cemetery Road (now Cedar Road). It was predicted that eight of the houses would be ready by early July. The London Housing Board proposed rents, inclusive of rates, of 17s 4d for the smaller type and 21s 6d for the larger, despite the fact that the average controlled rent in Enfield, to which these rents, under the 1919 Act, should have been comparable, was between 11s and 12s. 'What is the use of putting up houses for ex-servicemen who will have to pay 21s 6d', it was asked 'when many are only drawing £1 a week?' The housing shortage was causing grave difficulties to those employed in the area. The Associated Society of Locomotive Engineers and Firemen complained to the Council in February 1921 that seven engine drivers stationed at Enfield could not find a place to live and, being unable to get back to the dormitory at Stratford, they were often forced to spend the night in the engine sheds.[11]

The scheme for Ponders End continued to be held up. At first it was because of changes demanded by the London Housing Board, but then came a communication from the Ministry of Health ordering that no further expense should be incurred by the Council in connection with the scheme. The year 1921 had seen the country immersed in the worst depression it had ever known. Curtailment of government expenditure was adopted as a remedy and a decision was taken to halt local authority house building. The housing crisis remained however and the moratorium was short-lived. A contract for fifty houses at Ponders End was won by the Guild of Builders, a co-operative of building trade-unionists with a headquarters in Oxford Street. It claimed that because it was able to call upon the services of all building trade-unionists, its work could not be held up by any shortage of labour, nor could it be stopped by strikes or lock-outs. The guild was organised, it was asserted, 'not for profit

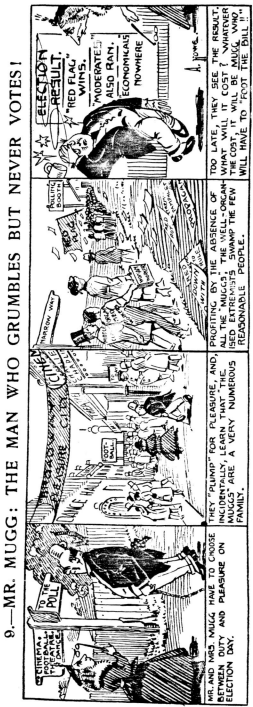

9.—MR. MUGG: THE MAN WHO GRUMBLES BUT NEVER VOTES!

WILL HE REMEMBER AT THE FORTHCOMING ELECTIONS?

but for Public Service'. Thus it would be able to build or contract cheaper than any private contractor. A local branch of the guild had been set up in October 1920 with offices at 44 Warwick Road Edmonton. Its proposals had been received favourably by the Labour controlled Enfield Council and when tenders had been received for building the fifty houses, the guild's estimate was found to undercut those of fourteen private builders. The guild now agreed, with unwarranted confidence, to complete the contract by September 1922. December 1921 saw three or four army huts erected at the eastern end of Southbury Road to accommodate men taken on, and building was begun near the school. In September 1922 however the guild was forced to ask for an extension. The inspector from the ministry complained that no effort was being made to get the work finished and that the clerk of works appeared to be in no great hurry. The inspector asserted that too many men were employed on the job and some were discharged. By this time six hundred applications had been received for the fifty unfinished houses. The ministry was proposing rents of 10s 6d and 12s 6d, exclusive of rates.[12]

High rates were the issue when the local elections were held in April 1922. All the seats were contested by the Ratepayers' Defence Association and their candidates swept every Labour councillor out of office. Following the election J.Norton, the former Labour chairman, gave a careful analysis of the reasons for Labour's defeat. The old Council had come into control in a difficult period, it was the aftermath of the war and costs were rising. He pointed out that the Ratepayers' Defence Association was not as independent as it pretended to be, having originated in the Constitutional (ie Conservative) Club. Three years ago, he went on, drawing attention to Labour's achievements and difficulties, there had been no street lamps and the roads had been bad. Relief for the unemployed had imposed a heavy burden. 'Don't be misled by what Mr Mugg has to tell you', he continued, 'but reason for yourself'. This was a reference to a series of cartoons in the highly partisan *Gazette*. They featured a Mr Mugg, the man who did not vote and found himself, too late, saddled with a Labour administration and high rates. Mr Norton continued his catalogue of Labour's achievements in office. The Council had completed thirty houses in Lavender Gardens and had placed a contract for fifty at Ponders End, it had spent £51,000 over the three years on the sewage farm but, despite this, improvements had been unable to keep pace with the growing population. An efficient ambulance service had been established, and public conveniences had been built by direct labour at the Woolpack Bridge and at the foot of Lavender Hill. Three years ago, the Ratepayers' Defence Association retorted, the rates were 9s 4d in the pound; for the year 1922/3 they would be 20s 8d. The new RDA administration came in to reduce the rates and by the following March they were down to 19s. The Labour Party was unable to regain control in Enfield until 1929.[13]

The Conservative Party won the general election in November 1922. Colonel Henry F. Bowles had stood down as Conservative parliamentary candidate in Enfield. He was presented with a portrait of himself upon his retirement. His place was taken by T. Fermor Hesketh (later Lord Hesketh) who was returned with a majority of nearly two thousand over his Labour opponent. The election gave the newly formed BBC (British Broadcasting Company) an opportunity to broadcast the results as they came in throughout the night until one o'clock in the morning. The transmission was picked up on a four-valve receiving set in the offices of the *Enfield Gazette*.[14]

81.   Colonel Sir Henry Bowles of Forty Hall.

Among the problems facing the new local administration was the poor performance of the guild at Ponders End. It was becoming a joke in the local press. 'Just think of it', said the *Gazette* (22 October 1922) 'fourteen houses nearly ready after twelve months work, out of a total of fifty being provided to meet a demand for six hundred.' Work at this time was at a standstill because of a dispute between the guild's men and the tar paviours who, they insisted, should only be allowed on the site upon production of a trade union ticket. The sub-contractor protested that he had observed trade union rules and conditions; stalemate ensued. Very few of the houses were occupied by January 1923 and there were complaints in April about jerry-building in Aberdare Road.[15]

The new Council at once offered the Ridgeway site for sale, stipulating that the purchaser must develop it for middle-class houses having a rateable value of not less than £50. The condition was accepted by the builder, A. Ingram, who offered £4,200 for the site, which was the price originally paid by the Council.[16]

A scandalous state of overcrowding persisted in the eastern part of Ponders End and at Enfield Wash. There were four-roomed houses with a family in each room. Many who had come into the district to work at the shell factory and at other arms factories during the war had been unable to get away, their children were growing up and getting married, and this added to the congestion. E. J. Spackman (vice-chairman of the Urban District Council) gave a graphic description of a house in South Street where a husband, wife and three children were living in a single room. Of course it may have paid people to convince the vice-chairman that overcrowding was worse than it really was, as it was one way of getting a council house.[17]

The standard of comfort available in working-class homes in the early 1920s

82.   The contract for council houses near Southbury School was given to the Guild of Builders in 1922. Building progressed slowly. Fourteen houses were nearly ready after twelve months work, out of a total of fifty being provided to meet a demand for six hundred and the men were on strike. Photograph shows Brecon Road 1992.

is hardly comprehensible to those who know only of conditions in the late twentieth century. Sid Robinson, recalling the time, in his autobiography *Sid's Family Robinson*, relates: 'My homework was done in the kitchen, the only room in our cottage with a table, chairs, heating and lighting. This kitchen was the centre of activity and leisure for our family of eight .... There was a coal-fired kitchen range alight summer and winter on which all the cooking was done and the water heated, as well as the flat-irons for the fortnightly wash. On the metal fireguard there was always washing airing or clothes drying ... The table was near the wall and alongside it stood a home-made wooden form used by the children ... Dad and Mum had two wooden armchairs and these, with two ordinary kitchen chairs, filled up the space available .... On a flypaper, hung quite low from the chain on the gasmantle light in the centre of the room, captured flies buzzed away, struggling to free themselves ....'

The life of the Slater family too was lacking in luxury. The imminent arrival of a third child forced Richard Slater's parents to leave the little house in Government Row where they had lived with the grandparents, for a cottage at Forty Hill. The two older children rejoined their parents a few days after the birth. It was 14 December and it had been freezing hard. Mrs Slater was still in bed upstairs with the new baby, while downstairs Mr Slater and the children frantically endeavoured to deal with a burst pipe. Not long afterwards, the grandfather, now sixty-five, had to retire and give up the house in Government Row and the grandparents moved in with the family at Forty Hill. To add to the difficulties Mr Slater got the sack from the Ordnance Factory, a victim of the Geddes economy cuts. There were no wages coming in, rent arrears began to mount and money was owing for groceries. The grandfather took odd gardening jobs at the big local

83.　Cottage Place, Forty Hill, where the Slater family and the grandparents moved from Government Row. Mr Slater and the grandfather were both unemployed but they scraped a living of sorts, the former as a bookmaker's runner, the latter on odd gardening jobs at the big local houses. Photograph 1992.

84.　Young Richard Slater found work at Elsynge Cottage, half a crown a week, polishing the shoes, chopping the firewood, and cleaning the knives in the basement.

houses while the father managed to earn a few shillings as a bookmaker's runner. Sixpennyworth of pieces from Ansell, the local butcher, stewed up, now had to last several days. Occasionally it was supplemented from the same shop by a rabbit which had probably been surreptitiously shot and usually had the lead pellets still inside. These when found by the children were placed in triumph around the rim of the plate as they competed to find the most.

Richard got himself a job at Elsynge Cottage, occupied at the time by Major Ball, his wife and young daughter. They employed a cook and a governess and needed a boy for half an hour or so in the mornings to polish the boots and shoes, chop the firewood, and clean the knives. He worked there in the basement before going to school, also on Saturdays and Sundays and got half a crown a week of which he gave two shillings to his mother; he was allowed to keep sixpence for himself. His small stature, ragged jersey and patched short trousers, together with his general appearance of an undernourished street urchin, must have touched a chord in the hearts of the governess and cook for they regularly gave him 'cakes and other titbits from the kitchen'. During the summer holidays he worked as a relief butcher's boy at Banks's shop in Lancaster Road, riding a bicycle with a huge basket on the front filled with parcels of meat.

The Council proposed, in October 1922, to put up a hundred or more houses on the north-east portion of the Southbury Road site. Tenders were accepted for two types, at £570 and £620 each, thus building costs were falling slowly; the houses built at Lavender Hill had cost £1,000 each. The government was obliged to provide a subsidy if the net annual loss per house to the Council was more than £12, but the Geddes committee was now beginning to restrain government liberality. Local wage rates were such that most working people were able to afford rents of no more than 13s a week. It looked certain that the cost of building would continue to fall, for the wages of building workers had undergone a substantial reduction over the previous twelve months. The price of building materials however remained high.[18]

The 1923 (Chamberlain) Housing Act sought to extend owner-occupation further down the social scale by providing, to private builders, a subsidy of £6 a house over twenty years on houses built to standard dimensions. It also gave local authorities power to advance money to prospective purchasers. More importantly it offered the same subsidy for local authority housing, but only if it could be shown that the houses would not have been provided by private enterprise. Further the 1923 Act reduced the superficial area required in houses built to qualify for such a subsidy. The Wheatley Act, under the Labour Government in 1924, offered a larger subsidy amounting to £9 a year for forty years, and also required that £4 10s be added from the rates. Thus a subsidy of £13 10s a year became available which meant that the local authority could fix the rents for houses built under the Wheatley Act at £7 10s a year lower than similar houses built to receive the £6 subsidy under the Chamberlain Act. Furthermore, under the Wheatley Act, the Council was again required to ascertain average rents in the area before fixing the rents of new council houses, and since the average rents paid to private landlords were still held artificially low by statute, the Council was forced to build cheaper terraced houses. Some now built were of the non-parlour type, and cheaper land was sought on which to build them. Land at Scotland Green Road was acquired; it cost much less than the land near Southbury Road. A block of ten low-cost houses was begun at Scotland Green Road in February 1924 by Forward and Sons. The committee was so impressed by the firm's performance that it recommended that it be awarded the contract for a further block of six. Later that year however Forward and Sons ran into cash flow problems. Bricks were so scarce that brickmakers refused to supply them on credit; this difficulty held up work for so long that the firm went bankrupt. The workmen applied to the receiver for their wages, he

85.   Low-cost housing built by Forward and Sons for the Council in 1924. Land was cheaper in Scotland Green Road, but the builder went bankrupt because the brickmakers refused to supply bricks on credit. Photograph 1992.

referred them to the Council which declined to pay. The Council surveyor, in a vain endeavour to secure a supply of bricks to complete the work, in June 1924 approached both the brickmakers Plowman and the London Brick Company. Plowman regretted that owing to a strike he would be unable to supply stock bricks before the end of August and the firm already had a large accumulation of orders for the cheaper Flettons. The London Brick Company told him that they were returning, by the dozen, orders which they were unable to meet. Further delays threatened because of a shortage of bricklayers. The local brick industry was only now beginning to return to life.[19]

Enfield Council planned to build more low-cost four-roomed cottages at Albany Road, others already built in that road were of the six-room, bay window type. The Gazette told its middle-class readers that it feared that these dwellings would become slums. With 1,007 names still on the Council's waiting list for housing in April 1924, tenders were accepted for forty-two council houses in Baker Street at £444 each, they were to be in blocks of six, but would have three good sized rooms on the ground floor and three bedrooms and a bathroom on the first floor. The rent was expected to be about 15s a week. Tenders were accepted for sixteen houses in Glenville Avenue (off Brigadier Hill), of the non-parlour type, which would cost £404 each and would let at about 15s a week including rates. Thirty houses were to be built in Eastfield Road of brick covered with roughcast at a cost of £400 each. The Council hoped to build 418 extra

86.   *Low-cost cottages built by the Council in Albany Road. Photograph 1992.*

87.   *The Council accepted tenders for 42 houses in Baker Street to be built in blocks of six. Photograph 1992.*

houses by September 1924. It had sites for a further 188 but had not the money to build them. The Ministry of Health, under the new Labour government refused in September 1924 to sanction plans to build at eighteen houses to an acre, insisting on twelve to an acre and semi-detached (see cartoon p.126).[20]

The Conservatives had been defeated in the general election of December 1923 and Baldwin had subsequently resigned. W. W. Henderson (the son of Arthur) became the member for Enfield with a majority of 1,162 over T. Fermor Hesketh the Conservative candidate, in a straight fight. The Conservatives

GENTLEMAN'S ROW.

AN ENFIELD EXPLORER DISCOVERS THE DISTRICT COUNCIL CHAMBER.

HIS IMPRESSIONS.

88. The Labour Party in opposition nationally and locally continued to attack the building of smaller low-rent council houses such as those in Scotland Green Road, Albany Road and Glenville Avenue. Gazette *23 October 1925.*

regained power nationally following the 'Zinoviev letter' election in October 1924 and their candidate, Colonel Applin, won back Enfield with a majority of two thousand. There were 16,717 men and 12,754 women on the Enfield parliamentary electoral roll.[21]

The Council now reverted to building semi-detached houses. Sanction was secured in December 1925 to borrow £163,298 to build 164 more houses at Ponders End and 158 at Bush Hill Park. The following February saw bricks in scores of thousands carted into the area north-east of Southbury School for the extension of the estate begun there by the Labour council. The style was changed; whereas the original blocks were stuccoed, the new ones would be brick. The Billocks estate in Green Street was nearing completion. The old house called Billocks remained standing but shorn of its lovely garden and orchard. 'Many will remember', said a correspondent in the *Gazette* (12 February 1926) 'the hundreds of lilac trees in bloom'.[22]

Enfield was still suffering from overcrowding, conditions at Ponders End were deplorable. A case was cited of a man and women with five children in one room, the man and his wife and a two year old sleeping on the table and the other four children on the floor, the wife was expecting. There were 277 families, some with as many as five children, living in single room accommodation; 219

families, twenty of them with five children or more, were living in two-roomed accommodation. The Council had to pay £485 for the houses at Bush Hill Park, £502 for those at Southbury Road; all of these were semi-detached and built twelve to an acre, to let at 18s. One tenant in Leighton Road (Bush Hill Park) finding himself, in July 1927, owing £16 7s rent, wrote to the Council to ask for a cheaper house. He suggested Scotland Green Road where council houses could be had for 11s a week, and offered to pay £1 a week until he had cleared off his arrears. The houses at Baker Street were let at 15s 6d. Council house rents were too high for the poor; 10s to 12s a week was about their limit. The trade union rate for a labourer was £2 16s 9½d a week. Building in blocks of six was again advocated, each would have a fourteen-foot frontage, but the surveyor pointed out that the ministry was unlikely to grant a subsidy for small houses; there was in any case some uncertainty about the continuation of housing subsidies.[23]

The high cost of council houses and the high rents which the Council had to charge for them was causing considerable concern to councillors. Monopolies and 'brick rings' were blamed for the high cost of materials. The surveyor was instructed to get particulars of houses at Easton near Middlesborough, built for £285. It was stated that houses put up for Northaw Rural District Council were let for 8s 6d a week. Church Army houses at Barrow Close Winchmore Hill were offered at from 7s 6d to 9s 2d, plus rates; Neville Chamberlain had been invited to open them. There were 513 council houses occupied by December 1926, but 839 families remained on the waiting list, 123 of whom were thought unlikely to be able to pay the rents demanded. The high rents gave rise to sub-letting, estimated to be taking place in up to seventy-five per cent of council houses. Sub-letting was sometimes tolerated by the Council. Permission was given, for instance, to a man and wife, with two small children, taking a married couple as lodgers in their council house in Swansea Road, but tenants often took in lodgers surreptitiously. One family in Mayfield Road (off Green Street), a man and his wife with four children, had taken in a poor family from Wales, with two

89.   Early in 1927 the Council began building 488 houses and eight lock-up shops on the Albany site, each house to cost £383. There were 926 applicants of whom 413 were earning less than £3 a week. Photograph, 1992, shows The Link.

children. They explained that the Welshman had arrived late at night and had nowhere to go. The tenants were ordered to give their lodgers notice. Many couples felt unable to marry with nowhere to set up home and many who had married had to wait for council houses before they could have children, yet the ministry went blindly on insisting upon houses with three bedrooms, parlour and living room. The Council was also experiencing some difficulty in getting sites large enough to build four or five hundred houses; any site chosen had to be either near to the factories or to public transport.[24]

Early in 1927 the Council began building 488 houses and eight lock-up shops on the Albany site, of some forty acres; each house, it was estimated, would cost £383. There were 926 applicants of whom 413 were earning less than £3 a week. Labour members advocated building under the Wheatley Act, by which the local authority would be faced with an annual subsidy of £4 10s from the rates to each tenant. The Council compromised by building 250 under the Wheatley Act and 250 under the Chamberlain Act. The tenants of these latter would have to pay £4 10s per annum more for a similar house. Thirteen sites, including three big estates, were being developed at this time, and the Council was soon completing one house a day. Mr Edwardson, chairman of the housing committee, was opposed to the allocation of houses according to the number of children. Worthy tenants should be chosen, he said, their ability to pay the rent should be taken into consideration. Council rents were £400 in arrears by 1927. Some tenants, through a combination of ill-fortune and improvidence, in varying proportions, were forced to abandon, by night and without notice, both their homes and their debts, as did one man from Scotland Green Road. He owed £6 12s rent. A Council representative subsequently discovered on the premises two bedsteads, a spring- mattress and a quantity of loose bedding, somewhat verminous, also a treadle sewing-machine and a cabinet gramophone. This latter was claimed immediately by the Broadway Music Stores where a note had been received asking them to call at the house to collect their property. 'The keys will be at the Council offices', it said, 'having to give up house through unemployment', signed 'Yours brokenly'. Fortune occasionally smiled, even on lodgers. One tenant in Lavender Gardens left his rent arrears and his house very early one summer morning in 1924 to try a new life in Australia. His lodgers had been paying him 7s 2d a week, he had been given notice to evict them, but on his departure they were allowed to take over the tenancy.

The Labour Party was only slowly regaining its foothold on the Council, they gained five seats in April 1925, none in 1926 and two more in 1927.[25] In 1929 women were at last given equal rights to vote in parliamentary elections; 6,725 young women between the age of twenty-one and thirty were added to the Enfield parliamentary register. Colonel Applin, of course, had been adamantly opposed, he pointed out with ponderous and monumental irrelevance

'You find no women in the stokehold of a ship or in the Navy, you find no women down the coal mines and I thank God for it. You find no women in blast furnaces. Women cannot physically perform these duties. Therefore it is a very dangerous thing for a woman to demand a vote on equal terms with men …. It must mean taking on grave responsibilities which would perhaps be too great a burden for women'.

Labour did well in the local elections in 1929 (with assets like Applin you can't

90.   *Enfield Highway Conservative Club with the Ordnance Road 'Young Britons' assembled outside for Empire Day celebrations in 1928. Unity Building was erected that same year. Photograph by George Oldbury of Ordnance Road.*

ENFIELD'S THREE PARLIAMENTARY CANDIDATES

AS SEEN BY AN ENFIELD ELECTOR.

91.   *Col. R. V. K. Applin*
Conservative

W. W. Henderson
Labour

C. H. Durrand Lang
Liberal

92.   W. W. Henderson (middle row on left) was elected to represent Enfield in June 1929. His more famous father, Arthur Henderson, can be seen in the middle of the centre row.

wonder at it), gaining control for a second time with ten members to the Rate-payers' nine. Labour retained control of the Council the following year, still by a single seat and their candidate, W. W. Henderson, won the election for Parliament in Enfield in June 1929 with a majority of 258 over Colonel Applin in a three-cornered fight. Labour emerged from this election as the largest single party in the House and, with the support of the Liberals, formed a government.

Following the defeat of the Ratepayers Defence Association in 1929, the Enfield Municipal Association held an inaugural meeting. Five hundred invitations were sent out but only sixty attended. Mostly they were former members of the RDA, now disbanded, with some members of the Conservative Party, the Manufacturers' Association and the Chamber of Commerce, though this latter regretted, or said it did, the commitment to politics. The new organisation aimed to return anti-socialist candidates in council elections. Dr R. L. Ridge, president of the Enfield Liberal Party, declined to be associated.[26]

Private enterprise in 1923 at last resumed the building of houses, but they were either to order, or offered for sale at a high price. Over a period of two months in the late summer the only plans submitted in Enfield were for twenty-two villa type dwellings to be sold at from £900 to £1,400. The Ministry of Health had issued model by-laws in January 1923. It was hoped that their adoption might induce private builders to put up lower-cost houses and factories. It was thought at the ministry that previous by-laws had been too restrictive, and that there were moreover builders standing idle who might now be encouraged to speculate. Mr Bowyer, in February, had sold land in Enfield and this, he said, showed that life was beginning to stir in the building trade.

The rents of houses owned by private landlords had been frozen since 1915 at 1914 levels, with only a forty per cent increase in 1920. New houses, if built to let, would not be subject to rent control, nor were new tenancies, but private enterprise still considered it unprofitable to put up houses to rent to the working class, unless the work was subsidised. The Housing Act of 1923 offered builders a subsidy on houses of standard dimensions, built either for sale or to let. A scheme put forward by the then Labour Council, and approved by the Ministry of Health, offered to builders of houses, costing no more than £600, either a lump sum grant of £75, or an annual grant of up to £6 for twenty years. No payment would be made until completion. By mid-October applications had been received in respect of forty houses, and in January in respect of a further twenty-eight houses. The offer was publicised in the local press.[27]

A question asked in Parliament in July 1926, bringing attention to the serious state of overcrowding in Enfield, elicited from Neville Chamberlain, Minister of Health, the information that Enfield Council had undertaken to pay a subsidy in respect of 171 houses to be built by private enterprise. The Westmoor estate of eighteen houses in Green Street was completed early in 1927 and was built with a government subsidy. The houses, for sale freehold at £600, comprised three bedrooms, two reception, a tiled bathroom and had long gardens. Purchasers could pay for them £75 down, the balance at 21s 6d a week. Seven subsidised houses were planned in the Kingsway by Percival Hart; two were completed by October 1924, but work on the remainder was held up by a shortage of bricks. Hart sought permission to increase the density of his building but the Ministry objected. Their modifications to his plans, said Hart, would so increase his costs that he would be unable to sell at £600 and a higher price would not 'meet the pocket of the thrifty working man'. He still sought the

93.   *Houses built by George Walker in Catisfield Road with a government subsidy. The price was not to exceed £600. Photograph 1992.*

94.   The builder A. Ingram laid out an eleven-acre site on the Ridgeway in 1924 for seventy semi-detached houses with three bedrooms, bathroom, separate lavatory, dining room, drawing room and a kitchen and scullery combined, they were to sell at £980 freehold, a garage would cost £100 extra. Photograph 1992.

subsidy and offered to advance £500 to purchasers under his 'early payment system', on better terms, he claimed, than could be obtained under the Small Dwellings Acquisition Act. Another builder seeking a subsidy, but demanding to build at higher density, was George Walker who planned to build five houses in Catisfield Road to sell at a price not exceeding £600. It was a working-class neighbourhood, he said, where most of the houses had six rooms and no bathrooms. They had been built at a density of twenty-five to the acre and were let at inclusive rents of about 11s 6d a week.[28]

Most builders however remained interested only in the middle-class market, but even here they faced difficulties. A. Ingram, in October 1924, laid out the eleven acre site on the Ridgeway (south of Hadley Road) which he had purchased from the Council. He planned to erect seventy semi-detached houses with three bedrooms, bathroom, separate lavatory, dining room, drawing room, a kitchen and scullery combined, electric light and gas laid on, with fittings to install a geyser in the bathroom and a gas stove in the kitchen. The price, freehold, would be £980 (leasehold £800), garage £100 extra, but Ingram was not able to complete the estate until January 1928, more than three years later. Jones, Peters and Co., a builder in Cecil Road, had purchased ten acres in Old Park Avenue early in 1925, intending to erect sixty houses, each to have a rateable value of £40; he proposed to lay out five tennis courts there for the use of the householders. After twelve months he had built only ten houses. 'Building today is done under great difficulties', he complained.[29]

95.   *Bush Hill Parade was built about 1926. The shops shown in this postcard belonged, in 1931, to Wilson a confectioner, Eastman and Son dyers, the United Dairies, Walton, Hassell and Port grocers, the Village Road post office, Frederick Cottingham newsagent, Miss Hall a milliner, and Dewhurst the butcher.*

The Labour-controlled Edmonton UDC added to those difficulties. H. G. Stacey proposed to build 250 houses on the Golf Links estate opposite St Stephen's Church, early in 1924, but his plans were repeatedly thrown out by that Council because some of the houses, even though built at the generous density of 10.9 to an acre, would be a little smaller than others in the vicinity. Those fronting on the main road, at 7.47 to an acre, had been approved and were being built. The builder offered to make some of the smaller type houses available for rent. He pointed out, with perhaps some exaggeration, that the estate would eventually provide homes for two thousand people, and would bring in some £9,000 in rates. The Edmonton Council remained adamant and would not even allow the builder to lay the sewers, but permission was eventually given and building was well underway by July 1925. Prices ranged from £690 to £770. The houses consisted of a dining room, drawing room, kitchenette, three bedrooms, bathroom and lavatory, with a spacious hall. Front gardens were 33 feet by 33 feet, back gardens 70 feet by 33 feet. A nine-foot driveway was provided beside the house, big enough 'for a large touring car'. There was also a 15-foot driveway at the back to facilitate deliveries. Private house building was planned, in May 1924, in Graeme Road Enfield which was being extended eastward across Cherry Orchard Lane (Churchbury Lane). The more affluent middle class was beginning to seek homes beyond Enfield. One hundred large and elegant houses, by the summer of 1924, had already been built at Potters Bar. The estate there covered four hundred acres, a hundred of which had been let to a golf club. The average cost of the houses was £1,250. Roads were completed before occupation and electricity was supplied from a power station on the estate.[30] Expensive houses were being put up in Halstead Road, Winchmore Hill in

£775 House. Shewing Drive (9ft. wide).

Corner of the   awing Room.

Dining Room. Note fireplace at the back of which is the boiler which
supplies the house up and down with a constant supply of hot water.

£690 House. Same size as £775 House but not semi-detached.

*96.   Golf Links Estate Bush Hill Park, opposite St Stephen's Church, built by H. G. Stacey. The
semi-detached were sold for £775; a similar house but in a block of four cost £690.*

97.   Ingleborough on the Ridgeway.

February 1926, at £1,000 freehold; they were semi-detached, having a tiled bathroom and scullery, separate lavatory and three bedrooms with fitted wardrobes. All the houses were occupied by 1928.

More land became available on the Ridgeway with the sale of Ingleborough and, following the death of H. Corbin Weld, the sale of its neighbour Dunraven. These were followed by the sale of the Rectory at the corner of Baker Street and Parsonage Lane in August 1926. The developer, A. Harston, not quite understanding the distinction between a rectory and a monastery, misnamed the site Monastery Gardens. The houses were to be built in pairs and in blocks of four or six. Wardrobe cupboards with robing mirrors were to be fitted in the principal bedrooms. Prices freehold ranged from £825 to £875 (leasehold £700-£750) payable £100 down, the balance over fourteen to eighteen years. Houses in Southbury Road, of solid stock brick, were offered for sale at £925 (£100 down and 30s a week). Southgate UDC erected houses for sale in the Fairway in 1927 at £675, £50 down and repayments of 24s per week over twenty years. Freehold houses were built by Morris and Son in Old Park Avenue, overlooking the golf course, constant hot water was provided and room for a garage; they were advertised for sale at £1,100.[31]

Much land, ripe for use for house building, was coming on to the market in the late 1920s. Developers were casting covetous eyes on Pennyfather's allotments and Shorey's Field, about twenty acres east of Chase Side Enfield. They were part of the estate formerly belonging to Sir Alfred Somerset and his executors were offered £800 an acre. The leases of the allotment holders were due to expire in October 1928 and plans were submitted for houses on the site in 1931. More valuable freehold land came onto the market at Grange Park adjoining the Bush Hill Park golf course. It had frontages on Old Park Ridings, the Chine, Green Dragon Lane and Bush Hill. Marshall Hood, the builder, proposed building in blocks of four and a hundred and forty Grange Park

98.   The last of Enfield's ancient Rectory House at the corner of Baker Street and Parsonage Lane, following its sale in August 1926. The developer, not quite knowing the difference between a rectory and a monastery, misnamed the site Monastery Gardens.

99.   Monastery Gardens. Prices freehold ranged from £825-£875. Wardrobe cupboards with robing mirrors were fitted in the principal bedrooms. Photograph 1992.

residents immediately protested against building houses at a density of eight to an acre as against the prevailing density in the area of six. The residents of Bycullah Park at this same time petitioned the Council not to allow the building of small houses on that estate. F. J. Lawes offered houses in Southbury Road at from £795 freehold, and at Hillfield Park, Bourne Hill (Winchmore Hill) from

100. The gates of the Rectory.

(The Old Rectory).

101. Freehold houses in Old Park Avenue overlooking the golf course, with constant hot water, room for a garage, £1,100. Offered for sale in 1927.

£990. Harston was building houses on the Mayfield Road estate in Green Street in 1928 for sale at £725 freehold, £25 deposit and 29s a week. He had his show house at 22 Vista Avenue. The Park Nook estate, of nine and a half acres at Clay Hill, was purchased by Eaton Estates Ltd., a new local company, in August 1929, and there were proposals to widen the northern end of Browning Road. Park Nook adjoined the company's Clay Hill estate, so comprising about twenty-two acres altogether. They proposed to build 240 houses, semi-detached, offering

102. *The New River winds its way alongside Pennyfather's fields while beyond, in Chase Side, the glorious spire of Christ Church indicates the way to heaven. The leases on the allotments expired in 1928 and developers offered £800 an acre. Christ Church spire in all its glory is still there, somewhere ...*

103. *... 'if it wasn't for the houses in between'.*

in most cases, garage room, gas coppers, gas fires and geysers. Diplock's were building twenty houses on the site of the former Clock House at Bush Hill. The properties were of 'the better class variety'; some backed onto the New River, others faced the Bush Hill Park golf course. These were large detached residences and were available at between £2,000 and £3,000.[32]

104. Rose Cottage and Ivy Cottage were demolished about 1930. Rose Cottage was the low wooden building on the left where dwelt Mrs Torbay who sold sweets to the children, often a farthingsworth at a time. She was always spotlessly dressed. The cottage faced on to Saddlers Mill brook. Charles Welch can be seen standing in the garden of Ivy Cottage (in 1992 the site of Jewson's), opposite in Chase Side was a beer house known as the Vine.

105. Harston was building houses on the Mayfield Road estate off Green Street, £725 freehold, a £29 deposit would secure, repayments would be 29s a week. He had his show house at 22, Vista Avenue. Photograph 1992.

106. Park Nook House on Clay Hill, in grounds of nine and a half acres, came on the market in September 1928.

4. Twenty One Years of Change

Enfield market, since its revival, had never appealed to more than a small number of traders. 'On most days of the week', said the *Gazette* in 1919, 'the Market Place seems to be regarded as an arena for trick cycling'. It might have been thought that, with so many market gardens locally, fruit and vegetables would have been cheap, but the growers sold into the London markets from where local supplies had to be obtained. The only time the Enfield market came to life was when there was something scarce going, or something cheap. One Friday morning at the beginning of October 1919 an enterprising trader announced bacon for sale at sixpence and a shilling a pound. Women arrived on foot and by tram from all over the district, frantic buying persisted until late that night. It resumed first thing on Saturday, continuing again throughout the whole day. February 1920 saw the inauguration of the Enfield Chamber of Commerce, which replaced the Enfield Tradesmen's Association. The Council, anxious to improve shopping facilities, asked the Northmet to erect four six-hundred candlepower lamps in the Town and Church Street.[33]

Shops in the Town and Church Street in 1921 were mostly held by local tradesmen. Along the north side of the Town was Odell's stationers, White the basket maker, Fountain the coach builder, Warren a coal merchant, Hart the butcher, Bonfield's blouses, F. F. Smith the oilman, Newby tobacconist, Fuller the iron-monger, Clarke a coal merchant, Frederick Smith a confectioner and Bradshaw's provisions. South from the Nags Head (on the corner of Southbury Road) was Gomm the butcher, Beaven the grocer, Walter's dressmakers, Singer Sewing-Machines and Yates dyers and cleaners. West from London Road was Freeman the baker, Laing furnisher, Fensen fancy goods, Ebben's baker and confectioner (two shops), Pearson the draper (on both corners of Sydney Road), Harold Moyse the photographer, the International Tea Co., and Charles Lamb the butcher. Thus only three of the twenty-eight shops were held by multiples.

Even in 1930 Enfield Town retained something of the air of a provincial town centre, although the decade had seen the intrusion of Saxone Shoe Co., the A.B.C., Dunn the hatter, the Fifty Shilling Tailor, and that inevitable concomitant of middle-class shopping, a Lyon's tea shop.

All over the country local communities, unwilling to appear forgetful of those who had died in the war, looked around for ways to pay respect. In Enfield however a meeting held in April 1919 to consider the erection of a war memorial was poorly attended. One speaker urged that the least the town could do would be to provide a plate bearing the name and number of every man from Enfield who had lost his life. The vicar thought that the memorial should be inside the parish church. McGrath, the union leader at the RSAF, argued that the most appropriate war memorial would be an extension to the Cottage Hospital. It 'would stand for ever', he said hopefully, 'as an expression of parental and fraternal affection'. Tottenham proposed to spend £30,000 on a new wing for the Prince of Wales Hospital. The project of commemorating those who had died in the war was also pursued by the Enfield Patriotic Committee which set up a shilling fund, proposing to erect two cenotaphs, one on Chase Green, the other in Durants Park. Fifteen to twenty thousand shillings would be enough, but it was not forthcoming and the committee was forced to abandon half its plans - the Durants Park half. The cenotaph on Chase Green was to be erected on the former site of the bandstand.[34]

107. *Enfield market continued to languish, and was used only by a small number of traders. 'On most days of the week', said the Gazette in 1919, 'the Market Place seems to be regarded as an arena for trick cycling ....'*

108, 109.   Most shops in Enfield have changed hands time and time again over the last sixty years,
but there is the odd survivor. Both Hammond's and Furncrafts opened in London Road in 1933.
Furncrafts specialized in french polishing which was the proprietor's trade; they also dealt in
hardware.

110. Some local shops held their own against the multiples even into recent times. Here is Peter Collier, owner of number 60 Church Street. The shop looks much the same here in 1960, as it had done in 1920.

The YMCA, in 1919, brought a large hut from Enfield Lock and erected it on the wooded ground between the New River and the Presbyterian church; it was to be used as a Red Triangle Club for ex-servicemen and others. A verandah was constructed overlooking the river and a billiard room was provided with six tables. The project involved the destruction of many ancient trees and the rookery which for so long had sheltered high among the branches.[35]

111. Tom Howard outside his home-made sweet shop in Baker Street; it lay between the present Monastery Gardens and Cheviot Close. The shop had previously belonged to his father Tom, nicknamed 'Toffee Howard'. The family also kept a stall in Enfield Market. Photograph 1928.

112. Tingcombe's was a broad fronted general and drapery store in Baker Street opposite the Jolly Butchers. Nora Crane started work there in 1935 at the age of fourteen at a wage of 5s (25p) a week. Miss Derry was then in charge. When Mr A. C. Tingcombe sold the business he retired to his native Camelford in Cornwall and presented to that town a park which is called Enfield Park.

113, 114.   The Enfield Patriotic Committee set up a shilling fund, proposing to erect two cenotaphs, one on Chase Green, the other in Durants Park, but insufficient money was forthcoming and the plans for Durants Park were abandoned. Above, the war memorial, looking east along Church Street (from a postcard dated 1927); below, looking west across Chase Green.

Frank Goldby, in August 1918, gave up his chemist shop near the George where he had presided since 1896. Some of the fittings were dated 1780, others had originated only a few years later, though from this of course it does not follow that a pharmacy had existed on the site since 1780. The shop, which had been described a few years earlier in the *Pharmaceutical Journal*, had formerly belonged to John Tuff the local historian. After Mr Goldby left it was purchased by Mr Gange his assistant.[36]

115. Frank Goldby gave up his chemist shop near the George in 1918. It had formerly belonged to John Tuff the local historian. Some of the fittings were dated 1780.

Old houses which for so long had graced the parish were being abandoned and pulled down or converted to other uses. Fir Tree House in Silver Street was demolished in March 1919, the date 1778 was marked on a lead cistern there; a new house with the same name was built on the site. In July 1919 Enfield stood and gazed upward in admiration at that magnificent airship, the R34, which had just crossed the Atlantic. Causeyware Hall, a fine old mansion in Cuckoo Hall Lane, was offered for sale in September, following the death of the occupant J. Doe, a Justice of the Peace. The house was advertised as suitable for conversion to a factory, part of the grounds was to be developed for building. The *Gazette* in July 1920 announced the sale by auction of the Rectory in Baker Street, with vacant possession. The gates in the front and in the garden, bearing the arms of the Nightingale family, had been beautifully restored in 1910; they can now be seen at Cambridge, in the university. The Rectory had been the home in the early eighteenth century of Sir Robert Nightingale from whom it had passed to Joseph Gascoigne Nightingale whose daughter and heiress had married the Earl of Lisburne. Following the death of Lady Somerset in 1920, the future of Enfield Court was in doubt. The house had been built in 1690, and it was much enlarged in 1864 by Colonel A. P. Somerset. He had succeeded to the property on the death of his father Lord John Somerset, who had received the estate as a gift from General Martin, a Waterloo veteran, upon his death in 1852. The house and grounds were now secured by Middlesex County Council for secondary education.[37]

116. *Fir Tree House in Silver Street, built in 1778, was demolished in 1919. It had been the home of Ebenezer Gibbons who died in 1911.*

117. *Rear of Fir Tree House, Silver Street.*

The fine residence called Suffolks standing in grounds of thirteen acres, and overlooking Durants Park, was advertised for sale in November 1922. It had been occupied for many years by John Josiah Wilson the market gardener. Old Park at this time was let to a number of tenants who each occupied three or four rooms. Fuller House in South Street, owned by Denis Cranne, contained a fine

118. A new Fir Tree House which was erected on the site, was demolished to make way for the Civic Centre.

119. On the death of Lady Somerset in 1920, Enfield Court in Silver Street, built about 1690 and enlarged 1864, was secured by Middlesex County Council for secondary education. The school there opened in 1925.

carved oak staircase on which the Tudor rose figured prominently. It was said once to have been the residence of the Earl of Derwentwater.[38]

The British Land Company in 1922 offered to sell the ancient moat in Seaford Road (Oldbury) to the Council for £550 but the Council evinced a total lack of interest, although the site was known to be of great antiquity. By 1926 the moat had been almost filled in with street sweepings and every summer there

120. When the 'Palace' site was auctioned in July 1918, lot one comprised two old shops belonging to Goodman the saddler and Watts the barber. The purchaser was Pearson whose premises adjoined. Watts moved to Genotin Road where the business continues.

were complaints about the unpleasant small given off by the foul water lying in the bottom. Years ago, wrote a correspondent regretfully, it had been possible to skate round three sides, in some parts it had been twelve feet deep. The Council, acting with its customary urgency when fulfilling its duty to protect the town's heritage, purchased the site in 1928 (long after the ancient moat had been obliterated) to use as a recreation ground, but it has now been built over.

In July 1918 E. S. Gibbons announced that he was to dispose of the 'Palace'[39] site at a public auction. H. Dugdale Sykes again urged the Council to purchase the building for a museum but the Council declined and it was acquired by the Leggatt brothers for £7,000. Their agreement with the vendor stipulated that they should not sell it for two years, unless it was to the Council, or to the National Trust which had expressed an interest. It was said that Gibbons had already rejected one very good offer, knowing that it would have lead to demolition and wholesale redevelopment. Lot one in the 1918 auction comprised two old shops belonging to Goodman the saddler, and Watts the barber. The purchaser, Pearson's, proposed to demolish both and rebuild the frontage within two years following the end of the war. Both shops were demolished in August 1920. The site on the east corner of Sydney Road was purchased for a bank. The other properties in the sale, standing on either corner of Vine Lane, were occupied, one by the International Tea Company (it was taken over by Messrs Lyons the well-known caterers for a tea-shop in March 1932) and the other by J. Gomm the butcher.[40]

The Leggatt brothers, by 1920, were finding their 'Palace' expensive to maintain; it was costing them £200 a year. Although the value of the land had

121, 122.   Trams in Enfield Town in the early Twenties (above). The scene still overlooked by Dr Uvedale's cedar. An extension to Pearson's demanded the demolition (shown below) of the 'Palace' and shops along Church Street belonging to Augustus William Young photographer, Stapleton's dairy, Charles Lamb the butcher, James Neilson auctioneer, and the offices of the Metropolitan Water Board (open Tuesdays 11am to 1pm).

increased, they offered the property, at the 1918 price, first to the Council, then to the tenant which was the Enfield Constitutional Club, imposing a condition that the building would not be altered or demolished; both declined to purchase. The Constitutional Club's lease was not due to expire until 1927, nevertheless Pearson's made an immediate offer to purchase the property for

123. Enfield Town from the air about 1931 showing St Andrew's Church, Enfield Grammar School, the Rialto and the Gas Company offices on the corner of the Market Place.

124. *The house now known as Little Park came into the hands of the Leggatt family in 1864. The five Leggatt brothers were well-known in the art world. Four of them remained bachelors and lived at Gentleman's Row throughout their lives. Dudley the youngest survived until 1952. Standing, Ernest and Martin; sitting, Percy and Dudley.*

£5,500, the price to include the Oak Room and other fittings. The Club, meanwhile, had taken an option on land in Old Park Avenue.

Enfield manorial court met for the last time on 3 June 1925 in the 'Palace'. There it appointed a jury and a homage and elected, for the ensuing year a constable, a headborough and an ale-conner in each of the four divisions, also a leather-sealer for the manor. Thus within the precincts of the manor court nothing had changed since the seventeenth century. The year 1926 however saw an act passed through parliament to eliminate copyhold property and with it even the formal justification for holding manor courts in Enfield. It was as though Enfield's historic manor house had lost its last reason to live. It gave up the ghost and declined slowly into the grave. By 1927 the manor house was in a sad condition; 'Time has played havoc with the structure', lamented the *Gazette* (8 July 1927) 'the walls are bulging, the ceilings bending, the floors unsafe'. It was thought that 'the wonderful oak panelling' might find a home in a London museum. Many of the valuable contents had been removed by December. This building, the manor house of the manor of Enfield, was timber framed with uprights in oak fifteen inches or more square, tenoned into wooden sleepers with pegs. The sleepers rested on a brick foundation raised eighteen inches above the ground. The spaces between the timbers were filled with miscellaneous bricks, inside was wattle and daub. The woodwork was in good condition. Behind the Tudor panelling they found the mummified remains of a rat and a jackdaw. The removal of a wooden overmantle in one room revealed a stone

125. *Enfield's ancient manor house, known to locals as 'the Palace', was in a sad condition in 1927. 'The walls are bulging.' wrote the* Gazette, *'the ceilings bending and the floors unsafe'.*

fireplace carved with a Tudor rose. It had all gone by June 1928 and Dr Uvedale's great cedar had been laid low. Some fine panelling, an ornate ceiling, and a magnificent overmantle and fireplace were installed in the Tudor Room which had been designed by the architect Donald Hamilton and erected at 5 Gentleman's Row. Thus a little of Enfield's past glory survives in private hands into the late twentieth century.

The proposal of Pearson's that 'the dirty alley-way known as Vine Lane should be closed' and Sydney Road widened to compensate, was accepted despite opposition, and building proceeded across Vine Lane. Pearson's new store opened in December 1931.[41] An ancient tenement west of the Rummer was demolished early in 1923. It was owned at the time by F. A. Fountain (car builder, formerly coach builder) who had purchased it thirty years earlier. A building had been on this site (possibly the same building) since the reign of Queen Elizabeth I. The Co-op in London Road opened in August 1923. The *Gazette* complained of 'the haphazard architecture which was filling the Town with incongruous buildings'.[42]

'We learn', said the *Gazette* (29 July 1927) 'that valuable interior fixtures from the Clock House (formerly called Bush Hill Park) are being taken out and sold', some had already been sent to the United States. The decorative doorposts and pediments had been removed from the entrances front and back. Demolition quickly ensued and once the house was demolished the developers proceeded to fill in the boating lake with earth from the adjacent building site.[43]

Local shopkeepers were strongly opposed to market trading on any day but Saturday. When it was discovered, in 1926, that fruit and flower sellers had set

126. *This ancient tenement west of the Rummer, which was then called the Railway Inn, was demolished in 1923. It may well have been in existence when Edmund Twynhoe made his survey of Enfield Parish in the reign of Queen Elizabeth I. Through the gap separating it from the Vestry House can be seen Logsden's Yard.*

127. The market in about 1926.

128. Enfield Town about 1928.

up stalls during the week, the police were called. Many costermongers, it was alleged, were trading in the Market Place without paying, but the police refused to intervene. From May 1930 car parking was allowed there, which relieved the problem caused by parking in the streets around. In November 1932 electric lighting replaced the naphtha flares in the Market Place.[44]

A disastrous fire in November 1931 gutted the Bycullah Athenaeum, the roof collapsed and the whole building was a blazing inferno before the Enfield or the Ponders End fire brigade even arrived; by the time the fire was extinguished

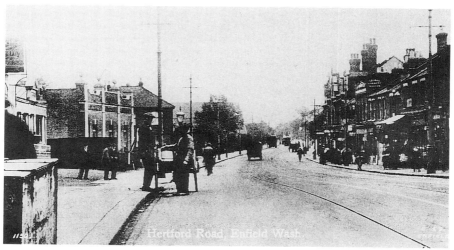

129. Enfield Wash 1927.

only the shell remained. The owner was W. C. Bennett of Adelaide House, proprietor of the Admiral Bus Company. Twenty-seven trees in London Road had to be removed in 1930 to allow double-decker buses (route 27) to get into the Town. A scheme was proposed in February 1932 to demolish all the properties along Southbury Road from the Nags Head to the Wallpaper House in Genotin Road. These properties would be replaced by seven shops which would be set back in order to widen the road, the work would cost £29,400. The widening was completed by November and the new Nags Head opened that same month. Courtney Pope, the shopfitters, were of the opinion that Enfield Town was underdeveloped as a shopping centre. As a consequence, they said, much of its trade had been lost to Palmers Green. Church Street was too narrow for buses and other traffic and it was therefore decided, in April 1933, to demolish the Rising Sun and the premises adjoining; new properties would be set back to widen the road.[45]

It was revealed in August 1933 that the Metropolitan Water Board was about to abandon the Enfield Town New River loop. The Council demanded its retention as an amenity and the board offered to hand over the whole loop as long as the Council was prepared to maintain the banks and the bridges. On this condition the Council accepted a free conveyance in June 1935 of the New River loop from Wilsons bridge in Southbury Road to the district boundary at Bush Hill Park. The board offered to provide water, but not free of charge.[46]

The forge on Chase Green went out of business in September 1933. More than a thousand people in January 1935 signed a petition in protest against a proposal by the Council to build a town hall on Chase Green. A meeting was held in the Tudor Room with Henry Ferryman Bowles in the chair, the Council bowed to public pressure and withdrew the proposal.[47]

Nobody though that Forty Hill would suffer change. The roadway was lined with great elms. Cattle might be seen leisurely refreshing themselves at the village pond on their way to their ultimate destination in Percy Ansell's

130. Following the widening of Southbury Road in 1932 tramlines were laid to enable the trams
to come into the Town, but the lines could never have been used for no overhead wires were provided.
The shops on the north side of the Town were the Aerated Bread Company (ABC), John Tranter
tobacconist, William Roberts hairdresser, Henekey's, and Hammett the butcher.

"HOME, JAMES AND DON'T SPARE THE HORSES"
(This night has NOT been ruined for me)
(Popular Song)

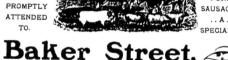

131. More than a thousand people in January 1935 signed a petition in protest against a proposal to build a town hall on Chase Green. The Council bowed to public pressure and withdrew the proposal. Gazette (1 March 1935.)

PERCY ANSELL [4]

HIGH-CLASS
Family Butcher

ALL ORDERS
PROMPTLY
ATTENDED
TO.

PORK
SAUSAGES
.. A ..
SPECIALITY.

Baker Street,
.. ENFIELD. ...

132. Percy Ansell's shop from 1908 until 1956. The butcher's name is immortalized by the name of Ansell's Green.

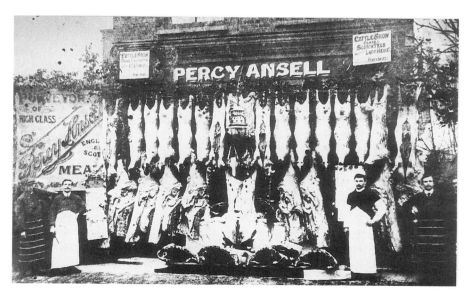

133, 134.   Richard Elston, the farrier and general smith at Forty Hill, appears to be busy. The business survived there until about 1923. The forge on Chase Green lasted a further ten years.

slaughterhouse. The butcher's name is immortalized in Ansell's Green. Richard Slater recalls sitting as a boy outside the forge watching Mr Ives the blacksmith at work. He was a small man in a leather apron. It filled the boy with fear and admiration to see him lift up the leg of some great cart-horse between his knees and slap a red-hot horseshoe on the hoof. For a moment the blacksmith would be hidden in a cloud of acrid-smelling smoke, but he would inevitably reappear, unperturbed.

135, 136.   Even Forty Hill suffered change. The Goat at the end of Goat Lane became a private residence in the late Twenties, the village pond was drained and a new neo-Tudor Goat public house was built on the site, with a sunken garden where the gravel pit had formerly been.

In the Twenties the Goat at the end of Goat Lane became a private residence. The pond was drained and a new neo-Tudor public house was built on the site with a sunken garden where the gravel pit had formerly been. Soon the blacksmith ceased to operate, for the age of the horse was drawing to a close.

The old parish lock-up at Enfield Highway remained standing on the west side of Hertford Road a short distance north of Green Street. It was a small unpretentious building marked with the letters E. P. (Enfield Parish) and the date 1819. The roof was falling in and the door was broken down. Middlesex County

137. The Old Bakery at Forty Hill was demolished in 1968 despite the fact that it was on the supplementary list of buildings worthy of conservation, and in spite of the opposition to demolition of Enfield Council and strongly worded pleas from the Enfield Preservation Society.

Council purchased it from the churchwardens in 1936 for £35; it was pulled down for road widening, apparently without any consideration being given to its re-erection on another site. At Ponders End High Street the fine Georgian house formerly occupied by Dr Agar was demolished in January 1936. In Chase Side the White House was pulled down in March 1937 to make way for Foresters Hall.[48]

Three acres in Silver Street were purchased in 1939 for £18,000, for municipal

138. The photograph shows the rear of Eagle House at Ponders End. It survived until 1957 and
had been home, at various times, to the Revd John Harman vicar of St James, T. P. Whitley JP and
Dr H.Barnes. The entrance hall had a white marble floor and there was a fine oak staircase. When
the house was demolished many of the bricks were used in the restoration of Forty Hall.

offices. Important council departments were by this time housed in timber sheds and in the bedrooms of private houses. J. W. Ingham, the deputy engineer, retiring in December 1938 after forty-one years' service, recalled that when he started in Enfield the Council had a staff of seventeen; three in the clerk's department, three in the sanitary department, seven surveyors, two in the library and two in education. There were now ten times as many staff.[49]

A new telephone exchange had been built at Bourne Hill (Palmers Green) in April 1925 and fifteen hundred subscribers were transferred there. Enfield had 1,174 working lines at this time at the old exchange in Church Street. A new telephone exchange was built in July that year in Cecil Road. A telephone exchange for Ponders End, to be known as 'Howard', was opened in 1937. It would serve eight hundred subscribers who would be able to dial direct.[50] The Enfield exchange remained manual until 1960.

Sliced bread became available early in 1931 from the Golden Crust Bread Company at Ponders End. The firm had installed what was said to be the first fully automatic bread slicing machine in England. Stapleton's were milking by machinery in the summer of 1931; the firm introduced aluminium milk bottle tops in October 1932. November 1934 saw the advent of the 'Fifty Shilling Tailor' in the Town. He promised his customers that 'whatever their special requirements the price would still be 50s'. That year a Murphy radiogram could be purchased for £24, a table-model radio for £14 10s. The large blue Police boxes which were installed in Enfield in April 1935 have now disappeared from our streets. Northmet offered electric refrigerators for 2s 6d a week (reduced in 1938 to 2s) including free maintenance for five years after purchase. Teleradio, which had a shop in Church Street, offered in 1939 to deliver and install a television, including the aerial, on payment of a £3 deposit.[51]

139. Stapleton's farm (the site is now occupied by Elmscott Gardens) where aluminium milk bottle tops were first used in Enfield in October 1932. The cattle are dairy shorthorns.

"Was it a vision or a waking dream?"—Keats.

Television Demonstrations Are Now Being Held In Enfield

140. The 1930s were to see the birth of that pervasive phenomenon the television. (Gazette 20 November 1926).

Tottenham and Wood Green Burial Board opened a crematorium on the Cambridge Road in 1937, nevertheless, in October 1938 Enfield went ahead with a £30,000 scheme to extend Lavender Hill cemetery; only a small percentage of people, it was said, look to cremation. The Gas Company premises on the corner of the Market Place were demolished in August 1937 and a block of shops was built; they were occupied by Burton's, Mansfield's (boot and shoes), Jay's (furniture) and Clara Reid the milliner. [52]

The Council, in August 1937, took a decision to sell the Library Green for commercial development. It had formerly been the site of Chase Side House, the home of Philip Twells, a partner in Barclay, Beavan, Tritton, Twells and Co., now Barclays Bank. The estate had comprised thirty-five acres when Philip Twells died in 1880 and after the death of his widow in 1901 it was sold. The Council purchased twenty-three acres for the Town Park, paying £13,000, and in 1902 paid £5,200 for the Library Green, where they then planned to build a town hall.

The plan was never carried out and the site remained derelict for a while; it was eventually fenced and laid out as a garden. The 1937 proposal to sell it met with strong opposition from the Enfield Preservation Society; the Council argued that it had been elected with a strong mandate to cut the rates. Middlesex County Council however, wanting to see the garden retained, offered a contribution for this purpose; Enfield Council, facing hostile public opinion, hastened to accept. The Enfield Preservation Society had been set up in December 1935 at a meeting convened by the Enfield Rotary Club; Dudley Leggatt had offered the Tudor Room as its headquarters.[53]

The Townspeople v. The Ogre

141. *The Council in August 1937 took a decision to sell the Library Green for commercial development. The proposal met strong opposition from the Enfield Preservation Society and was finally abandoned.* (Gazette *20 August 1937*).

142. *Church Street in the late Thirties; Spikin's the jeweller's shop stood on the eastern corner of Palace Gardens next to the Maypole Dairy. On the western corner stood Parkes' the chemist, then, in order, the Wallpaper Stores, H. E. Randall the bootmaker, Willmott's 'perm shop', French Cleaning and Dyeing and Dorothy Perkins.*

5. The Fire Brigade

The equipment of Enfield's two volunteer fire brigades, when the First World War ended, was out of date and in disrepair. Because it was estimated that it would cost £200 to repair the steam-engine at Ponders End, the Council in 1919 purchased a sixty-horsepower Dennis motor engine at a cost of £1,470. The Enfield Town brigade continued to work with two horses of which only one was available at any given time. One horse by itself was unable to pull the steam-engine which had perforce been abandoned. Now the Enfield Town area had to depend on the motor engine at Ponders End. This unfortunately was unavailable because of repairs when a disastrous fire occurred at East View on Windmill Hill in the summer of 1925. The brigade, having no pump available, had tried to use the mains, but the water pressure was too low and the firemen were left standing by helplessly while valuable merchandise was consumed by the fire. The Ponders End and Town brigades remained separate organisations; there was a little co-operation but no co-ordination. At every minor conflagration up would come a miscellaneous collection of trucks and vans accompanied by much bell ringing. Twenty firemen, no less, turned up on one occasion to a chimney fire and, in the confusion, put the water down the wrong chimney to the annoyance of a neighbour who had his dinner on the range. Other authorities in the area employed paid fire-fighters. Edmonton had a motor fire-engine capable of reaching Bush Hill Park in four minutes. Because of this they had been able to close their sub-station there adjoining the railway station in 1921. Not until September 1925 did Enfield decide to purchase a motor fire-engine for the Town. It cost £1,760, and a driver-mechanic was appointed.[54]

The old manual engine, said to have been built in 1790, languished in the council depot at Lincoln Road. A more elaborate manual, purchased in 1854 was at this time stored at Little Park; the first steamer, a one-stroke, had been returned to Merryweather's when a new steamer was purchased in 1899.[55]

The Council, in December 1930, decided to appoint a full-time paid officer to take charge of both fire stations. The volunteers threatened to strike, but offers of assistance in case of emergency from the Edmonton and the LCC brigades enabled the Council to stand firm. A professional superintendent, J. Dickinson, appointed in February 1931, was replaced almost immediately by A. H. Johnstone who was to take charge of both the fire brigades and the ambulance service. The position was particularly difficult at Ponders End where, because of business commitments, it was often impossible for volunteer firemen to answer a call. The superintendent asked for the appointment of five full-time officers, two for the ambulance service and three for the fire service. The full-time firemen were to be paid 75s a week, rising over seven years to 90s. A new Dennis fire pump was purchased for £1,469, a tender and hose for £370 and a Dennis trailer pump for £370. There were of course protests against this new extravagance, particularly voiced by a former first officer of the volunteer brigade. The protest was taken up by a number of Conservative councillors including W. H. Bishop and S. H. Fussell, also of course by Colonel Applin. A public enquiry had to be held and there the superintendent pointed out the clear necessity for modernization; the population was now (June 1933) 71,000, there were 190 factories and there had been 153 fires since 1931. One of the existing tenders was eighteen years old and was so slow that, as it crawled up Windmill Hill, the children ran round it in circles. The rateable value of the

143. It was estimated that repairs in 1919 to the Ponders End steam fire engine (top) would cost £200; it was decided therefore to replace it with a sixty-horsepower Dennis motor engine (below). The handsome brass helmets worn in both photographs were withdrawn in 1934 and utilitarian black leather ones were issued.

district had increased by £62,000 since April 1930 and the value of new property, including over three thousand new houses, amounted to more than £2m.[56]

Enfield's fire coverage at this time was divided into three areas; the east served by the Ponders End brigade, the central area served by the Town brigade, and

144. *The Ponders End fire station on the corner of Nags Head Road was built when the Ponders End brigade was reconstituted in 1891. This building also housed a branch of the Enfield Public Library from 1894. Photograph 1932.*

144a. *The funeral in August 1932 of Capt. Edwin T. Roberts of the Ponders End brigade was attended by over two hundred firemen. The photograph shows the cortege halted outside his house in Alma Road, and the disconsolate figure of 'Jock' the brigade mascot (extreme left). People lined the pavements with bowed heads as the cortege made its slow way along Nags Head Road past his fire station to St James Church.*

145. *The fire station in Holtwhites Hill was opened by Sir Henry Bowles in June 1936; it cost £42,000. Photograph 1992.*

the west served by an arrangement with the Barnet fire brigade. An important factor which limited the effectiveness of the Enfield service was the lack of a fire alarm system. The superintendent urged that a system should be installed with eighty-three alarm points to cost £7,000. There were 134 fires in the year 1933/4 and losses had amounted to £82,000, although this included £80,000 from one disastrous fire at Yager's in Wharf Road.[57]

Plans were put forward in June 1934 for a central fire station at Holtwhites Hill. The firemen's handsome brass helmets were replaced with lighter, more utilitarian, black leather; brass helmets were a disadvantage when dealing with electrical fires. It was proposed that the brigade personnel should be increased from thirteen to twenty-four, the superintendent and twelve men at the Town, and eleven men at Ponders End. Over the three years 1931-34 expenditure had risen by 125 per cent. The new fire station at Holtwhites Hill was opened by Sir Henry Bowles in June 1936; it had cost £42,000. Enfield, claimed the *Gazette,* was being equipped with the most modern fire alarm system in the world.[58]

In the years following the appointment of a professional in charge of the fire service the proficiency of the Enfield Brigade became so widely recognised that seven of the men received senior appointments in other brigades. At the time of the appointment there had been only four professional firemen and three ambulance drivers. Two of the officers serving in 1938 were former members of the volunteer brigade. There were now plans to build a new fire station in Carterhatch Lane to serve eastern Enfield, but these plans were not achieved until the 1960s.[59]

6. Enfield Town Plan and the Green Belt

Since the Town Planning Act of 1925, Enfield UDC had been discussing the formulation of a town plan, which, by the terms of the Act, had to be ready by 1929. The Council applied to Messrs Adams, Thompson and Fry who offered to prepare a plan for £2,350. The North Middlesex Joint Town Planning Committee in 1929 issued proposals which aimed to control the growth of London by the creation of 'a ring of open space ..., a green girdle' between Ruislip reservoir and Epping Forest. The 'girdle' would extend for about five miles through Enfield, and would include much of the former Enfield Chase. The Enfield town plan designated areas for industry between the King George reservoir and the railway, and between the Cambridge Arterial Road and the Hertford Road. The greater part of the frontage on the east side of the Cambridge Road would be available for factories, a very wise policy in view of later growth in the volume of traffic. The plan further proposed that housing density should nowhere exceed twelve to an acre. Large tracts of land in Enfield were being offered for building by 1929, brickfields, shops and houses encroached on the orchards and vegetable gardens. Overcrowding remained the most pressing problem facing the Council. The problem would not be solved by the Council's housing schemes in progress, even though when completed they would provide twelve hundred homes. Private enterprise, in the Twenties, had failed to meet the demand for working-class housing.[60]

The Enfield town plan, adopted in 1927, had been approved by the Ministry of Health in February 1928, and had reached map form by February 1930. James Neilson was of the opinion that it would cast a blight upon the town, robbing large areas of the prospect of development, for the proposals allowed for two thousand acres of open space and parks and this amounted to an average of one seventh of an acre to each house. Enfield, Neilson postulated, would become a barren area with only four houses to an acre. There were 12,602 acres in the parish, 8,509 were covered by the plan. The remainder, belonging to the Duchy of Lancaster, was exempt. Built-up land in Enfield comprised only 738 acres; Enfield Urban District Council owned 260 acres of parks and open space, the New River occupied thirty acres, the railways 202 acres, the Cambridge Road 58 acres, 94 acres were taken up by existing main roads and 255 acres by district roads. Whitewebbs, Forty Hall and Trent Park, some one thousand acres, were designated as private open space. The *Gazette* thought that there was a hint of coercion about this reservation for all time of other people's property; it was of the opinion that the scheme would have to undergo modifications before the Minister of Health would give his assent. The Clay Hill area, it pointed out, was largely covered by market gardens and glasshouses and it was unlikely therefore that it would ever become a populous centre. If this town plan was adopted, said Mr Neilson, Enfield would be doomed to a sparse population. The Greater London Regional Planning Committee sought to create, in perpetuity, 143 square miles of open space. Neilson questioned whether trade in Great Britain was in a position to warrant such extravagant schemes. Sir Henry Bowles asserted that the town planning scheme for Enfield, if adopted, would cost £750,000 in compensation.[61]

A rapid increase in the population of western Enfield was anticipated following the extension of the Piccadilly line, meanwhile eastern Enfield looked likely to grow because of the expansion of industry. The scheme proposed that

146. *The Green Belt in Enfield includes much of the beautiful countryside of the former Enfield Chase. The view shown here is from Cuckolds Hill on the Ridgeway looking south-west across the valley of Salmons brook towards Hadley Road.*

147, 148.   North Lodge (above), later known as St Nicholas House, was built about 1730 near Old Pond on Enfield Chase, but it was never a keeper's lodge like West Lodge, South Lodge and East Lodge. The present building on the site of East Lodge is shown below.

the industrial area should not encroach west of the Cambridge Road, thus it would be restricted to 1,050 acres. Housing was allotted 4,330 acres, some at three houses to an acre, some at eight and some at twelve, this might eventually result in a population of 250,000. Enfield, it was thought, was likely to become more and more a dormitory town. Thus the plan set a limit to the density of new housing.[62]

The outlying areas in the north and west of the parish remained largely occupied by private estates. Little development was expected there, though land at Beech Hill Park, owned by the Hadley Wood Golf Club, was zoned at two houses to an acre, and land owned by Sir Philip Sassoon at four to an acre. Mrs Ashley Cowen, the owner of an estate of fifty acres called Wildwoods, objected strongly to the greater part of her land, the lake and the area adjoining White-webbs, being zoned as open space, although the frontage of the estate along Theobalds Park Road was zoned to allow houses at six to an acre; such houses would have to be sold at around £2,000. The Theobalds estate comprised some three thousand acres but only ten per cent of it lay within Enfield. It was one of the largest private estates near London, encompassing almost the whole of the park which King James I had enclosed within a brick wall in the early seventeenth century. It had extensive frontages on Whitewebbs Road and Cuffley Road, but Mr Neilson, who represented the estate owners, saw no immediate prospect of development because of the lack of services, particularly sewerage. This same difficulty would impede the development of all these outlying estates. Negotiations were in hand in June 1930 to convert Theobalds House into a high-class residential hotel; it opened in July 1931 with telephones in every bedroom, but it was not successful. The house, with the furniture and fittings and seventy-seven acres, was offered for sale by auction in May 1937 but it was withdrawn at

149. The lounge at Capel Manor when the Warrens lived there.

150. *Whitewebbs had 14 bedrooms, three reception, five bathrooms and a self-contained sewage plant 300 yards from the house. Orr Lewis bought the estate from Sir Hedworth Meux for £15,000 and had spent lavishly on improvements; it was purchased by Middlesex County Council in 1930 for £23,000.*

£74,000 and was subsequently purchased by Middlesex County Council with a view to using it as a hospital during rebuilding at the North Middlesex. The Capel House estate, zoned at four houses to an acre, was unlikely to be developed until Mr J. Warren ceased to live there.[63]

Members of the UDC visited Whitewebbs in May 1930. The estate had been designated as private open space and the Council was hoping to purchase it with a grant from the Regional Town Planning Committee. Mr Orr Lewis had paid £15,000 for Whitewebbs when he bought it from Sir Hedworth Meux before the First World War. Since that time large sums had been spent improving the house. It had fourteen bedrooms, three reception rooms, five bathrooms and a self-contained sewage plant three hundred yards from the house. Middlesex County Council now purchased the estate for £23,000, seventy-five per cent of the cost was to be met by the County. The park of 254 acres would be preserved as regional open space, and would be leased to the UDC for 999 years at one guinea a year. The County proposed to use the house as a home for old people.

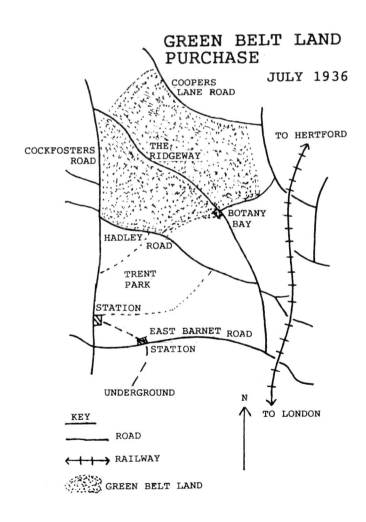

GREEN BELT LAND PURCHASE
JULY 1936

KEY

——————— ROAD

◄─┼─┼─► RAILWAY

▨▨ GREEN BELT LAND

April 1932 saw the sale of the household furniture at Claysmore, in Clay Hill.[64]

It was the designation as public open space for use as playing fields, of large areas of potential building land within the built-up area, like Bury Farm, which most annoyed the developers. This land, they claimed, was ripe for building. It had been acquired for that purpose between 1898 and 1901 but development at that time had not been as rapid as had been hoped. Now there was a strong demand for houses in the district, a hundred had been built there since 1928 and they had almost all been taken up. The builders, wanting to extend Ladysmith Road as far as Carterhatch Lane to provide a further 218 homes, purchased sixteen acres at the very low price of £350 an acre, because the laying of a sewer would cost £4,000. Twelve houses to an acre were to be permitted.[65]

Enfield in 1930 was subject to two town planning schemes; the one prepared by the UDC as the planning authority under the Ministry of Health, and the County scheme. The scheme prepared by the Middlesex County Council was to be used as a guide so that the local schemes might fit together as a homogeneous whole. It was the County which undertook the creation of the Green Belt. The *Gazette* reported (3 April 1936) that a large tract of land in western Enfield was likely to be included. The paper warned that, if the project materialised, hundreds of acres would be sterilised. Middlesex County Council, in July that year, purchased 2,005 acres in Enfield from the Duchy of Lancaster for inclusion in the Green Belt. It paid £315,000 of which the LCC contributed £105,000 and Enfield UDC £31,000. The Duchy agreed that parts of the land could be used for playing fields, and that the public should be given access by means of footpaths. The land included farms and private tenancies which produced rents amounting to £4,000 a year; no tenancies were to be disturbed. This land was the last remaining portion of Enfield Chase in the hands of the Crown; it was described as 'a beautiful open tract of particularly English countryside'. The Duchy was given assurances that the property would be preserved from building development.[66]

MR. JAMES NEILSON,
of Enfield Town.

151. Gazette 1 July 1936.

Enfield Council, in January 1937, was informed of the intention of the County to acquire, from Trinity College Cambridge, 586 acres near the Ridgeway. This would link up the two thousand acres already purchased, with the area of Whitewebbs and Hillyfields. This new land would include the Crews Hill golf course of 109 acres, also several dairy farms; Rectory Farm (244 acres), Parkside Farm (136 acres) and Botany Bay Farm (80 acres). Enfield Council however demanded the resale for residential purposes of part of this land, some ninety-five acres, although Trinity College pointed out that it had accepted a low price as a contribution towards the Green Belt. Negotiations at this time were in progress with Sir Philip Sassoon for the purchase, as open space, of 153 acres of Trent Park. Sir Philip objected, but a compromise was reached through arbitration whereby no conveyance would be made within thirty years unless Sir Philip should cease to reside at Trent. Sir Philip died in June 1939.

In March 1937 Middlesex County Council acquired a further fifteen hundred acres for Green Belt purposes at Potters Bar. The County by this time had taken possession of some four thousand acres in the area. Some people remained firmly opposed to the creation of a Green Belt. Councillor Nielson reiterated his strong objections to so much land being sterilized as open space. He thought that Enfield ought to expand, the district should be able to provide space for two or three thousand more houses.[67]

7. Council Houses and Politics in the Thirties.

The Housing Act 1930 came into operation in August that year. Arthur Greenwood, the Minister of Health, urged local authorities to get on with the job of slum clearance. Enfield's problem however as not slum clearance but

152. *The Suffolks estate of four hundred houses between Brick Lane and Carterhatch Lane. It was intended that they should cost £273 each. Photograph 1992.*

overcrowding, more houses at low cost were required, for rent arrears on council estates at the end of the year 1930 amounted to £1,200. The new Labour Council, in January 1930, made a compulsory purchase of fifty-eight acres between Carterhatch Lane and Brick Lane for the Suffolks estate. It was proposed to erect four hundred council houses there, and Councillor Collier urged that the land should be used for cheaper homes. He cited a man with six children who got 30s a week on the dole and had to pay 16s rent. In eastern Enfield, he said, many men were out of work and nearly a thousand names remained on the housing list. Priority, it was decided, should be given to families, with children, living in one or two rooms. A hundred and sixty of these families had only a single room, some with as many as five children. A further 271 families occupied only two rooms, one such couple had eight children. Houses on the Suffolks estate, it was decided, should cost £273.[68]

The 1931 census shows that the population of Enfield was 67,869, an increase of 7,219 in the ten-year period, or 11.9 per cent. The population of Southgate had increased by 16,448 or 42 per cent (this was among the highest increases in Middlesex) Edmonton had grown by 16.2 per cent, Tottenham by 7.5 per cent. There were 14,800 houses in Enfield in June 1931 but only 1,135 were council houses; 1,739 houses were overcrowded. Overcrowding in eastern Enfield was made worse by the expansion of industry, causing a constant influx of labour from the depressed areas in the north of England. Four hundred and twenty-four houses were built in Enfield in 1930, but all were by private enterprise and for sale as were a further 550 in course of erection at the end of that year; plans had been submitted for many more. Some of those who came here and found work, bought newly built houses which they could ill-afford and took lodgers in order to repay the mortgage. The Ministry of Health was of the opinion that three thousand new houses for rent were required in Enfield. Land values now began to rise at a faster rate and the Ministry suggested that the Council should secure sites for council houses before they became too expensive.[69]

The year 1931 was a disastrous one for the Labour Party, both nationally and locally here in Enfield. At the national level its leader, Ramsay MacDonald, led a coalition of Conservatives, National Labour and National Liberal into a general election against the Labour Party and inflicted a devastating defeat on it. The Labour Party was not again to govern Britain till 1945. In Enfield, in the April 1931 Council elections all Labour candidates standing for election lost. The working class had deserted Labour in droves mainly, it is true, by absten-tion, but also by voting for anti-socialist candidates. Among those who did remain loyal to the Labour Party, MacDonald was hated as a traitor. At a Conservative Association meeting in the Co-op Hall Enfield Highway, in Sep-tember, a former Labour councillor F. Knyveton, having courageously spoken in defence of the Prime Minister, found himself challenged to a fight. He even got as far as taking off his coat before peace was restored. In the October general election for the Enfield constituency Colonel R. V. K. Applin polled 24,532 to defeat William Mellor, the Labour candidate, who polled only 13,646. Seventy-nine per cent of the electorate voted.

Following the Urban District Council elections in April Labour's former majority of one on the Urban District Council had been reduced to a minority of three. The Enfield Municipal Association took office and E.W.Edwardson, the manufacturer, its chairman, became chairman of the Council.

153. *Councillor E.W. Edwardson, soap manufacturer, a progressive on the Board of Guardians and a radical on the Urban District Council, seen here at Chase Side School on Empire Day, perhaps 1930.*

Edwardson was a man with radical ideas which pleased neither Conservative nor Labour. He proposed that council houses should be built without subsidy, reasoning that before the war a four-roomed cottage, such as those in Fifth and Sixth Avenues, could be had for between 5s 6d and 6s 6d a week, while three-bedroomed houses, like those in Percival, Burleigh or Lincoln Roads, could be rented at 8s or 8s 6d a week. This latter class of house, under rent restriction, was now let at 13s 11d a week, yet most artisans were earning double their pre-war wages. Mr Edwardson had examined the earnings of those applying for council houses; eight of them were earning more than £6 per week, twenty-four of them between £5-£6, 156 of them between £4 and £5 a week, and 553 of them between £3 and £4. Thus there were 741 on the waiting list who earned more than £3 a week, whose rents, in his opinion, ought to require no subsidy from either ratepayers or taxpayers. Only the remaining 449, who earned less than £3 per week, had any right to be subsidised. He went on to point out that many young married couples were having to pay between 15s and 17s a week for two rooms usually having to share a lavatory, bathroom and kitchen. He even dared to suggest that a man with one child had as much right to a council house as a man improvident enough to have five.

Under Edwardson's administration there was a substantial increase in the salaries of Council officers. Salaries in Enfield were now thirty-three per cent higher than the average for local government officers in England and Wales. Edwardson's radicalism, and his prodigality, particularly annoyed Colonel Applin who wrote to Neville Chamberlain in November 1931 concerning the Council's debt which amounted to more than £1 million. He ridiculed the Council's plan to provide a golf course at Whitewebbs, pointing out that there were already three within the district. E. W. Edwardson was nonetheless re-elected chairman of the Municipal Association in November 1931.[70]

Almost every house on the Council's Suffolks estate had been allocated by October that year and, according to Edwardson, no more council houses were in prospect. Land owners were pushing up the price of their land whenever the Council wanted to purchase. The Suffolks estate included twenty-five flats for old people. Knifton was the contractor engaged to collect refuse for the Council. That summer (1932) there were complaints about his antiquated rubbish dump on Brown's former brickfield between Carterhatch Lane and Palmers Lane. The refuse had been left uncovered and it was giving forth a suffocating and poisonous stench of decay. Grime and ashes were being carried on the wind into people's homes in Old Road and a plague of crickets had invaded the houses on the new council estate at Carterhatch Lane.[71]

The Municipal Association took two more seats from Labour in the 1932 local elections, this gave them thirteen seats against Labour's six. Edwardson's next proposal was adopted by the Council despite being very controversial. He urged that council house rents should be graduated according to the ability of the tenant to pay. He proposed a rent of 8s for those earning £2 a week and, for every 3s below £2, a shilling rebate; for every 3s above £2 a shilling should be added to the rent. His scheme took no account of the number of children but the man with the large family would be given a bigger house.[72]

The following year (1933) a section of the Conservative Association broke away from the Municipal Association and put forward their own candidates under the label 'Anti-Socialist' one of whom, William Bishop, defeated Edwardson in the Town ward. Labour regained two seats that year, leaving the 'antisocialists' with a majority of three. Edwardson's position had become progressively more difficult. He had been constantly harrassed by the Conservative Association and ridiculed by the Labour Party for his attempt to keep politics out of local government. The EMA dissolved itself at a meeting in the Tudor Room in December 1933. The position of Sidney Hills, the ILP member, was also under attack, for neither the Conservative Association nor the Labour Party, from which he had seceded, would support his candidature onto committees.[73]

Dr Geffen, the MOH, continued to complain of the serious overcrowding. He cited one case of seven people living and sleeping in a single room. Those who had rooms to let unfurnished could expect a reasonable rent; two rooms in Durants Road, with a bath and a separate gas stove and meter, were offered at 11s a week; two rooms and a kitchenette in Nags Head Road cost 12s 6d; three rooms in Second Avenue, 16s, including light; an unfurnished flat of three rooms with a long garden, 'children taken', was offered at 15s a week.[74]

Southgate became a borough in September 1933. Enfield by this time was the largest urban district in the country except for Rhonda. A petition for incorporation could therefore be submitted with confidence, but the Council's expectations were marred by Sir Henry Bowles who, as president of the Chamber of Commerce, refused to give his support, for he objected to changes proposed to the ward boundaries. It was a matter of principle to him, he said. Population alone should not be allowed to decide, people who owned large estates (and Sir Henry was one) should not be penalised. Under these new projected wards,

Councillor S. G. Hills Has a Dream

Another "Codlin's-the-friend-not-Short" Story

154. 'At the annual meeting of the Enfield District Council to be held next Tuesday evening, much will depend upon the way in which Councillor S. G. Hills (Independent Labour Party) uses his vote. For the moment the "odd man" of the nineteen councillors becomes of some importance'. (Gazette 30 March 1934). Many will remember the respected secretary of the Federation of Enfield Residents' and Allied Associations who died in 1989.

eastern Enfield would have twelve representatives, the remainder of the parish only nine. Such a division (by population) would give an advantage to the 'socialists'. The Labour Party responded with a threat that it would withdraw support from incorporation if the proposed ward boundary changes were not accepted. Thus the petition for incorporation was withdrawn.[75]

The Labour Party regained two seats in the 1934 election so that the state of the parties was : 'anti-socialist' nine, Labour nine, Independent Labour Party one. That one was Sidney Hills of the ILP. He might be expected to vote with the Labour Party, though no one could quite tell with Sidney Hills, especially after the way he had been treated. Labour took power precariously, nevertheless the new Council had ambitious plans including a large fire station on a new site, an extension of the sewage farm, and a town hall, a civic amenity which Enfield had not previously enjoyed. Application was made in April to borrow £35,000 to extend the sewage farm, although Enfield was growing so rapidly that any extension was likely to be inadequate before it was completed. An east Middlesex sewage disposal scheme was by this time under consideration by Middlesex County Council, but Enfield UDC was in no position to wait.[76]

There was a serious problem of bugs on the council housing estates. The prosecution of offending householders was demanded by anti-socialist members of the Council, and it was urged that incoming tenants should have all their belongings disinfected. Dr Geffen said that 679 council houses were verminous. He proposed a few houses of reception where incoming tenants could stay for

155. *There were serious problems; bugs in the council housing estates and unmade-up roads everywhere; on the Orchard estate at Ponders End the roads were 'worse than cart tracks', while at Morley Hill a milk float toppled over into the mud. There was also the problem of Enfield's sewers which were now full to capacity.* (Gazette *18 January 1935*).

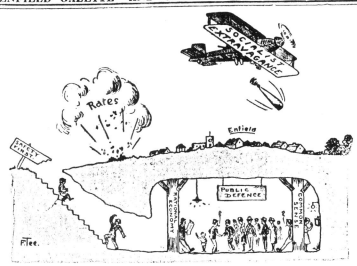

THERE IS TALK ABOUT PROVIDING SHELTER FROM AIR-RAIDS

156 Labour gained two seats in the 1934 local elections and held power precariously, the state of the parties was Labour nine, anti-socialist nine, Independent Labour Party one. The shadow of the impending war was already looming on the horizon.

"WHAT! ALL THESE?"

157. Labour in power, the Gazette *campaigns against high local government expenditure. (5 January 1935).*

one day while their furniture and bedding were checked for vermin. Respectable people must have found this treatment humiliating. The use of wallpaper by tenants made disinfestation difficult, as did the wooden skirting boards.[77]

The differential rent scheme had come to an end in March 1934, thus many council tenants had their rents increased. The Albany tenants association was discussing a rent strike and, although the strike proposal was rejected by a tenants' ballot following a sixpence a week reduction, there was a petition to reduce and equalise council house rents over the various estates. The petition was supported by the tenants at Ponders End, Green Street, Enfield Wash and Bush Hill Park who asserted that their rents were too high compared with the more recently built council housing estates. The Council proposed a comprehensive review of all their rents. Seventy-eight houses had been built under the 1919 Act, 563 under the 1923 Act, the rents of these houses were disproportionately high, and tenants on these estates were paying fifty per cent more than those in later built houses. They were paying 15s 8d at Bush Hill Park and 14s 8d at Baker Street.[78]

High rents and large families could create real difficulties for tenants. One family, a man, wife and four children paid a rent of 17s 4d for a house at Ponders End; the man's average weekly earnings amounted to £2 1s 3d.

The family spent:	£	s	d	
		3	1½	on meat
		2	10	on bread
		3	7½	with the grocer
		2	5	with the greengrocer
		5	4	with the milkman
			7	on fish
Rent and electric light		18	4	
Clothes, fuel and gas (1s)		5	0	
Total	2	1	3	

With the milkman they spent:

eggs		6d
margarine		3½d
Cookeen		3d
butter	1s	6d
cheese		3½d
milk	2s	6d
Total	5s	4d

On grocery they spent:

tea	9d
sugar	6d
tinned milk	9d
sultanas	4d
oatmeal	3d
salt	1d
rice	1½d
cocoa	2d
soap etc	8d
Total	3s 7½d

All the cooking was done on a kitchen range which was considered more economical than gas. The washing was done in a gas copper. The family had to be extremely careful, nothing was spent on recreation, no visits to the cinema or football, no cigarettes, no pocket money for the children, nothing on insurance. Their daily menus, shown below, indicate however that, if they could maintain this extraordinary degree of parsimony, they certainly would not starve.

Monday	*Breakfast*	Fried bread, tea.
	Lunch	Orange.
	Dinner	Cold meat, mashed potatoes, tomatoes, rice pudding
	Tea	Bread and butter, cake, tea.
Tuesday	*Breakfast*	Porridge, bread and dripping, tea.
	Lunch	Orange
	Dinner	Liver and bacon, onions, potatoes, Yorkshire pudding with jam.
	Tea	Lettuce, bread and butter, tea.
	Supper	Cheese and tomato.
Wednesday	*Breakfast*	Steamed fish, bread and butter, tea.
	Lunch	Milk
	Dinner	Stewed marrow-bone with vegetables and dumplings.
	Tea	Bread and jam, tea, cake.
	Supper	Soup and toast.
Thursday	*Breakfast*	Porridge, bread and dripping.
	Lunch	Orange.
	Dinner	Roast breast of mutton, mint sauce, potatoes and greens.
	Tea	Bread and jam, tea.
	Supper	Cocoa and cake.
Friday	*Breakfast*	Banana, bread and butter.
	Lunch	Milk
	Dinner	Tomato soup, dumplings, potatoes, rice pudding.
	Tea	Watercress, bread and butter, tea.
	Supper	Cocoa, cake.
Saturday	*Breakfast*	Bread and butter, egg, cocoa.
	Dinner	Chops, greens, potatoes, sultana pudding.
	Tea	Bread and dripping.
	Supper	Kipper, bread and butter
Sunday	*Breakfast*	Bacon and tomatoes, bread, tea
	Dinner	Roast mutton, mint sauce, greens, potatoes, left-over sultana pudding, custard.
	Tea	Celery, bread and butter, cake, tea.[79]

Lunch would have been taken mid-morning, dinner at mid-day, tea round 5 o'clock and supper later.

The 1935 local elections left Labour still holding power. The balancing act by Sidney Hills came to an end; he was defeated in Ordnance ward by a Conservative but at the same time Labour gained a seat in Bush Hill Park. The *Gazette* continued to attack Council spending. The rates, at 12s 6d in the pound, were the highest in Middlesex, even so December 1935 found the estimates already overspent by £3,000. Expenditure was rising at an alarming rate; the Council appointed an economy committee.

Colonel Applin was 66 years old and no longer wished to retain his seat in Parliament; he was replaced by Bartle Brennon Bull. In the election of November that year Bartle Bull retained the seat for the Conservatives with a majority of 5,503 over William Mellor the Labour candidate. Frank Broad retained Edmonton for Labour.[80]

An annual abstract of accounts, published for the first time in March 1936, showed that Enfield's debts amounted to £1,284,942 (£17 4s 2d per head of the

"WEIGHT" AND SEE!

158. 'Consternation is being felt among the doctors of Enfield at the fatness of a number of school-children. They, and most of us, are also concerned at the growth of other things in Enfield' (Gazette 14 August 1936). The rates (1935-6), at 12s 6d in the pound, were the highest in Middlesex. Labour did badly in the local elections April 1936.

159. A. J. Standbrook, the well-known landlord at the George.

population), of this £818,882 was owing on housing. The proposed seven hundred houses at Bullsmoor Lane, to be built without government subsidy, would add a further £500,000. It was pointed out by Councillor Anderson that in the three years nine months ended December 1935, sixty-three per cent of new building in Enfield had a rateable value of £20 a year or less. He asserted that the rate received on houses assessed at less than £30 did not pay for the services provided. He predicted that this trend would lead to bankruptcy and

160. The Church Army built thirty-four cottages and eight flats in Green Street, but offered them to tenants on the Edmonton Council waiting list. Rent for a three-bedroomed cottage, including rates, was 11s 7d. Photograph 1992.

therefore proposed that western Enfield should be reserved for larger, more highly assessed properties.

Labour did very badly in the local elections of April 1936, losing five seats of the six contested, even including the two at Ponders End. This left the Conservatives with fourteen and Labour with five seats. The annual abstract for the following year confuted Councillor Anderson's gloomy prognostication for it now predicted that Enfield's rateable value would rise more rapidly than council expenditure, promising an eventual decline in the level of rates.[81]

The decision of the Conservative Council in July 1936 to impose a new scale of council house rents (to become operative in October) was met by pandemonium in the Council chamber. There were shouts of 'We will fight to the bitter end', and 'Come and collect the rents yourselves, you haven't got the guts, you dirty lot of tykes'. The Council had aimed to remove disparities between tenants with similar accommodation, there were reductions and some rises, though none of more than 2s 6d. The Council backed down and the motion was rescinded. Labour regained one seat in April 1937.[82]

Edmonton was becoming so crowded that in June 1937 Edmonton Council sought to purchase land for housing in Enfield; six acres in Carterhatch Road, twenty-seven acres in Hoe Lane and six acres in Bell Lane. Sanction to purchase the land in Bell Lane was refused. The Church Army, building thirty-four cottages and eight flats in Green Street, offered them not to Enfield but to Edmonton Borough Council (Edmonton became a borough in October 1937) requesting particulars of large families in Edmonton living in overcrowded conditions. The estate was completed in May 1938 and was opened by the Duchess of Kent. The rent for a three-bedroomed cottage was 7s 6d plus 4s 1d rates, the inclusive rent for a four-bedroomed house was 13s 8d.[83]

Overcrowding persisted in 151 privately rented properties in Enfield. The occupants were offered council houses though only sixty-six accepted. Dr Geffen, Enfield's long serving Medical Officer of Health, was of the opinion that some people felt that there was a stigma attached to becoming a council tenant, just as, he explained, certain persons would suffer pain and discomfort rather than risk being sent to the North Middlesex Hospital because it had once been a poor law institution, although treatment there was as efficient and sympa-thetic as possible. Probably the good doctor was right about the hospital but he was surely wrong about the council houses. The truth was probably that neither the tenants nor the lodgers in controlled rented private property wanted to pay the higher council rents. Indeed some of the more expensive council houses during the Twenties had been occupied by middle-class tenants; many factory workers and most labourers could not afford the rents.[84]

Enfield was divided into new wards in June 1937. West ward was to be represented by six councillors, central ward by nine, north-east ward by six and south-east ward by six. The first local elections using the new wards was in April 1938. Enfield local elections at this time re-elected one third of the councillors in each ward every year but, presumably owing to the re-organisation, three seats were to be contested in the wards which now returned six councillors and six in the central ward. The election resulted in a Council comprising seventeen Conservative councillors and ten Labour. The Labour party won all the seats contested in the east, the Conservatives held those in the centre and west of the district. The population of Enfield was estimated, in the annual abstract of statistics for the year 1938, to be 87,200, but another estimate put the figure at 95,000. Following this, in March 1939, S. J. Dabbes the town clerk, claimed that the population was 102,000 and that it was increasing at the rate of a thousand a month. The local elections in April 1939 reduced the Conservative majority to one. The Labour Party adopted Ernest Davies, 'a much travelled journalist' as its parliamentary candidate.[85]

8. Houses and Owner-Occupiers

Private enterprise in 1930 still made no attempt to build for the less well-off; new houses were designed and priced to meet the needs of the middle class. On the summit and northern slopes of Bush Hill 'very attractive …. houses were erected' and existing trees were being retained wherever possible. At First Avenue Bush Hill Park, houses 'with leaded lights in the front windows' were available for £795 (£50 down and 26s a week). Morter and Forster were building houses in Sketty Road for £795 with gas fires in two bedrooms, a geyser over the bath and room for a garage. Houses off Windmill Hill (£840 freehold) were provided with an automatic gas copper having a wringer attached.[86]

Grange Park resumed its growth in the Thirties. There were plans for 536 houses at eight to an acre north of Green Dragon Lane and some 450 on the Vera Avenue estate. Marshall the builder was to plant trees along the roads; he had agreed to assign land to widen Green Dragon Lane to sixty feet. He emphasised in his brochure that development in the district had been limited to good class private residences, claiming that there was no slum area for miles in any direction, that the Enfield golf course was near at hand, the Bush Hill Park and Crews Hill courses were within easy reach, and there were tennis-courts on

Plan of
FREEHOLD LAND.
GRANGE PARK. N.21.
For Sale by Auction by
STANLEY PARKES & BROWN.
NOVEMBER, 1933

the estate. His houses were provided with garages. In order to keep up the status
and character of the area Marshall declared that he would accept no low
deposits, and in future mortgages would be limited to a maximum of 87½ per
cent. A high-class private high school for girls was established in the Chine, it
incorporated a kindergarten and a boys preparatory. A small estate of 108
houses was planned at Crews Hill and 350 south of Parsonage Lane. Rowley Bros
had houses for sale on their Windmill Hill estate costing between £695 and
£1,000 and described, most honestly, as 'eight minutes uphill to the station'.
Plans were submitted for 193 houses south of East Barnet Road (now Enfield
Road), also on thirteen acres north-east of and overlooking Enfield golf course.
Houses at Brimsdown were being offered for sale by Austin at £5 down and 32s
a week for two years, then ten years at 28s, an arrangement which, it was hoped,

161. The world we have lost; this photograph, about 1880, shows dilapidated dwellings in what
is now Trinity Street. Round the corner in Chase Side stood the Vine, a bow-windowed beerhouse.
Ivy Cottage can be recognised by its dormer windows and through the gates lie Pennyfather's fields.

162. *Plans were submitted in 1931 for 86 houses on Pennyfather's fields. The footpath from Chase Side to the bridge over the New River along which, a hundred years before, Danby's murderers had staggered homeward, became Parsonage Gardens. Photograph 1992.*

163. *Said the* Gazette, *2 October 1931; 'Kilvinton Hall, the well-known private school at Clay Hill will move to North Lodge next term'. The area, it was thought, was deteriorating owing to the extensive building of small houses. Kilvinton Hall was a preparatory school for boarders and day scholars, teaching boys between the ages of five and fourteen. The house, which stood on the south side of Clay Hill, was demolished in 1932.*

would prevent the buyer putting a millstone around his neck.[87]

Potters Bar was rapidly becoming a dormitory town and was losing its rural appearance, Ideal Homes offered houses there at £850 and £885, and the extensive Oakmere estate of five hundred houses continued to grow. A large percentage of the Potters Bar inhabitants travelled daily to the City. The area, the South Mimms Rural District, became the Potters Bar Urban District for local government purposes in 1931.[88]

Plans were submitted for eight-six houses on Pennyfather's fields east of Chase Side Enfield. The footpath leading from Chase Side to the bridge over the New River, along which, a hundred years before, Danby's murderers staggered homeward, was now transformed into a pleasant suburban road. The site of a private school at Kilvinton Hall (Clay Hill), which closed in October 1931, looked likely to be developed.

In view of all the housing developments mentioned above it is not surprising that the Council had before it in October 1931 proposals for four thousand houses; they were to be built for sale at an average price of £750. Road construction had failed to keep pace with house builders and many roads remained in a scandalous condition. At Morley Hill a milk van toppled over into the mud, a pantechnicon was bogged down for twenty-four hours and over-laden dust-carts perilously swayed, dropping the garbage in the mire.[89]

"Roll Along, Covered Wagon, Roll Along!"
(House building in Enfield proceeds at a more rapid pace than road building.)

164. Unmade roads gave rise to persistent complaints by householders and ratepayers' associations. Houses in Enfield were being built at a rate of 2,500 a year (Gazette 29 November 1935).

165. *Peachey had his show house open until eight o'clock at night every night including Sunday. (*Gazette *April 1933).*

166. *George Reed offered 'enamelled Ideal boilers, shower bath fittings... coloured leaded lights and garage accommodation'. (*Gazette *April 1933).*

167. Building was begun on the Orchard estate at Ponders End in 1929. Five years later the roads 'were worse than cart tracks' and parts of the estate had no street lighting. There were sewer smells, rubbish and rats. The photograph of Orchard Road, 1992, shows that it is pleasant enough there now.

Business was beginning to pick up for local building societies. By 1932 more people were using them as savings banks; they were offering five per cent tax-free. With lower mortgage interest and lower building costs, house sales looked set for a boom. Houses were being offered in May 1932, in Lincoln Road, at £645 freehold. The houses in Ladbroke Road, built by Peachey, cost £695 and could be secured for £35 down, repayments would then be 27s 3d a week including rates. Peachey had a show house furnished by Drage's. Houses at Farr Road and the Drive cost £875, those on the Chase Side estate, built by George Reed in Nunns Road and Chase Side Avenue, sold for £835 freehold or £645 leasehold (£30 down and 20s 4d a week). The local paper advertised more houses in June 1932 at £595 freehold in Carterhatch Lane. Only three of the houses built by A. Tracey, offered at £675 freehold, were left on the Bridgenhall estate. Despite the increased building activity there were still 746 local building workers out-of-work in October 1932. Almost all Diplock's new houses at Morley Hill were occupied by October that year, but the residents still had to plough their way through mud, slush and stagnant water to reach their gates. Unmade roads gave rise to persistent complaints from householders' and ratepayers' associations in the area. Building had been begun on the Orchard estate at Ponders End in 1929; five years later the roads were 'worse than cart tracks' and parts of the estate had no street lights. There were sewer smells, rubbish and rats, the backways and ditches, especially between Orchard Road and Allens Road, were in a filthy condition.[90]

The Bill to establish the London Passenger Transport Board came before Parliament in 1932. Considerable disappointment was felt in Enfield as it became apparent that there would be no tube station near the Town. The planners were held responsible because they had sterilised so much land in the area of Whitewebbs and Forty Hall. Cockfosters station, it was said, would serve no one, half the area within a mile radius was occupied by Trent Park, and much of it was scheduled as private open space. Of the remaining land within a mile of the station site, only 267 acres were available for house building. Of this 58 acres were zoned at four houses to an acre and 209 at eight to an acre. Beech Hill Park was now Hadley Wood Golf Club and thus unlikely to be made available for building, Hadley Wood was common land and would never be built upon, nor would the North London cemetery. The existing density of population in the Cockfosters area at that time was one person to two acres. As yet there was no mention of a station at Enfield West, later called Oakwood; Southgate

168. The site chosen for Enfield West Station (now Oakwood) lay in open country. Eastpole farm, opposite the northern end of Chase Road, barred the line of the track.

169. Eastpole Farm

looked likely to profit most from the Piccadilly extension.[91]

Tenders for the tube railway were submitted in July 1930, the contracts were worth £5 million and the work would employ twenty thousand men. The Arnos Grove estate was being cut up for high-class housing development by September and Southgate Council had acquired land there for a park. Also at Southgate 103 acres were offered for sale in January 1931 with frontages on High Street, Chase Side, Osidge Lane and Crown Lane. Construction of the new railway was under way by November 1930 and building was in progress on the station sites at Arnos, Southgate, Enfield West and Cockfosters. Twenty-five per cent of the tunnelling had been completed by April 1931, all by manual labour. Work was carried on twenty-four hours a day, seven days a week. The site chosen for Enfield West, like the sites for Arnos and Cockfosters, lay in open country. A farm opposite the northern end of Chase Road barred the line of the track. It was demolished and new farm buildings were erected five hundred yards away. Towards Southgate the foundations had been laid for an eight hundred feet viaduct; five spans, fifty feet high, had been completed by January 1932. The line was scheduled to be in operation as far as Arnos Grove in May, and to Enfield West by October; by that time the railway would have cost £5.3 million.[92]

Power was switched on from Arnos Grove to Southgate in February 1933. The stations at Southgate and Enfield West opened in March; trains left every ten minutes from 5.50am. Two bus services (routes 306 and 307) gave a ten minute service from Enfield Town. The East Barnet Road, from Enfield West to the foot of Slades Hill, was renamed Enfield Road in April 1932. It was Southgate Council which pressed, unsuccessfully at first, to have Enfield West given what the councillors called 'a more suitable name'. With a flash of pure local government inspiration members suggested 'Southgate North', but since this would have been unacceptable in Enfield a compromise was reached and it was called Oakwood. Twenty-five acres adjoining the station were sold to building contractors in March 1934.[93]

Cockfosters station opened at the end of July 1933 and development of the area began, but progressed slowly, perhaps because of the absence of sewers. Little Grove at the foot of Cat Hill had been demolished early in 1932. This house had originally been built in 1553 and rebuilt in 1719. One room retained its Jacobean oak panelling. Cockfosters had been expected to develop rapidly, but four years after the opening of the railway there were still only 184 houses within a radius of a quarter of a mile from the station and 98 of these stood empty; of the fifty shops built, only twenty were occupied. The greater part of the Cockfosters area, amounting to 184 acres, was transferred from the Enfield to the Southgate local authority in August 1933, with a resulting loss (to Enfield) of rateable values amounting to £2,595. At the same time ten acres at Worlds End, rateable value £5, were transferred from Southgate to Enfield.[94]

It was not until 1933 that a high demand for small and medium-sized houses developed. That demand was encouraged by lower building costs and lower mortgage interest rates. The large-scale building contractors who undertook this work were to prove more efficient and more conscientious than some of the local builders. The Council, in January 1933, approved plans submitted by Hilbery Chaplin, one of the largest estate developers in the country, to build 216 houses in Stannards (now Clydesdale), Sedcote and Walters Roads at Ponders End, on land which had formerly been an orchard. The houses had long gardens with fruit trees well established, all the roads and paths were made up.

170. Hilbery Chaplin offered six-roomed houses at £390 freehold, with tiled fireplaces, glazed sinks, gas coppers, larders, dressers, bay windows and electric light. There were no legal fees, mortgage costs or road charges. The photographs, 1992, show houses in Garfield Road (above) and Clydesdale.

Both here and in Garfield Road, Hilbery Chaplin offered six-roomed houses at £390 freehold, with tiled fireplaces, glazed sinks, gas coppers, larders, dressers, bay windows and electric light. There were no legal fees, mortgage costs or other extras. Hilbery Chaplin was putting up more houses at £390 on the Grosvenor

171. Gazette *21 April 1933.*

PEEPS INTO THE FUTURE
What Enfield May Be

172.   *As early as 1933 developers like Hilbery Chaplin could offer houses for as little as £390. Deposits were low, there were no road charges, no mortgage costs, no legal fees and no other extras. Our cartoonist (Gazette* 20 September 1935) *wonders whether it will be like this in 1954. You know the answer.*

173. Wright's claimed, with a little
exaggeration, that those who
purchased their houses in Church
Road would have a good outlook
on Epping Forest and would be able
to reach the trams, buses and
Ponders End railway station in one
minute. Photograph 1992.

£40 GIVEN AWAY

TO EVERY PURCHASER OF

A Sound
Investment at
19/-
weekly

WRIGHT'S
WELL - BUILT
HOUSES

'Phone
Enfield 2891
NOW
and don't lose
time

in CHURCH ROAD, PONDERS END, at

£725 Freehold

Decorated to your liking at no extra cost.
Electric Shades and Lamps provided.   Nothing else to buy.
One minute Trams, Buses and Railway Station.
Good outlook on Forest.   Purchase Terms to suit all.
Show House :   Apply :
168 Church Road, Ponders End.   127 VILLAGE ROAD, ENFIELD

Gazette 21 April 1993

estate near the Red Lion at Enfield Highway, with considerable foresight, even
providing space for a garage. The buyer could move in for £5 down, his
repayments could be as low as 9s 6d a week. Other low cost housing was offered
on the Aylands estate, west of the Hertford Road at Freezywater, at £395
freehold. Jackson's houses on the Oakfield estate in Green Street were offered
at £575 freehold, £30 down and 16s 10d a week.[95]

Most houses continued to be priced at from around £700. Houses at Church
Road, off South Street, were for sale at £725; Wright the builder offered to
decorate to the liking of the purchaser and to provide electric light shades and
lamps. With perhaps a little exaggeration, he boasted 'one minute to the trams,
buses and the railway station' and 'good outlook on the forest'. He was also
building houses and bungalows 'on the Cuffley heights' served by a new bus
route from Waltham Cross. A. Morris and Sons were offering four-bedroomed
houses in Glebe Avenue at £1,150 upward; five months later only two (at £1,200)
were left. J. A. Roberts had houses for sale on the Slades Hill estate at £1,250,
featuring what he described as a 'unique entrance hall ..., three double bedrooms, a bathroom with a fitted square bath, cavity walls and a separate brick

garage'. Houses on the Old Park estate, built by Cyril W. D. Walden, were offered at from £975. Thirteen acres were sold in August 1934 for the Old Park View estate of seventy-five houses off Slades Hill. Gate's and Hunt's Orchard estate at the western end of Carterhatch Lane had houses for sale at £695. C.Meeker had acquired twelve acres, a former Cornish brickfield, in the angle between the railway and the Cambridge Road, to build a hundred and seventy houses on three roads connecting with Trinity Avenue. On part of this land, near Bush Hill Park station, chalet bungalows and houses, with coloured roof tiles to choice, were put up in Melbourne Way by Hugh Davies at £670 freehold; the deposit was £31 2s, repayments were 19s a week.[96]

Cheaper land on the perimeter of the parish was more likely to be used for bungalows. The Oaklands Park estate off Theobalds Park Road had 'charming freehold bungalows' for sale, 'no two alike'; the absence of sewerage was not mentioned. The dwellings were duly built and occupied, the householders formed a ratepayers' association which petitioned the Council for a sewer. It would cost £40,000, and the Council insisted that it could not be built unless the landowners and developers in the area were willing to share the cost. No sewer was constructed and within a year or two there were complaints of overflowing cesspools. A further development in the area took place in 1937. The situation posed a dilemma, for if the Council undertook to empty the cesspools on the Oaklands estate two additional cesspool machines (pumps) would have to be purchased at a total cost of £1,600, but even then the sewage could not be emptied into the sewerage system, for the sewers by this time (January 1938) were full to capacity. Money spent on any local scheme to dispose of the sewage had to be considered in the light of the probable introduction, before long, of an east Middlesex main drainage scheme which had been under consideration since 1933. The Council therefore continued to empty the cesspools charging the householders 7s 6d each time; 7s 6d was too much for some (or they were keen gardeners) and they distributed the sewage over their gardens, causing an unbearable nuisance on the estate. Enfield had borrowed £35,000 in 1934, and a further £100,000 in 1935, to extend the sewage works, but the district was growing so rapidly that any improvements were quickly overtaken by the rise in demand. A further application had to be made in April 1936 for sanction to borrow £145,000 for a new sewage disposal works to be constructed at Edmonton. Thirty-seven acres of the old sewage farm at Cuckoo Hall Lane were sold to Edmonton Council for £1,100 an acre to be used for housing. The County, by July 1937, had prepared the Bill for an East Middlesex Main Drainage Scheme but its construction was delayed by the Second World War and it did not come into operation until October 1957.[97]

With the expansion of industry and trade, eastern Enfield was ceasing to be merely a dormitory area; more and more people both worked and lived there. A great deal of building was going on, over three thousand houses were completed or started there in the years between 1931 and 1934. Completed in those years were: 286 houses on the Aylands estate, 234 on the Grosvenor estate, on the Carterhatch estate 274, on the Cedar Road (now Cedar Avenue) estate 50, at Church Road 150, at Scotland Green 216 and on the Southfields estate 33. The quality of the building had also improved. In order to sell their houses many of the builders were now making up the roads and even planting trees and shrubs. Corner houses were set back to avoid traffic blind spots. The Council had under consideration for approval, in July 1934, builders' plans for 554

174. This photograph, ingeniously dated by Stephen Sellick, shows Walter Aldous's tobacconist, confectioner and newsagents shop in 1935 at 168 Hertford Road (renumbered in 1936 to no. 738) at Freezywater. Modern Coaches had premises in Lancaster Road and ran daily excursions to many local seaside resorts.

houses on the Suffolks and Carterhatch Lane estates. The rate of house building in eastern Enfield was maintained throughout the remainder of that year. Semi-detached houses on the Tysoe Gardens estate, north of Ordnance Road near Enfield Lock station, were offered at £565 freehold in 1934.[98] Homemakers were building 115 houses on the Sunnyside estate at Carterhatch Road. Houses cost £449 on the Mapleton estate in Hoe Lane, the deposit was £29 4s and the weekly repayments 13s 6d. Building had recently begun or was about to begin, in July 1934, on a number of estates: at Bullsmoor Lane and Hertford Road 162 houses, on the Unity estate 142, in Turkey Street on the west side of the railway 57 and on the Enfield Wash side of the railway 282, on the Grosvenor estate an additional 40, in Brick Lane 54, at Green Street 39, at Mezens meadow 132, in Falcon Road 40 and in Lincoln Road 62.[99]

Sites were more expensive west of the Cambridge Road. The Drapers Company had sold twenty-two acres in Baker Street and Churchbury Lane, but it still retained sixteen acres between Baker Street and the footpath to Forty Hill (later the Kenilworth Crescent site). It was thought that land prices would soon reach £1,000 an acre. There was some talk of building 'a model town' of 2,500 houses on 1,300 acres in the northern part of the district, in the area west of the Rose

175. Ernest Owers Ltd purchased 74 acres of Trent Park in 1935 for £116,000. The plan envisaged shopping areas on the north side of Bramley Road and on the east side of Cockfosters Road. The houses were expected to sell at about £1,000. The photograph, 1992, shows the north side of Westpole Road.

and Crown in Clay Hill, for the land there, at this time, was still zoned as residential. The Council however placed an order in 1934 restricting the development because of the absence of sewers and the incapacity of the sewerage system. The landowners were informed that if they offered a substantial contribution to the cost of improvements, the Council might be prepared to reconsider.[100]

Southgate Borough Council in September 1934 made application to borrow £19,260 to provide sewers in that part of the Cockfosters area which had been recently transferred from Enfield. The cost would inevitably be very high in relation to the number of properties served, and because the sewers would enhance the value of neighbouring land, the Ministry felt that the land-owners and developers ought to share the cost; it therefore refused to sanction the loan. The difficulty was overcome by an arrangement with Ernest Owers Ltd. The firm purchased seventy-four acres of Trent Park in May 1935 and agreed to provide sewers on their estate large enough to take all the sewage from Cockfosters into the sewers in Bramley Road. The land was purchased for £116,000, more than £1,500 an acre. The estate plan provided for shopping areas on the north side of Bramley Road and on the east side of Cockfosters Road. This area was zoned for house building partly at ten to an acre and partly at eight. Oakwood and Cockfosters stations would occupy the two corners of this estate, known as Westpole Farm. The houses were expected to sell at about £1,000.[101]

Another area of Enfield Chase near Oakwood station was taken for house building when Chamberlain and Willows sold South Lodge and Farm on behalf of the Duchy of Lancaster in March 1935. The mansion, whose earlier history

176. *John Laing and Son set out to build a beautiful estate. Four eminent architects were employed to provide variety of design (three designs are shown here) and eleven acres of public open space were provided.*

177. Laing's 'de luxe' kitchen contained a large cabinet fitted with a pull-out table with a folding double seat on one side, also a put-away ironing board. The kitchen was fitted with a gas copper, a hot-water boiler and had a red tiled floor.

178. Bincote Road was intended as part of a bypass to take traffic from Green Lanes along Green Dragon Lane, Worlds End Lane across Enfield Road, Hadley Road and the Ridgeway to join Cattlegate Road. Trentwood Side continued the bypass a little way north of Enfield Road before the project was abandoned.

is described by David Pam in *The Story of Enfield Chase* had been used for some years as a preparatory school. This use was to continue until the end of the summer term and then the house would be demolished. Nobody at that time

179. The park at South Lodge was developed by John Laing from 1935. Much fine woodland and two lakes were preserved to embellish the new housing estate. Boxers lake (top) and Lakeside (below).

seems to have thought of conversion, but at least it was hoped to retain much of the beautiful timber and ornamental trees in the park. Eleven acres of public open space were to be provided, including two fine lakes and much woodland. The purchaser was John Laing and Son. Four eminent architects were to be employed to ensure that there would be no monotony in design, and the landscaping was excellent. Development was to begin at the north-west corner nearest the tube station; 939 houses were to be built.[102]

East of the South Lodge estate 145 houses were planned on the Old Park estate near the bridge at the foot of Slades Hill. Through this estate a section of a proposed sixty-feet wide Enfield bypass would be constructed, to be known as

£1030

NO ROAD CHARGES   NO LEGAL FEES

ACTUAL PHOTO. PAIR OF (A) TYPE.

Purchase Price, Freehold £1030
Deposit 10% £103

Building Society Repayments, 21 years, £1 6s. 9d. per week
Ratable value £33 at 13/- in £ and
Water Rate 6% of nett access. approx.   9s. 0d. per week

35/9 PER WEEK   Including Rates and Water

A few of this type are available with independent Garage Drive and wider frontage at £1,070. Brick Built Garage, £60.

Other Terms to suit Purchasers

180 (above and opposite).   High quality houses in Bincote Road.

Bincote Road. This was intended as part of a link from Green Lanes Winchmore Hill, along Green Dragon Lane, thence by Worlds End Lane, across Enfield

Lounge of
A Type
House
Note Large
Bay & Tiled
Fireplace

View of
Hall and
Lounge
with
Folding
Doors open
A Type

Road and Hadley Road to cross the Ridgeway west of Oak Avenue, then across East Lodge Lane to join Cattlegate Road. The road was continued fifty or so yards north of Enfield Road (Trentwoodside) but was then abandoned.[103]

Land prices were still rising. Eight and a half acres fronting Southbury Road

ENFIELD TOWN, MIDDLESEX

Having frontages to Southbury Road of about 412 feet, and Eaton Road of about 475 feet and a total area of about 8½ acres, which will be offered for SALE BY AUCTION by Messrs. BOWYER & BOWYER at THE GEORGE HOTEL, ENFIELD TOWN, on THURSDAY, the 8th day of NOVEMBER, 1934

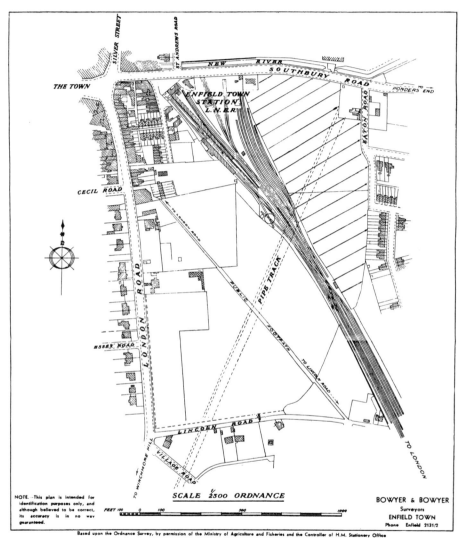

The eight and a half acres shown here (broad hatching) were sold in November 1934 for £17,300 (£2,000 an acre). The New River, buried in pipes, crosses the land.

and Eaton Road were sold in November 1934 for £17,300 (£2,000 an acre). It was to be developed as shops and houses by E. H. Stephens, who also planned to develop the Glebe Estate of twenty-four acres in Churchbury Lane where 270 houses were proposed. Houses on the Enfield Town estate were of three types.

ENFIELD TOWN ESTATE - 1934

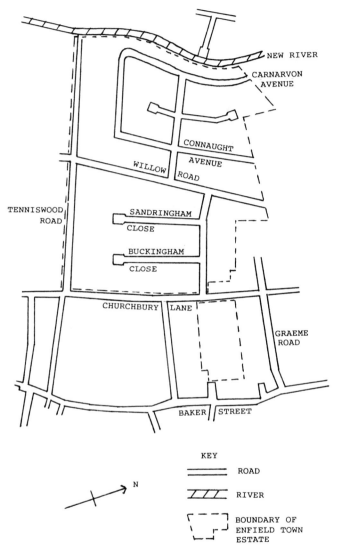

KEY

═══ ROAD

▨▨▨ RIVER

⌐ ─ ┐
⌐ ─ ┘ BOUNDARY OF
└ ─ ┘ ENFIELD TOWN
        ESTATE

The 'A' type cost between £450 and £495, a £25 deposit would secure and repayment could be as low as 11s 8d a week plus 3s 5d a week rates. The 'B' type sold for £550 and the 'C' type for £520. All the 'A' type houses had been sold by January 1935 except six in Sandringham Close and two in Churchbury Lane. Seven hundred houses on this estate were sold in less than two years.[104]

An application was submitted for the development of the Adelaide House estate (205 houses) in May 1935. It was planned to continue Carterhatch Lane

*181. Gazette 13 July 1934. 700
of these houses had been sold by July
1935, that is in less than two years.
Trees were being planted along the
footpaths and the walk to the
railway station had by then been
reduced to seven minutes.*

*182. Orchard Crescent 1934
shows unfinished houses from
number 28 downward and the
surviving remnants of the orchards.*

in a direct line to Forty Hill by a road known as Myddelton Avenue. A scheme
was proposed for 130 houses in Turkey Street and 182 in Ordnance Road. Bricks
and mortar were rapidly covering the orchards which had given the name to
Cherry Orchard Lane. The old barn there stood forlorn, awaiting demolition.
The farm, tended for years by the Ironside family, would soon be but a memory.
Houses on Goodchild's Pembroke estate, east of the Cambridge Road in Carterhatch Lane, offered at £435 freehold, could be secured for £25 deposit,
repayments would be 10s 8d a week. Sterling Homes on the Hillview estate in
Medcalf Road (off Ordnance Road) were sold in September 1935 for £499 and
£525, £2 secured a house, repayments were from 12s 11d plus 3s 1d rates. The
firm was also building on the St Gildas estate in Duck Lees Lane. [105]
Martyn was building houses on the Ridgeway estate (near Drapers Road) in

183. Thomas Currey offered houses off Willow Road in 1935 at £775 freehold, built on land formerly Gibbons' orchards. Where possible the fruit trees were left in the gardens. A monthly return from Enfield Town to Liverpool Street then cost 32s 9d. Photograph 1992 shows Carnarvon Avenue.

December 1935 and had opened a show house. Houses on Thomas Currey's estate in Willow Road were offered at £775 (deposit £40 repayments 22s 3d), others were offered at only £715. This land had formerly been used as orchards by J. Gibbons, and wherever possible the fruit trees were left standing. Currey advertised the estate as lying close to Enfield Town railway station from where a monthly season ticket to Liverpool Street could be bought for £1 12s 9d (1935). The houses had long gardens ranging from 110 feet to 220 feet, ample space for garages was provided and Crittall metal windows were fitted; there were no legal costs or road charges. Neville J. Reid was building bungalows in Cuffley for £685. Land in Enfield still found ready purchasers. Bowyer and Bowyer, in July 1936, sold 5.2 acres at the junction of Baker Street and Clay Hill for £8,950 (£1,725 an acre). Sixty-six houses could be built on the site under the town planning scheme. This might be compared with twenty-one acres of land zoned for agriculture, on both sides of Theobalds Park Road, including eight cottages and two nurseries, sold at the same time for £5,650 (£270 an acre) and six more acres of agricultural land on the Ridgeway Cuffley sold for £1,575 (£262 an acre). Bowyer also had for sale eight acres of land and farm buildings on the west side of Churchbury Lane, part of the Somerset estates, but the land was immediately acquired for the Council by compulsory purchase; Chase School and playing field now occupies the site. In the six months ending 30 September 1936, 1,174 new houses were built in Enfield. [106]

Land values remained high, 5¼ acres of the Somerset estate in Baker Street, facing Enfield Court, were sold in April 1937 for £10,100 (nearly £2,000 an acre) to the Bury House estates. The Council intimated to the purchaser that it was intended to construct a wide road through the estate as a continuation of Parsonage Lane and Willow Road; it was to be part of another Enfield Town

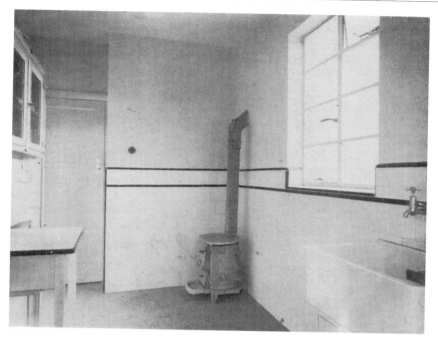

184. The kitchen, in the Currey houses, contained a 'Hygena' cabinet with glazed dresser cupboard together with an enamel-topped table which ran on rubber wheels and contained a concealed wringer and drainage tank. 'The tradesmen's entrance', it was pointed out, 'leads out of the kitchen'. Below is shown the drawing room which was at the back of the house.

JULY 12, 1935.

A FEW EXAMPLES OF

GORDON'S

SALE BARGAINS !

COME TO-DAY!
SEE OUR WINDOWS
FOR SPECIAL KEEN
OFFERS !

Save Pounds
BY BUYING NOW

SPLENDID 4ft. OAK BEDROOM SUITE, comprising Wardrobe with large mirror, ample hanging room; Modern Dressing Table, triple mirrors; and Linen Chest.

BARGAIN PRICE

10
GUINEAS

THREE - PIECE SUITE, covered in Rexhide and Velour. The Suite consists of luxurious Settee and two roomy Armchairs.

BARGAIN PRICE

10
GUINEAS

GOODS
STORED &
DELIVERED
FREE

Complete OAK DINING ROOM SUITE, comprising 4ft. Oak Sideboard, 5ft. Extending Dining Table, and four Chairs.
BARGAIN PRICE

9
GUINEAS

ALL SALE BARGAINS
ARE OBTAINABLE ON
OUR

**1, 2 or 3
YEARS
CREDIT
TERMS**

GORDONS

52 CHURCH STREET, ENFIELD
196-198 HOE STREET, WALTHAMSTOW, E.17

Please ask for our Sale lists.

Name......................

Address......................

....

185. Readers are advised not to send for the sale lists.

bypass leaving the Ridgeway at Lavender Hill, using Holtwhites Hill and Parsonage Lane to link with Southbury Road. This would enable traffic from the Great North Road to reach eastern Enfield, on its way to the docks, avoiding the Town. For this purpose the Council made a compulsory purchase of twelve acres

ALAS! POOR CISSY!

186. Land prices were still rising.
Land on the Somerset estate,
opposite Enfield Court in Baker
Street, sold for housing in April
1937 for nearly £2,000 an acre.
(Gazette 30 April 1937).

187. Traffic through the Town
was increasing so rapidly by 1937
that the Council purchased land to
build a wide bypass as a continuation of Parsonage Lane and Willow
Road into Southbury Road.
Photograph 1992.

from the trustees of Sir Alfred Somerset. Traffic was increasing rapidly. In 1931,
21,000 vehicles in seven days had used Windmill Hill; by 1935 the number was
36,000, a seventy per cent increase. In the same period traffic using Southbury
Road increased by forty per cent. Another piece of the Somerset estate, 7½ acres
with a frontage of 270 feet on Churchbury Lane, was sold for £9,575; at twelve
to an acre it would accommodate ninety houses.[107]

There were 23,000 dwellings in Enfield by May 1936. Houses were now being
built at a rate of 2,500 a year, yet the MOH report shows 341 families living in
overcrowded conditions, including 110 in council houses. The Council proposed to erect four, five and six-bedroomed houses to alleviate the problem.
Many large houses built before the turn of the century were falling vacant and
it had become difficult to find purchasers or tenants. There were so many
mansions empty on the Bycullah estate that the town planning officer spoke in

188. *Frederick Hills stands in the doorway of his shop at number 30 Southbury Road in 1929. He was a newsagent, tobacconist and confectioner. His business prospered with the spread of the housing estates in the Thirties when he developed a delivery service to hundreds of local households.*

favour of wholesale redevelopment; the town planning profession has always had an unfortunate predilection for this sort of action. The well-off preferred modern superior residences, costing anything between £3,000 and £8,000, like those available at Winchmore Hill, Southgate or Cockfosters. [108]

Although estate developers in eastern Enfield were beginning to experience a shortage of suitable land, Enfield west, which contained 6,544 acres and included much Green Belt land, had 3,550 acres zoned for building in 1937 of which 2,850 acres remained undeveloped. Five hundred and seventy-five acres were still available for building in central ward, 311 acres in the north-east ward, but only 54 acres remained for house building in the south-east ward, where most of the industry lay.[109]

The vast new William Girling reservoir on the Lea marshes, south of and adjacent to the King George reservoir, was begun for the Metropolitan Water Board in September 1935 by the contractors Mowlem and Co., to improve the water supply in the Lea Valley; it was completed in 1951. Parliamentary powers for two reservoirs had been secured by the East London Water Co. in 1900; the first, the King George, had been completed in 1913. The River Lea was now diverted into channels each side of the new reservoir. Fifty miles of railway tracks were laid there by December 1936. No doubt the reservoir was necessary, but it involved the sad loss of a lovely walk from Edmonton, over the marshes from Picketts Lock to the Ha'penny bridge and thence across the 'seven fields' to Epping Forest.[110]

Fifty-three thousand cubic yards of refuse were collected each year and dumped among people's homes in eastern Enfield by the Council. One dump lay between Hoe Lane and Carterhatch Lane and another between Osborne Road and Goldsdown Road. Demand for an incinerator grew, yet in February 1936 the Labour Council began negotiations to acquire for a rubbish tip a twenty-three acre gravel pit, south of Carterhatch Road, near the Westmoor estate off Green Street. The move was, as might be expected, highly unpopular in eastern Enfield and as a result the Labour party lost five seats, including two at Ponders End, in the local elections that April. The new Conservative Council wisely abandoned the unpopular proposal, but the difficulty of finding a place for refuse disposal remained. As an emergency measure it was decided to use the Council's Carterhatch Lane gravel pit, although it had capacity for a further eight months dumping only. At the same time Heath's pit in Goat Lane was offered for twelve months at a shilling a load. By February 1937 a Ministry of Health inquiry was set up to consider a request to borrow £32,160 to construct a refuse disposal plant in Carterhatch Lane; this began operating in July 1938. The old method of controlled tipping within the urban district area had been rendered impracticable by the rapid growth of the population.[111]

Enfield's twenty-nine year old electric tram service came to an end at an hour past midnight one Sunday morning in May 1938. The last tram from Enfield Town was mobbed by a wild crowd of souvenir hunters; guard rails were ripped off, seats dragged out, men were clinging to the front and the rear and there was an escort of hundreds of cars and motor-cycles. Trolleybuses were quietly introduced later that morning. The tram service from Edmonton to Waltham Cross ended in October; the last journey was again marked by drunkenness and hooliganism. One wonders why nobody thought of making the change-over when the pubs had been closed. Before a month was out, complaints were being made about the trolleybus service.[112]

There were 26,254 inhabited houses in Enfield by the end of the year 1938, yet there were still estates where every tenant sub-let. Sub-letting, though controlled in Council property, was virtually unchecked in private property. A tendency for landlords to pull down old poor-class houses, in order to erect modern houses on the sites, was encouraged by the high price of land.[113]

The Council's debt stood at £1.5 million in 1937; over £1 million was owing on housing and education. On the other hand the rateable value of the parish had almost doubled since 1928, from £369,000 to £714,000. Over the preceding

189. The electric tram service to Enfield Town ended at an hour past midnight, one Sunday morning in May 1938. The last tram, shown here, was mobbed and torn apart by souvenir hunters.

190. Feltham tram, Enfield to Tottenham Court Road, in the Town, 1938.

191. *Trolleybuses were introduced on the route to Enfield Town in May 1938. Within a month there were complaints about the service.*

192. A plan was submitted in May 1939 for nine hundred houses on the north side of Clay Hill. It had perforce to be rejected because the Council's sewers could take no more. (Gazette 28 July 1939).

four years the type of property erected in Enfield had been improving. The average rateable value of new houses built in 1934 was £18, in 1937 it was £23.[114]

Plans were submitted in May 1939 for the development of the Claysmore estate in Clay Hill, some forty-five acres on which nine hundred houses were intended. The plan was rejected by the local authority by virtue of the temporary building restrictions which it had imposed to cope with Enfield's sewerage difficulties. Nevertheless proposals to build more houses kept pouring in to the Council offices, including eighteen houses in a new street off Alexandra Road and fifty-five in new streets off Durants Road at Ponders End. Also before the Council were plans to build forty-six houses in a new street off Addison Road and fifty-six houses on the west side of the Cambridge Road north of Bullsmoor Lane. [115]

The growth of Enfield in the ten years preceding the war had thus been enormous, more than twelve thousand houses had been built and each required sanitary provision. The existing sewerage system by 1939 had reached its capacity and the Council was forced to reject plans for new houses until it could improve its sewers. It was feared that an epidemic might break out if the system failed, nevertheless developers continued to appeal to the Ministry seeking to override the restrictions. [116]

Notes to Chapter Three

1. Alan A. Jackson, *Semi-detached London*
2. *Gazette* 13 My 1921, 19 My 1922, 31 Oct 1919, 16 Mr 1923, 10 Ap, 16 Oct 1925, 8 F 1924
3. *ibid* 9 Ap, 5 N 1926, 28 Ja 1927
4. *ibid* 24 D 1926, 5 Au 1927, 20 Ap, 15 Je, 11 My, 13 Jl 1928
5. *ibid* 16 Mr 1923, 20 N 1925, 14 Ja 1927, 22 N 1929
6. *ibid* 2, 30 My 1924, 27 D 1927
7. *ibid* 22 N, 28 D 1918, 11 Ap 1919
8. *ibid* 6 My, 5 D 1919, 9 Ap 1920, 1 Ap 1921, 9 Ap, 4 Je 1920
9. *ibid* 21 F 1919, 12 Mr 1920
10. *ibid* 19 S, 16 My 1919, 30 Ja 1920
11. *ibid* 26 N 1920, 27 My 1921, H & T P minutes

12. *Gazette* 22 Ap, 17 Je, 9 D 1921, 8 S 1922, H & T P minutes
13. *Gazette* 3 Mr, 7 Ap, 14 Ap, 31 Mr 1922, 30 Mr 1923
14. *ibid* 23 N 1923, 17 N 1922
15. *ibid* 13 Ap 1923
16. *ibid* 12 My 1922, 12 Oct 1923
17. *ibid* 22 S 1922
18. *ibid* 19 Ja, 2 Mr 1923
19. *ibid* 6 Oct 1933, 11 F 1924, H & T P minutes 5 Je, 9 Oct 1924, 12 F 1925, 12 Je 1924, 26 My 1925
20. *Gazette* 28 Mr, 25 Ap, 5 D, 23 My, 13 Je, 26 S, 31 Oct 1924.
21. *ibid* 14 D 1923, 31 Oct, 17 Oct 1924
22. *ibid* 11 D 1925
23. H & T P minutes 26 Jl 1927, *Gazette* 17 S, 25 Je, 2 Jl 1926
24. *ibid* 17 S, 15 Oct, 19 N 1926, H & T P minutes 28 S 1926, *Gazette* 17 D 1926
25. *ibid* 14 Ja 1927, 29 Je 1928, 11 F, 5 Au, 16 S 1927, H & T P minutes 26 Jl 1927, 5 Je 1924, *Gazette* 8 Ap 1927
26. *ibid* 6 Ap 1928, 29 Mr 1929, 11 Ap 1930, 22 N 1929
27. *ibid* 9 F, 19 Oct, 16 N 1923, 11 Ja, 31 Oct 1924
28. *ibid* 16 Jl 1926, H & T P minutes 8 Mr 1927, *Gazette* 21 My, 30 Jl 1926, H & T P minutes 9 Oct 1924, 12 My 1925
29. *Gazette* 9 Oct 1924, 27 Ja 1928, 13 F 1925
30. *ibid* 24 Ja, 1 F, 16 My, 27 Je, 1 Au 1924
31. *ibid* 6 Au, 24 S 1926, 4 Mr, 18 Mr 1927
32. *ibid* 15 Ap, 22 Jl 1927, 20 Jl, 13 Jl, 10 F, 17 Au, 14 S 1928, 30 Au, 2 Au 1929
33. *ibid* 13 F 1920
34. *ibid* 18 Ap, 6 Je 1919, 9 Ja 1920, 11 F 1921
35. *ibid* 11 Ap, 8 Au, 3 Oct 1919, 19 Mr 1920
36. *ibid* 23 Au 1918
37. *ibid* 21 Mr, 1 Au, 12 S 1919, 6 Au 1920, 8 S 1922, 3 Je 1921
38. *ibid* 24 N 1922, 25 S 1925
39. *ibid* 30 Je 1922, 10 Je 1927, 4 Mr 1932
40. *ibid* 19 Jl, 9 Au 1918, 11 Mr 1932
41. *ibid* 10 D 1920, 15 D 1922, 2 Ja 1925, 3 F, 11 My, 3 Je 1928, 11 D 1931
42. *ibid* 30 Mr, 8 S 1923
43. *ibid* 26 Au 1927
44. *ibid* 23 Jl 1926, 6 Jl 1928, 2 My 1930, 25 N 1932
45. *ibid* 4 D 1931, 12 F, 13 My, 18 N, 10 Je 1932, 7 Ap 1933
46. *ibid* 4 Au 1933, 2 Mr 1934, 2 Je 1935
47. *ibid* 15 S 1933
48. *ibid* 10 Ja 1936, 5 Mr 1937
49. *ibid* 2 D, 9 D, 23 D 1938, 28 Jl 1939
50. *ibid* 25 Jl 1925, 26 F 1937
51. *ibid* 6 F 1931, 28 Oct 1932, 23 N 1934, 10 Je 1938, 19 My 1939
52. *ibid* 28 Oct 1938, 6 Au, 10 D 1937
53. *ibid* 17 S, 5 N, 27 N 1937, 28 Ja 1938, 20 D 1935
54. *ibid* 21 F, 16 My 1919, 15 Au, 25 S 1925, 25 Je 1926
55. *ibid* 15 Oct 1926
56. *ibid* 5 D 1930, 27 F 1931, 4 Mr, 30 D 1932, 26 My, 9 Je 1933, 28 Jl 1933
57. *ibid* 7 S 1934, 28 Jl, 22 S 1933, 9 Mr 1934
58. *ibid* 8 Je, 27 Jl, 7 S, 21 S, 12 Oct 1934, 8 Mr 1935, 19 Je, 26 Je 1936
59. *ibid* 28 Ja, 25 N 1938
60. *ibid* 27 N 1925, 30 S 1927, 2 Au 1929, 28 D, 1 Mr 1928
61. *ibid* 14 F, 16 My, 7 Mr 1930
62. *ibid* 10 Oct 1930
63. *ibid* 6 My 1932, 20 Je 1930, 17 Jl, 23 Oct 1931

64. *ibid* 9, 16 My, 20 Je, 4 Jl, 26 S, 7 N 1930, 22 Ap 1932
65. *ibid* 14 Mr 1930
66. *ibid* 31 Jl 1936
67. *ibid* 28 Ja, 5 F 1937, 18 Au, 9 Je 1939, 5 Mr, 31 D 1937
68. *ibid* 10, 31 Ja, 14 F, 10 Oct, 12 D 1930
69. *ibid* 10 Jl 1931, MOH report 1930, *Gazette* 5 D 1930, 12 Je 1931
70. *ibid* 30 Oct, 3, 24 Ap, 11 Jl, 20 N 1931
71, *ibid* 9 Oct 1931, 4 Mr, 26 Au, 25, 30 S 1932, 31 Mr 1933
72. *ibid* 5 F, 19 F 1932
73. *ibid* 17 F, 7 Ap, 1 D 1933, 12 Ja 1934
74. *ibid* 25 N 1932, 1 D 1933
75. *ibid* 12 Ja, 16 F 1934
76. *ibid* 30 Mr, 13 Ap 1934
77. *ibid* 14 S 1934
78. *ibid* 16 Mr, 20 Jl, 14 S, 16 N 1934
79. *ibid* 11 Oct 1935
80. *ibid* 5 Ap, 12 Ap, 22 F, 8 N, 22 N 1935
81. *ibid* 6 Mr, 4 D 1936
82. *ibid* 31 Jl, 11 S 1936, 9 Ap 1937
83. *ibid* 4 Je, 10 S, 26 N 1937, 3 Je 1938
84. *ibid* 13 Au 1937. Many of the residents in my own street on an Edmonton Council estate were middle class.
85. *ibid* 8 Ap, 9 D 1938, 6 Ja, 17 F 1939
86. *ibid* 11 Jl, 4 Jl, 1930
87. *ibid* 28 N 1930, 10 Jl 1931, Enfield Marshalls Estates sale cat. 1933
88. *Gazette* 5 Je 1931
89. *ibid* 2 Oct, 27 N 1931
90. *ibid* 18 Mr, 28 Oct, 24 Je, 11 N 1932, 24 Au, 12 Oct 1934
91. *ibid* 17 Ja 1930
92. *ibid* 11 Jl, 26 S 1930, 16 Ja, 10 Ap 1931, 8 Ja 1932
93. *ibid* 10 Mr, 22 S 1933, 25 Mr 1932, 9 Mr 1934
94. *ibid* 21 Jl 1933, 18 D 1931, 6 My 1938, 18 Au 1933
95. *ibid* 31 Mr, 6 Ja, 19 My, 21 Ap, 22 S 1933
96. *ibid* 21 Ap, 6 Oct 1933, 15 Je, 20 Jl, 10 Au, 31 Au 1934, 2 Je, 21 Jl 1933
97. *ibid* 28 Jl 1933, 21 D 1934, 3 N 1933, 15 Au 1938, 29 N 1935, 1 My 1936, 2 Ja, 2 Jl 1937, 1 Jl, 7 Ja 1938
98. *ibid* 10 N 1933, 13 Jl 1934
99. *ibid* 26 Oct, 16 N 1934
100. *ibid* 2 N 1934
101. *ibid* 5 Oct 1934, 29 Mr, 31 My 1935
102. *ibid* 29 Mr 1935
103. *ibid* 31 My 1935
104. *ibid* 16 N 1934, 24 My 1935
105. *ibid* 31 My, 6 S, 20 S 1935
106. *ibid* 13 D 1935, 17 Ap 1936, Enfield Auct. Cat. 1935, *Gazette* 17 Jl 1936, 2 Ap 1937
107. *ibid* 1 My 1936, 23 Ap 1937
108. *ibid* 15 My, 29 My, 4 D 1936
109. *ibid* 18 Je 1937
110. *ibid* 6 S 1935, 9 N 1934
111. *ibid* 15 My 1936, 26 F 1937, 29 Jl 1938
112. *ibid* 13 My, 21 Oct, 9 D 1938
113. *ibid* 12 Au 1938
114. *ibid* 27 Au, 22 Oct 1937
115. *ibid* 2 Je 1939
116. *ibid* 28 Jl 1939

Chapter Four

Religion, Pleasure, Health and Education Between the Wars

1. Introduction

The twentieth century has seen a dramatic decline in organised religion in England, both in the number of its adherents and in the influence of its teaching. Even in the mid-nineteenth century it had become apparent that urbanisation tended to diminish the role of religion in the community and that the larger the aggregation of population, the smaller the proportion which attended church or chapel. Before the First World War the rivalry between the established church and the Nonconformists had been reflected in the struggle between the Conservative and Liberal parties, but the Liberal Party declined in the period between the wars and class replaced religion as the dividing issue in politics.

In the Twenties and Thirties the churches had to compete for people's time on Sundays with many distractions. As more and more families became owner-occupiers, gardening, shopping, home decoration and repairs took up much of each week-end. Yet the nation, with the help of the Lord's Day Observance Society and Lord Reith's dictatorship at the BBC, retained, to some extent, the sedate British Sunday. Families still donned their best clothes, but they no longer went to church in them. Few would admit to being atheists, but churches were only for the big occasions, weddings, christenings and funerals. Many people based a belief in pacifism upon a vague Christianity, others followed with fervour the false creed of Marxism and painfully devised or swallowed, convoluted arguments to justify each and every one of Stalin's atrocities.

The Roman Catholic Church continued to grow, for unlike the Nonconformists, the Romans managed to retain separate denominational education. Many of the smaller sects succeeded in retaining the loyalty of their members by insisting upon a high level of commitment and by threatening exclusion against those who fell below their rigid self-imposed standards. Thus the Jehovah's Witnesses, the Seventh Day Adventists, the Reorganised Church of Jesus Christ and the Society of Friends survived virtually undiminished. The Salvation Army soldiered on doing good work among the down-and-outs and caring for expectant mothers. The Jews too, despite their growing prosperity, continued largely to retain their adherents and to build synagogues in places like Golders Green and Southgate as they deserted the East End for a better life.

In suburbs like Enfield, increasing spending power financed a growing

193. A wedding in 1937, Leonard Newman to Dorothy Wheeler at Christ Church Chase Side. The minister, third from the right, was the Reverend Ebenezer Rees.

194. The Embassy in Eaton Road, a leisure centre incorporating a dance hall and theatre, was completed precisely at the outbreak of the Second World War, but the building was immediately requisitioned by the government.

market in entertainment, while with shorter working hours, paid holidays and smaller families, people had more time to enjoy themselves. The super cinema dominated the Thirties. It provided lush carpets, luxurious decor and seats suitable for a millionaire, which contrasted impressively with the mundane interiors of most working-class homes. On the screen was paraded a dream world of handsome men and beautiful women who moved in resplendent settings quite unlike the High Road into which the audience would emerge when the film was done. But it was a family entertainment and it was cheap; you could get in for sixpence, and only fourpence at the Alcazar or the Premier. Also attempting to provide a glamorous setting was the local dance hall, like the Royal in Tottenham or the Imperial at Waltham Cross; there were also dances in the town halls, church halls and in the parks. The names of bandleaders like Henry Hall, Harry Roy, Roy Fox and Bert Ambrose were known to everyone who listened to late night dance-music on the wireless.

Professional football had a huge following and countless working men placed their hopes for a better future on the football pools every Saturday. Amateur clubs were well supported as was Sunday morning football in the parks. The names of the leading cricketers, Hobbs, Sutcliffe, Larwood, Hammond, Hutton and Bradman were upon every boy's tongue. Some schools, particularly the grammar schools, had fine cricket pitches. Good class professional boxing was widely presented at small arenas like the Alcazar and, for the even less sophisticated, there was all-in-wrestling.

Apart from the football pools there was extensive betting on horse-racing and the dogs, despite the fact that off-course betting was illegal. Even people who didn't bet knew who the bookie was and where a bet could be placed. Numerous local dog tracks were set up like the ones in Town Road, Edmonton and near Tramway Avenue, on which the crowds converged, some with their greyhounds, every Sunday morning and on certain evenings in the week.

With shorter opening hours and higher taxation, drinking decreased, but smoking, particularly cigarette smoking, increased. Thousands sought an early death to get gifts from Kensitas and Ardath. Boys collected cigarette cards, especially of footballers and cricketers. There were innumerable excursions by train and charabanc which were extended late into the autumn by trips to Southend to see the lights.

The middle class joined tennis clubs and later the council provided tennis-courts in the parks. Middle-class men played golf and wore plus-fours. They also purchased cars and went out for rides along the new arterial roads. Those who could not afford a car might buy a motor-cycle and sidecar. People took more interest in their gardens and in their homes where entertainment was provided by the wireless and the gramophone. People read a great deal and the number of branch libraries expanded rapidly; long queues would form at the 'in' counter on Saturday nights between seven and eight o'clock.

The health of the country improved between 1914 and 1939. The death rate fell from 14.3 per thousand population, before the First World War, to 12 before the Second World War; the average expectation of life was increased by some ten years. Deaths from infectious diseases diminished drastically, especially deaths from tuberculosis after the Ministry of Health ordered the pasteurisation of milk in 1922. Infant mortality (the number of deaths of children under one, per thousand live births) is considered to be a guide to levels of poverty; in Greater London in 1935 the figure was 51, in Enfield 50, in Jarrow that year it was 114. The following year came the Midwives Act which required local authorities to provide trained midwives.

The National Insurance Act of 1913 provided a free general practitioner service to insured workers, sickness benefit was paid through approved societies. Others had to depend on private insurance and on sick clubs. The poor often sought treatment at the out-patients departments of the free hospitals. Hospitals were either voluntary, like the War Memorial Hospital in Enfield or were run by a board of guardians and subsequently by the county, like the North Middlesex.

Education to the age of fourteen became compulsory after the First World War. It was elementary education for most, only 7.5 per cent in 1923 received secondary education. Such educational changes as occurred between the wars were initiated by the Hadow Report of 1926; in the Thirties children over eleven went either to secondary modern or to grammar schools. The growing number of working-class children who received an education at grammar school has done much to modify the division of the nation into classes.

2. Religion

All the churches, except perhaps the Roman Catholic, lost ground substantially during the Great War, and the decline continued in the years that followed. The middle class acquired cars and went on Sunday afternoon drives. The working class took bus rides into the country, spent their Sundays in the parks, or in the garden, or if it rained went to the pictures (though not in Enfield until 1938). Despite this, new places of worship opened in Enfield and existing ones were expanded. Others closed; the Enfield Highway Congregational church, built in 1873, closed in May 1919 through lack of support, the building was subsequently purchased by the Co-operative Society. The last Congregational service was held

195. *Vast crowds attended armistice services at a temporary cenotaph erected in Church Street in 1919 and in 1920.*

196. The Small Arms Factory church belonged to the Board of Ordnance. It was licensed for services in 1846 and was closed as a government economy measure in 1921.

in the Baker Street chapel in April 1923, before it was taken over by the Salvation Army. The Wesleyan church by the New River, built in 1889, was destroyed by fire in 1919, the rebuilding was completed in April 1923. On the other side of Church Street pew rents were abolished at St Paul's Presbyterian church in July 1921. Vast crowds attended armistice services at a temporary cenotaph erected in Church Street in October 1919 and in November 1920.[1]

The frame supporting the bells at St Andrew's had shrunk during the summer drought of 1921, £180 had to be spent on the re-hanging. The RSAF church closed at the end of the year 1921 after sixty years; this was an economy measure taken by the Army Council. The little church stood within the factory site approached from Government Row by a wooden bridge over the back river. Worship was transferred to the former parish hall in Ordnance Road, and a new church was built there dedicated to St Peter and St Paul in May 1928. Services were still being held in the Countess of Huntingdon's chapel at Whitewebbs in 1922; it was destroyed by bombing in the Second World War. The Roman Catholics began to build a new church at Ponders End in October 1923. The Baptists planned to rebuild in Cecil Road after their tabernacle in London Road had been sold to Woolworth's, the foundation stone was laid in November 1925. With the resumption of middle-class house building a temporary church was erected in Vera Avenue at Grange Park in September 1927, and at St Stephen's, Village Road an expensive church hall was begun. The Reorganised Church of Jesus Christ opened a new place of worship at the corner of Lavender and Lancaster Roads in December 1929.[2]

Many churchmen were becoming despondent at the dramatic decline in church attendance, particularly in working-class areas like Ponders End where, at St Matthew's, the Reverend Harold Mullett, in 1930, wept over 'the sinking

197. At St Stephen's Church, Bush Hill Park the building of an expensive church hall was begun in 1927; its roof can be seen above the tramcar in the photograph. House building on the opposite side of Village Road was proceeding rapidly.

moral, spiritual and social degeneracy' in his parish. 'Formerly everyone went to church', he moaned, 'now nobody does … It was the saddest thing on earth' he lamented, 'to see a young girl waiting for her first job at the factory gate …, once inside she would come under the evil influence of her work-mates, her last spark of decency would be crushed, she would be left stranded on a heap of wrecked humanity.' The poor vicar obviously had little understanding of the inherent decency of most factory girls. 'There is no God in the factory', he went on, 'the Church is only for the funeral'. The Reverend Koch at Jesus Church was another who expressed alarm at the general decline in church attendance. Even at St Andrew's, the vicar bewailed the decreasing numbers who attended church day schools and Sunday schools, and he urged his congregation to give more freely to meet church expenses so that he would not have to depend so heavily on pew rents, the income from which looked, in 1930, likely to diminish.[3]

A faculty was secured in April 1930 to remove the monument to Francis Evington from the corner of the south gallery in St Andrew's church, to the south wall of the south chancel chapel, also to move the brass to John and Jane Smith from the floor of that chapel, where it had been worn down by the boots of generations of organ blowers, to the north wall of the chapel. Despite considerable opposition, another faculty was obtained in 1932 for the removal of the galleries from St Andrew's Church; a legacy from Miss Chambers (a daughter of Charles Chambers) helped to pay for the work. During the removal a fine oak board was discovered behind the organ case in the west gallery. It proclaimed the pious gifts which had formerly enriched the parish of Enfield. Made and put up with much acclaim in 1772, it is now displayed in the north aisle. Also found were the jambs of a doorway obliterated at the beginning of the last century, undoubtedly this was 'the littell dore to St Jamys chapel', mentioned in the will of Edward Causton, vicar of Enfield from 1466 to 1491. In 1932

Colonel Sir Henry Bowles gave permission to remove his great-grandfather's memorial from the north aisle to the south wall.[4]

The foundation stone was laid in March 1931 for a new Methodist church at Ponders End, it was to replace the chapel in South Street which was by now too large for the congregation. The former Congregational church in Baker Street, which for seven or eight years had been rented by the Salvation Army, was taken over by the Old Baptist Union in 1932 to be known as Emmanual Baptist. A stone-laying ceremony for Grange Park's handsome £10,000 Methodist church took place in June 1938, it was opened for worship in December. A church had been established there in 1919, meeting at first in members' houses. The Methodists were also planning to replace their church in Wellington Road in October 1938. The congregation had first met in Edenbridge Road about thirty-five years earlier.[5]

Thus churches continued to prosper in some middle-class areas, but in many poorer parts of the parish congregations were reduced to diminishing bands of the faithful gathered precariously around despondent ministers in large, cold and empty churches.

3. Pleasure

Cinema dominated the world of mass entertainment between the wars. The technical presentation of films in the early Twenties was much better than it had been pre-war and the public found the new purpose-built cinemas far more inviting than the small, crudely adapted premises of the early days. Progress was

198. *The Rialto was built in 1920. The photograph was taken early in October 1923 (dated by Stephen Sellick). The cost of building was so high that the owners were declared bankrupt in 1925. In the Market Place next to the Rialto was the shop of Leapman a clothier, next door was Henry Smith a confectioner who sold teas and ices, then the Gas Company showrooms.*

being made, through the summer of 1920, on a picture palace which was being built by W. Grenfell at Enfield Wash; it opened in September and they called it the Premier.

199. *Local cinemas in 1922 offered their customers whatever inducements they could think of, such as 'cycles stored free' or, children under twelve with an adult '3d only'. (Gazette 25 August 1922)*

232

Richard Slater recalled the Saturday morning children's programmes there in the early Twenties. 'After our spartan gas-lit surroundings at home, the inside of the cinema was a wonderland. For twopence we entered a palace of luxury with electric lights, tip-up upholstered seats, red and gold painted ornamental balconies and red velvet curtains. The films were all silent and in black and white. Most of the action took place in what appeared to be a continual downpour of rain ... films were accompanied by a piano player who varied his tunes according to the action taking place on the screen. Before the films started the place was a feverish hive of expectancy. Then came the magic moment when the lights dimmed and a great cheer rang through the cinema. More cheers as the curtains parted and a white searchlight beam streaked out above our heads illuminating the screen ... Charlie Chaplin, Harold Lloyd, Buster Keeton, the Keystone Cops, Chester Conklin and cowboy Tom Mix were some of the stars who kept us in raptures. As the films were silent we could let ourselves go whole-heartedly into the action and the place was a continuous uproar of cheers, boos and laughter'.

The Rialto in the Market Place was also built in 1920. Building costs were extraordinarily high at that time; in consequence the company found itself without the means to equip the cinema and had to borrow £8,000 from Allen Fairhead the builder. Bankruptcy followed and in 1925 the Rialto was sold for £31,000. It was completely remodelled by 1927 at a cost of £8,000 and a 'new wonder organ' was installed; a huge queue formed for the re-opening in August. The following year improvements were begun at the Queens Hall in London Road where the balcony was rebuilt to seat three hundred, this brought the capacity up to one thousand. It re-opened on 12 November 1928 with a 'talking

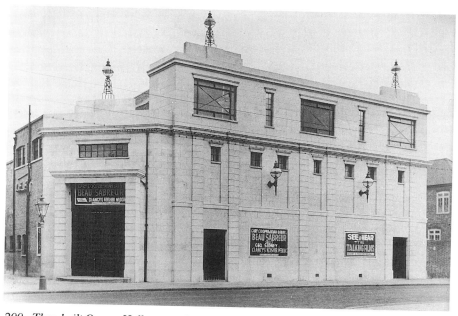

200. *The rebuilt Queens Hall re-opened 12 November 1928 with a talking picture,* The Luck of the Navy.

picture' *The Luck of the Navy.* The Wood Green Empire in August 1929 was showing Al Jolson in *The Singing Fool* as well as the British Movietone News. The Capital in Green Lanes opened on Boxing Day 1929. There were ninety-two applications for cinematograph licences in the county in 1929, thirty-one for talkies and sixty-one for silent. In the following year there were seventy-nine for talking and only ten for silent films; by November 1931 only one cinema remained in the county showing silent films.[6]

Sunday cinema was still banned by Middlesex County Council at this time but in November 1932 the councillors, throwing caution to the wind, announced that cinemas would now be allowed to show films on two Sundays every year. The Regal Edmonton opened in February 1934 with seats for 3,250. In addition to films it presented stage shows and employed a full orchestra supported by a Compton organ. A new cinema was planned in Southbury Road to seat 2,500. The demand for Sunday cinema was growing, advocates called for a plebiscite. A poll was finally taken in Enfield in 1938, the result in favour was by the narrowest of majorities, 6,904 for opening, 6,290 against.[7]

Throughout the summer months of 1921 a concert party played in the little gardens fronting the New River on the south side of Church Street. 'No place was more appreciated in the sweltering heat of that summer' wrote the *Gazette*, 'than George Betser's concert pavilion in Chase Gardens ... where the deckchairs and canvas armchairs were filled for every concert'. The previous week it had been the 'Melodies Concert Party', this week it was 'Charles Williams and his Frivolities'. Each season closed at the end of September. Late September 1922 saw an Anglo-Scots party with Suzette Tarri, Tony Copeland and others. The 1923 season opened at the end of April with the 'Humourettes'.[8]

Many of the local bands which had been so popular in the parks before 1914 had survived. Albert Plume had kept the Enfield Silver Prize Band going through

CHASE GARDENS PAVILION
Top of Church Street, Enfield.

Geo. Betser's POPULAR CONCERT

SATURDAY, AUGUST 26th, at 7.30.

THE CAPITALS CONCERT PARTY

My lease of the Gardens expires this year and the Committee of the Triangle Club have up to the present refused a renewal. I shall be glad to hear of a suitable site for next season. Particulars to 8/9 Great Pulteney Street, W.1. Phone: Regent 818

PRICES 2/-, 1/3 & 9d. (including Tax).
Seats booked in advance (no extra) Saturdays 12 till 7

201. George Betser's pavilion was set up in the gardens between St Paul's Presbyterian Church and the New River, where stood the Red Triangle Club house. (Advertisement Gazette 25 August 1922) The Red Triangle Club must have relented and allowed a renewal of the lease for the 1923 season opened there the following April.

202. Nearly five thousand attended a British Legion band concert at Hilly Fields Park in 1927 when they played the 1812 Overture with bomb and flare effects.

the war years with only eight members. He had been a bandsman for forty-three years by 1924 and bandmaster for twenty-five. The band season for the year 1921 began in the Bush Hill Park recreation ground on Whit Monday. The concert was disrupted, complained the *Gazette*, by the intervention of two Labour members of the Council. Determined not allow the band to play the national anthem, they threatened the bandmaster that he would receive no further engagements if he insisted. A massed band performance in the Town Park on May Day 1921 (a Sunday), in aid of the War Memorial Hospital, was heard by ten thousand people. On August bank holiday Monday that year there was an immense gathering at a band concert in the bandstand in Hilly Fields Park.[9]

The British Legion band was highly successful. Nearly five thousand people attended their concert at Hilly Fields Park in 1927 where they played the 1812 Overture with bomb and flare effects. The Council was less than generous to the musicians, it paid only £200 a year for the season of Sunday concerts in the parks; this worked out at £6 a performance and a band might comprise as many as thirty men. The London County Council offered £18 for afternoon and £24 for evening concerts. The Enfield Silver Prize Band, one of the finest bands in north London, felt so aggrieved that it refused Council engagements and played in the Market Place in June 1927, taking a collection, but then the Church complained. The following week they performed at the fountain in the Town. It was a delightful programme but it attracted so large an audience that the police had to bring the concert to a close. As many as eight thousand people attended a performance by massed bands in the Town Park in September that year.[10] As the cinemas became even more popular in the Thirties, interest in band performances sadly diminished. At one performance the *Gazette* reporter counted four people and a dog, at another the sale of tickets realised eleven pence.[11]

Motor cars existed before 1914 but were so rarely seen that they remained an object of curiosity to the wondering onlookers; mostly they were chauffeur driven and the chauffeur had also to be a mechanic. Mass production was not

A Car at a Price You · can afford

The POPULAR FORD

as illustrated *now* **£115** *at Works*

TAX NOW £6

The Popular Ford—now reduced in price—is a splendid choice because it is so economical to buy, to run and to maintain. On appearance and performance the Popular Ford is value far above the price you pay. We can arrange easy terms. Let us demonstrate.

CHASESIDE MOTOR Co., Ltd.

Depot and *Main Distributors:*
Service Stn.: **CAMBRIDGE ARTERIAL RD., ENFIELD.**
Telephone 3456.
Showrooms: **48 CHURCH ST., ENFIELD. Tel. 1907**

203. Gazette *18 January*
1935

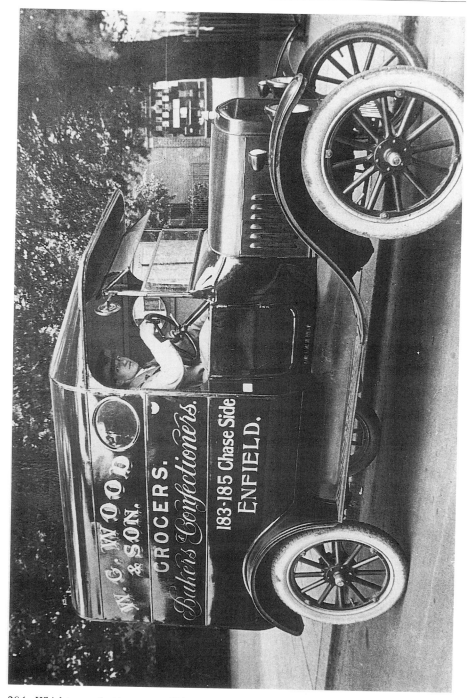

204. Which proves that progress could be made even in Enfield. Volume two displayed an illustration of the baker's horse and cart. By the Twenties he had this van, but the driver remained the same.

205. Enfield and District motor-cycle and car clubs rally at the Robin Hood on the Ridgeway (top).
Captain Edwin Roberts of the Ponders End fire brigade with his wife and youngest son (he had six sons and six daughters) on a fine combination motor-cycle in the Twenties (right).

yet under way in 1920, cars were still individually built. The price of petrol was reduced in January 1921 by 7d a gallon to 3s 5½d. Ford's opened an agency in an old cottage next to the former British School at Chase Side in April 1922 and in December the firm, Chase Side Motors, was given permission to erect petrol pumps, as was Graham Bros in Church Street. By that time a Ford runabout cost £140, a Ford delivery van £150, the touring car cost £157 and the sedan £260. Cars gradually became cheaper; a Ford touring car was advertised in 1924 at £110. An Austin Seven in March 1927 could be purchased for £145. The use of cars had increased so much by 1928 that a car park was opened on the former site of the 'Palace'. The last horse cab, a four-wheeler owned by W. Welch, ceased plying for hire at Enfield Chase station in April 1929. Lavender Hill garage on the Ridgeway advertised a twenty-four hour battery-charging service and offered conveyance by Daimler to any London station for 15s. The Chase Side Motor Company, in January 1930, took five acres on the Cambridge Road next to the Sangamo works. It was to be used for the sale, service and repair of Ford cars. By 1935 a Ford Popular could be bought for £115 and the police had to take measures to prevent parking in Church Street.[12]

Few people however had cars in the 1920s and excursions by charabanc were popular. The 'Enfield Belle' ran from Mr Tranter's tobacconist shop in Silver Street to Southend on Whit Sunday and Monday in 1920, at 12s a head. Redburn's of Green Street arranged charabanc trips up to seventy or eighty miles into the country; they also ran shorter trips into Hertfordshire and to Epping Forest. High Beech was a favourite place to go at holiday times, the 'swings and donkey rides there were an attraction for the children', said Doris Shuttlewood, 'and there would be coconut shies'. Redburn's of Ponders End had been laying on excursions for fifty years, in those early days they had used horse brakes. Seaside resorts opened up immediately after the war. Beaumont's in 1922 advertised trips to Brighton and Clacton. Graham Bros purchased a fine new twenty-eight seater charabanc in 1922. Many extra buses, laid on to Broxbourne and Rye House at Easter 1924, were crowded.[13]

Railways were freed from Government control by the summer of 1921 and began to advertise cheap excursions to the seaside. Before the war there had been three porters at Enfield Town railway station, by 1921 there were twelve. For the August bank holiday in 1924, excursion trains ran on the Sunday, Monday and Tuesday to Southend, from Gordon Hill, Enfield Chase and Grange Park, via Finsbury Park, Canonbury, Victoria Park and Stratford, for 3s 8d return. There were excursions available at Whitsun 1927, to Clacton (5s return) and to Skegness (7s return). Excursion trains caused problems for heavy drinkers, for non-corridor trains were used. Bed and breakfast at Southend might be had at a guinea a week, board residence at 42s.[14]

The Prince Omnibus Company in 1933 applied to renew its licence to run from Enfield to Bognor, Hastings, Folkestone, Bournemouth and Portsmouth. That summer there were Sunday excursions to Yarmouth on the railway at 7s return. A day return to Southend on the railway in August 1935 cost 4s; you could go to Clacton on the Crested Eagle for 5s. Modern coaches would take you to Margate from Lancaster Road for 7s 7d, Clacton 6s 6d and Southend for 3s 6d return.[15]

Throughout the war the upper middle class had enjoyed its game of golf, and the popularity of the game continued to grow. Enfield Golf Club in February 1920 received a surprise visit from a royal party when the Prince of Wales, Prince

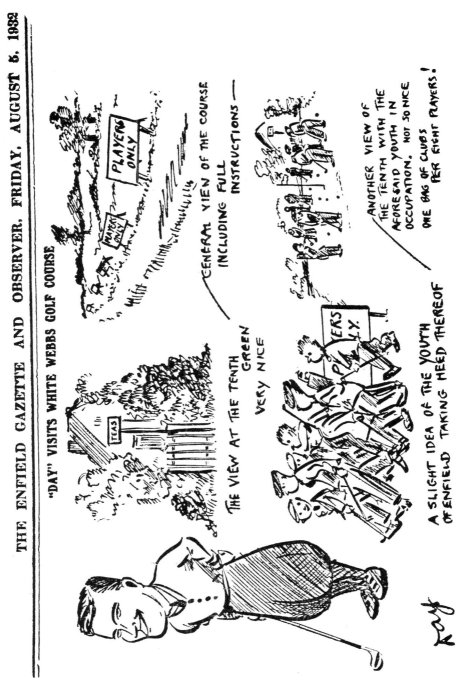

THE ENFIELD GAZETTE AND OBSERVER, FRIDAY, AUGUST 5, 1932.

"DAY" VISITS WHITE WEBBS GOLF COURSE

PLAYERS ONLY

MEMBERS ONLY

GENERAL VIEW OF THE COURSE INCLUDING FULL INSTRUCTIONS

ANOTHER VIEW OF THE TENTH WITH THE AFORESAID YOUTH IN OCCUPATION. NOT SO NICE. ONE BAG OF CLUBS PER EIGHT PLAYERS!

THE VIEW AT THE TENTH GREEN VERY NICE

TEAS

PLAYERS ONLY.

A SLIGHT IDEA OF THE YOUTH OF ENFIELD TAKING HEED THEREOF

206. Whitewebbs park, of 254 acres, was purchased by Middlesex County Council for £23,000, to be preserved as regional open space. It was leased to Enfield for 999 years at one guinea a year. The golf course of eighty-three acres was opened by Lord Derby in March 1932.

207. Whitewebbs golf course, photographed in 1990.

Albert and Princess Maud of Fife motored over from Trent Park where they were guests of Sir Philip Sassoon. Bush Hill Park Golf Club received a setback in October 1920 when their pavilion, a wooden structure with a corrugated iron roof, on Bush Hill, at the entrance to the Old Park estate, was burned down, but the club was doing well and was negotiating for the purchase of the Old Park mansion and grounds. Hadley Wood golf course at Beech Hill, opened in June 1922. Whitewebbs golf course of eighty-three acres opened in 1932. Both the Bush Hill Park and the Enfield golf courses, 195 acres in all, were purchased by the county for £102,500 in 1937.[16]

The Ponders End Cricket Club was wound up in February 1919. Their ground, adjoining the railway station in South Street, had been taken over early in the war for the building of the Shell Factory. The club was revived in 1921 using a ground at Scotland Green. A new sports club was opened on Shoreys field behind the Enfield County School in 1921. It provided facilities for tennis, cricket and bowls. The entrance fee was 10s 6d, the annual subscription one guinea. Enfield Chase Athletic and Social Club established tennis-courts and a cosy pavilion in the grounds of the Rectory by Parsonage Lane; it had a hundred members. Facilities for sport in Enfield parks in 1927 were described as woefully inadequate. Restrictions on cricket in the Town Park had recently been imposed, Chase Green at the time was practically derelict. There was a shortage of hard tennis-courts in the Enfield parks. Enfield Council, in this respect, lagged behind its neighbours in Southgate and Edmonton.

Hill Lodge at Clay Hill, formerly the residence of Mrs R. G. Porter and earlier of Sir Roland Stephenson, was acquired on lease for the Enfield Riding Club in 1937, to be used for riding, tennis, badminton and swimming, a full restaurant service was provided. The old Dutch barn standing in the grounds was converted into a gymnasium. It had formerly been used for cock fighting and its galleries and original floors were still there.

Pheasant shooting occupied the leisure time of the upper classes during the winter months. Richard Slater, when a boy, earned himself half a crown by serving as a 'stopper and beater' at Theobalds in the Twenties. He had to set out at half past six on a freezing cold December morning, with a pocket full of bread and margarine for his mid-day meal, in order to be in time to join the boys waiting with the gamekeeper at his cottage near Goffs Oak. He was stationed in a field at the edge of a wood, where it was his duty to prevent the birds coming out before the 'guns' arrived. The morning was dull and overcast with a bitterly cold wind blowing. For four hours he stood perished until the 'guns' arrived and he could precede them into the shelter of the woods.

Armed with a stick it was his function to walk in a straight line through the thick undergrowth to flush out the pheasants. Just as he was beginning to think that the birds had perhaps been forewarned in this part of the wood, one flew up from beneath his feet with a great whirring sound and behind him came the report of a shotgun. The pheasant plummeted to the ground, bounced once and then lay still. Richard, stared at it in bewilderment, from which he was released by a curt order to pick it up from the gentleman with the gun. The boy sauntered forward trying to look nonchalant, meanwhile fervently praying that the bird was really dead. He lifted it cautiously by the neck, the body still felt warm as he carried it back and handed to the gamekeeper. The shoot proved successful and the bag of pheasants steadily mounted. It was four o'clock and getting dark when the beaters finally assembled in the stable yard at the Glasgow

208. *Southbury open-air swimming bath created a great sensation when it opened in July 1932. Mixed bathing was to be allowed and this led to much foreboding among the older generation.*

Stud Farm, there he was given his half a crown and trudged off homeward in the dark.[17]

The Victoria Swimming Club (established in 1887, the year of Queen Victoria's Jubilee) held its annual championship in 1924 on Rammey Marsh watched by two thousand spectators. The club was to hold its fiftieth anniversary in 1937. Lady swimmers, it was announced in June 1925, were to have 'the privilege of the pond in Enfield Town Park' on Wednesdays. A scheme to provide an open-air swimming bath in Southbury Road was first proposed in March 1929; the baths opened in July 1932. Mixed bathing was allowed and this led to some speculation among the older generation as to where such goings on would end. Two daring young ladies wearing white bathing costumes, 'so abbreviated that they were kept on by little more than willpower', caused a commotion at Barrowell Green baths on the very first Sunday that bath was open in the summer of 1933. Driven on by the complaints of less stylishly clad female bathers, the baths superintendent was induced to request the young ladies to hire more adequate (though perhaps less elegant) covering; much annoyed they flounced out.[18]

Pigeon flying continued to be popular in the area, and homing societies were established in Enfield Wash, Enfield Highway, Enfield Town, Cheshunt, Waltham Cross and Edmonton. Locally owned birds were flown in long-distance races. P. Hobbs of Lancaster Road, in 1926, got a bird home from Lerwick in Shetland, repeating the triumph of one from Mr Wilson's loft in Baker Street in 1910. At the Enfield Fanciers' Association annual show in October 1930 there were 1,525 entries from all parts of the country.[19]

Thousands of working-class men watched professional football. Heroes, even legends, were created overnight, such a one was Jimmy Dimmock, a boy formerly at Montague Road School, who won the FA Cup for the Spurs in the

209. At Christmas 1934 Enfield were top of the Athenian League; at the end of the season they were runners-up.

final against Wolves in 1921. Forty thousand saw Spurs beat Arsenal three nil in 1923. The process which has led to the payment of astronomical sums for the transfer of star players, was beginning. Baden Herod, a full back, was bought by Spurs from Brentford for £4,000 in March 1929 and it was a record for the club. They were said to be negotiating for Barrett of Fulham, whose price was likely to be £6,000. In July 1931 Spurs made a coup, signing Willie Evans, Whatley and Burgess all from Chester. Enfield played at Cherry Orchard Lane in the Athenian League, their 7-2 victory over Leyton in 1927 was celebrated by a cartoon in the *Gazette*. Four thousand watched Enfield defeat Wycombe Wanderers, the Amateur Cup holders, 6-1 at Cherry Orchard Lane in November 1931. Enfield ended the season 1934-5 winning the London Senior Cup, and were semi-finalists in the Amateur Cup and runners-up in the Athenian League. The club faced a crisis in 1936 with the loss of its ground to housing development. The Council was demanding more rent than the club could afford for the new ground in Southbury Road; but a compromise was reached and Enfield started their programme there with a 2-1 victory over Golders Green. The season however proved a poor one and they finished second from bottom of the Athenian League. A record crowd at Holly Hill Farm watched the Enfield Chase Foxhounds point-to-point.[20]

A boxing booth was always a feature of the fairs held annually in Albany Park. The first professional boxing arena in the area was at the Alcazar Edmonton. It was very popular in the late Twenties and Thirties when Haydn Williams and Tom Benjamin were the great attractions, though Benjamin disgraced himself and was disqualified for biting Red Pullen's ear; Red Pullen was always a difficult one to hit.[21]

Victorian morality survived at least on the library committee, which voted in 1920 to protect its readers, particularly of course the ladies, from the corruptive

210. *Gazette* 5 *December* 1924

influence of Hardy's *Jude the Obscure*, Anatole France's *Penguin Island* and George Moore's *Esther Waters*. A reference library and museum was opened in April 1924. From 1925 readers were given direct access to the lending library shelves, which meant that they no longer had to choose their book from a list and inspect an indicator to see if it was available. Library expenditure had reached £2,372 by 1929 of which £618 was spent on books. Enfield's museum, formerly displayed in the Central Library, was packed up in boxes in December 1933 and it was to lie thus for many years. The remains of a boat, two feet wide and twelve feet long, found in the gravel pits at Sewardstone, was rejected by the librarian who suggested Essex County Museum. In 1936 the library committee took further strong action to protect the readers from the revolutionary influences of the *Daily Worker.* [22]

Drunkenness diminished after the war. There were sixty licencees in eastern Enfield in 1919 serving a population of thirty thousand, but there was not a single conviction for drunkenness: maybe the police took a lenient view. The Swan and Pike, which stood right on the towpath of the Lee Navigation, was demolished in the early Twenties. The Spotted Cow at Bulls Cross surrendered its licence in April 1923. The Holly Bush was rebuilt and reopened in June 1927. The White Lion in Old Road closed in February 1930; the licence was transferred to a new house at the junction of Carterhatch Lane and the Cambridge Road. At home the gramophone was all the rage in the 1920s; Saville's of Church Street had twenty thousand records to choose from.[23]

Parks remained popular in the Twenties, especially among those who did not have the money to go on excursions or to take holidays. O'Ryans field at Ponders End, which the Council had purchased in 1920 for a recreation ground, was ploughed and levelled in 1923. It had been used until then as allotments. Land at Strayfield Road was purchased in January 1924 for an addition to Hilly Fields Park. Thousands came out by bus to Forty Hill from Tottenham and Wood Green at Easter in 1928. A bowling-green was put down in Albany Park in 1924. The Council's proposal in August 1928 to allow games in the parks on Sundays aroused such widespread hostility, according to the *Gazette*, that the paper organised a poll of its readers, obviously expecting a wholesale reaffirmation of Victorian values, but a large majority voted to permit Sunday games. The measure proved popular and the tennis-courts and bowling-greens were regularly occupied. The use of parks by the public however began to decline. August bank holiday 1935 saw the parks in eastern Enfield deserted and the buses and trains crowded. Yet the Council continued to extend its parks. It laid out College Farm as an extension of Albany Park in 1937 and completed the Enfield Playing Fields in 1938. A golf course was completed there in 1939 only to be immediately ploughed up as war allotments. It was thought that the Council ought to allow Sunday football in the parks since golf and tennis were played on the Sabbath. Crowds of a thousand or more watched Sunday morning football at the Church Street recreation ground in Edmonton.[24]

May 1935 saw the Jubilee. Many streets put on parties for the children, music and fireworks attracted thousands to the Town Park and to other parks. In March 1937 came the Coronation. That June, after attending an air pageant, the King and Queen visited Sir Philip Sassoon at Trent Park. They arrived at six o'clock and spent the evening watching a firework display. A burst of cheering greeted the royal car as it emerged through the Cockfosters gates soon after midnight. When Sir Philip died in 1939 fighter planes circled and dipped over

Chorus of Councillors: "Now what shall we do with it THIS time?"

211. May 1935 saw the Jubilee. Enfield had hardly recovered from the celebrations when there came the Coronation in March 1937 (Gazette 5 February 1937).

Trent Park as they scattered his ashes from the air. He was a fifty-year-old bachelor and left a fortune amounting to £1,946,892. [25]

4. Health

The end of the war found the Cottage Hospital facing a crisis. The cost of each patient had risen over the previous four years from 24s to 34s a week, while subscriptions had declined. An overdraft had to be temporarily guaranteed by Colonel Bowles and Mr Hollington (presumably A. J. Hollington of the Clock House, Forty Hill) to allow time for steps to be taken to remedy the situation. The hospital had no secretary, treasurer or executive committee, and the public was warned that it might have to close unless new officials were found. Moreover many people felt that a twenty-five bed hospital was inadequate for a town the size of Enfield.[26]

The War Memorial committee at this point took a hand, inviting the acting council for the Cottage Hospital to co-operate to form a hospital board of management which would seek to establish and maintain an adequate hospital, to be known as the Enfield War Memorial Hospital. A public appeal was thereupon launched. The valedictory meeting of the Cottage Hospital committee took place at the end of March 1920, a new scheme of management was drawn up by the Charity Commission and the public was asked to contribute £10,000. A start was made on an extension to the building in December 1922. An old chapel, once Primitive Methodist, which had been used for many years

212. *The Cottage Hospital closed and the War Memorial opened in the autumn of 1924 with fifty-two beds. The extension had cost £12,000.*

as an annexe to the hospital, was demolished and the foundation stone was laid for the new extensions. Patients henceforth would be required to contribute according to means.[27]

It was hoped to complete the work without disrupting patient care in the old building, but this proved impracticable. The old wards became so full of dust and noise that the hospital was forced to close through the spring and summer of 1924. It reopened in the autumn with fifty-two beds. The extension had cost £12,000. There still remained a shortage of accommodation, 620 patients were admitted throughout the ensuing year, ninety-four per cent treated free and six per cent paying. The average cost per patient per week was £2 11s 2d, expenses exceeded income by £1,136. In 1926, for the first time, more than a thousand patients were treated and by the end of the year 1928 the accumulated debt stood at £1,768. The population of Enfield in 1931 was 68,000, yet the hospital still had only fifty-two beds and there was no adequate out-patients department. It needed £7,700 a year to keep going, most of the income came from the western side of the parish. During the year 1933 an Enfield Hospitals Contributory Scheme was instituted which proved able to meet forty-two per cent of the cost of treatment of its two thousand members; arrangements were also made for members to receive treatment where necessary at the North Middlesex. A revised scheme was introduced in July 1934 under which a subscription of one guinea a year was paid to cover a member, his wife and all his children under sixteen. It provided maintenance and medical fees up to £2 a week for five weeks in any one year, either in the War Memorial, or in any more appropriate hospital. Membership of the scheme had risen to four thousand by the end of the year 1937. There were plans in 1936 to replace the War Memorial Hospital with something larger on a five acre nursery site at Lavender Hill, opposite the junction with Gordon Hill, but another war intervened and the project was deferred.[28]

The Edmonton Military Hospital began to admit civilian patients in March 1920; it became known at this time as the North Middlesex Hospital. The poor were expected to pay according to their means, but even the better-off paid only for their maintenance at £2 9s a week. For this they were given separate accommodation with special crockery and cutlery and other privileges, yet some of them, the critics complained, underwent operations which would have cost up to £50 in a private hospital. Seven thousand patients a year were admitted by 1923 but this included only 103 private patients. The management of the institution remained in the hands of the Edmonton Union, an unfortunate inheritance from the nineteenth century, for the Guardians were still unable to make up their minds whether the hospital should be a poor-law institution or a general hospital. Mrs Mason's resolution at a meeting of the Board of Guardians, that no one should be admitted except poor-law patients, received considerable support from members in 1925. People on £700 a year, she complained, 'were swanking there'; she might also have mentioned that it was their rates which maintained the institution. There were plans, in 1926, to build a new maternity ward for sixty beds. Four thousand six hundred patients were admitted in the half year ended 31 March 1927, including 942 maternity cases. Colonel Mort demanded both a new operating theatre and improvements to the old one. A convalescent home at Woburn Sands was purchased by the Guardians to ease the overcrowding, but despite this the hospital remained so full that only acute cases could be admitted. Many doctors, unable to get their patients into voluntary hospitals, were sending them to the North Middlesex. The Guardians, in March 1929, spent £6,000 on a department for the treatment of cancer by radium.[29]

The Local Government Act 1929 gave counties the power to run public hospitals. It might have been hoped that, with the end of management by the Board of Guardians, patients would no longer be described as paupers, but Middlesex County Council was conservative and was determined, when it took control on 1 April 1930, to manage the hospital under the Poor-Law Acts. This was against the strongly expressed advice of Colonel Mort who urged that it be taken over by the public health committee, so 'striking a blow against class distinctions'.

The hospital was soon receiving 10,000 patients a year and over a thousand babies were born there annually. Most of the patients were people of small means who, apart from their illness, required no help from the poor-law. The hospital served an area of seventy square miles and a population of 516,360. There had been 9,797 admissions in 1929 and 988 births; 2,226 operations had been performed. Patients wanted to look upon admission to the hospital as a right, but many, even at this time, because it was a poor-law institution, would only enter when they were at death's door. This unfortunately accounted for the large number of deaths which occurred in the hospital, 1,599 in the year 1929, including 162 patients who died within forty-eight hours of admission.[30]

This part of Middlesex was not well served with hospital beds, thus it was that most of the serious cases, and many chronic cases which would have been rejected in other general hospitals, had to be treated at the North Middlesex. It took more sick and injured people than all the other general hospitals in Middlesex put together; the gates were never closed, patients were received at all times. The hospital claimed no right of refusal except for acute infectious cases. There was constant criticism of the hospital on the grounds of extravagance; it was accused of having practically one member of staff to every two patients.[31]

The matter of transferring the North Middlesex Hospital to management under the Public Health Acts was again deferred. It was difficult for county councillors to fundamentally change their attitudes to the hospital service. They were worried about the financial problems which they thought must arise when their hospitals were appropriated under the Public Health Acts, for then the law of settlement, for nearly three centuries uppermost in the minds of local administrators, would no longer apply. It was feared that the County Council would then be unable to transfer patients whose settlement lay outside the county, nor would they be able to charge maintenance on the area to which the patient's poor-law settlement belonged. At the same time those counties running their hospitals as poor-law institutions would still be able to charge maintenance on Middlesex patients in their hospitals. Thus the seventeenth century law of settlement survived incongruously and inconveniently into the twentieth century. Middle-class people, including some who urgently needed hospital accommodation, had as ratepayers in the former Edmonton Union been paying sevenpence in the pound for the upkeep of the North Middlesex, yet they were still unable to get treatment there unless they were prepared to pauperize themselves. Councillor Edwardson, as always thinking more logically than most of his fellow politicians, urged the establishment of general hospitals ready to render service without discrimination to all those who needed it. The North Middlesex and the other four county poor-law hospitals were at last appropriated under the Public Health Acts, but not until 1 April 1936.[32]

Colonel Spencer Mort died in November 1932. He had been in charge for twenty-two years and was a pioneer in the use of radium. The *Daily Express*, under the headline 'Secret of Dead Doctor', alleged some scandal. His widow over-come by shock, died soon afterwards. It was decided in May 1935 to transfer the remaining aged but healthy inmates of Edmonton workhouse to Chase Farm. The remaining workhouse buildings at Edmonton, although old and unsuit-able, were merged into the hospital.[33]

Enfield Council established an ambulance service in 1921, using, at Ponders End, an old military ambulance, until a new one was purchased in 1924. A charge was made for its use and this may have deterred the poor; no free ambulance service was provided until October 1930. The cost of the Enfield health service for the year ending March 1924 was £16,212. The Ministry of Health urged the appointment of a full-time medical officer of health, pointing out that there was no other district in England with a population over 45,000 which had not already made a full-time appointment. The post, said the Ministry, should incorporate that of school medical officer and a full-time assistant should be appointed. In October 1923 the Ministry refused to approve the appointment of a part-time MOH; despite this, in February 1925, Enfield proceeded to appoint Dr J. J. Robb part-time. It was not until November 1926 that the Council accepted that a full-time appointment should be made; the appointee was also to be the schools medical officer at a salary of £800 rising by annual increments to £1,000.[34]

Free treatment in hospitals was now a thing of the past, for voluntary contributions were no longer forthcoming to maintain the service. Branches of the Hospital Savings Association sprang up in many factories; a family contribu-tion of 3d a week covered the cost of hospital treatment and was considered good value for money. Most of the important hospitals in London and in the suburbs were covered by the scheme under which a patient, producing an HSA voucher, was passed straight through the almoner's department; even in those institutions not covered by the scheme the almoner would make a refund.[35]

The subject of birth-control remained taboo into the Twenties. Miss E. S. Daniels, a health visitor in Edmonton, was suspended and subsequently dis-missed in December 1922, with one month's salary in lieu of notice, for having given working-class women the address of a clinic at Walworth (either this or the one run by Dr Marie Stopes) when they had asked her how they could avoid unwanted children. A packed protest meeting in Edmonton Town Hall, with Frank Broad MP in the chair, demanded her reinstatement, but the Council remained insistent upon dismissal. Edmonton UDC in 1925 passed a resolution urging the Minister of Health to allow local medical officers to give birth-control information to mothers at maternity and child welfare centres. The matter was even discussed at Enfield during the following year, but there the Council merely asked the Ministry to issue instructions. It was not until 1933 that Enfield Council finally took the decision itself (by a small majority) to allow the medical officer to give lectures upon that still scarcely mentionable subject. Complaints about the poor facilities at the mortuary were constantly voiced in the police court, much of the trouble arose because the place was manned only by a part-time assistant who also had a job as a picture palace attendant.[36]

More care began to be taken in the Thirties of the health of both babies and mothers in child-bearing. A new clinic costing £4,500 was opened at Southbury School in March 1931. The school medical service had begun in 1907 but it really only became effective after the 1918 Act. Three further maternity and child welfare clinics were opened in 1935 at Rosemary Avenue (Baker Street)

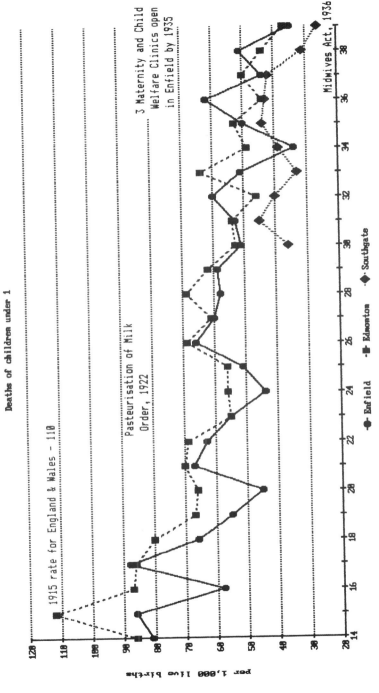

INFANT MORTALITY 1914 – 1939

Deaths of children under 1

per 1,000 live births

St Stephen's Road (Enfield Wash) and at Lincoln Road (Bush Hill Park). There was not a single death from diphtheria or scarlet fever in Enfield in 1934 and infant mortality was the lowest ever. It was urged that the Middlesex County Council maternity hospitals should be able to accommodate all women suffering financial necessity, all cases requiring admission on medical grounds and a proportion of those women whose home accommodation was not deemed suitable. A scheme for the provision of whole-time municipal midwives (under the Midwives Act 1936) was introduced in 1937. Five midwives were appointed by the end of the year 1937 and over two-thirds of pregnant women attended Council ante-natal clinics. Two hundred more beds were provided at the Isolation Hospital in 1938.[37]

Hospitals, both general and voluntary, general practitioners, ophthalmic and dental services, midwifery, maternity and child welfare, the provision of medicines, spectacles and dentures, all these were taken over and provided virtually without charge, by the National Health Service set up under the Act of 1946.

5. Education

The legacy of the late Prebendary George Hodson lingered on into the period which separated the two wars. For over twenty-five years, almost single-handed, he had battled to prevent the establishment of a school board in Enfield. In his heroic defence of the interests of his Church however, he had from time to time been forced to meet deficiencies in the number of school places by conjuring small schools into existence with the least possible delay and at the lowest possible cost. Many of these little schools and departments survived into the Twenties so that in 1925, whereas Edmonton had more than nine thousand children in thirty departments, Enfield had less than nine thousand in forty-five departments. Twenty-three of these had accommodation for less than two hundred children, yet each required the expense of a head-teacher's salary, £400 maximum for men and £330 for women. These small church schools still retained an above average proportion of uncertificated teachers. The authority had now begun (Vicar Hodson being a long time dead) to close some of his schools. St Andrew's in Gordon Road (subsequently used as a scout hall) and the former St Andrew's Upper Grade in London Road had been closed. The London Road school was currently used for infants but the playground was very small and there were only two toilets for the sixty-two children. Education committee members would have been glad to close more but approval was difficult to secure.[38]

Enfield was classed, for educational purposes, as a necessitous area, a penny rate produced about 2s 7d per child. The Board of Education was of the opinion that the local authority had done well in adapting its expenses to its circumstances although, compared with other necessitous areas, its proportion of certificated teachers to total staff, at seventy-four per cent, was low. The percentage in Edmonton was eighty, while the average for non-necessitous areas was seventy-seven per cent. Total expenditure per child in Enfield amounted to £10 6s 6d a year (eleventh in a list of twenty local education authorities) but of this as little as 7s 3d was spent on administration; only three of the twenty authorities kept their administrative expenses lower. Enfield

213. The National school London Road, on the right, opened in March 1840. It consisted of two schoolrooms each forty feet by eighteen and an infants' school. The Co-op in London Road opened in August 1923, this postcard must therefore precede that date. The photographer was looking north towards the Town.

employed no supply teachers, it used, in any emergency, assistant teachers currently undergoing training in a variety of schools with a view to ultimate promotion to headships. Large classes persisted. In March 1927 there were 117 classes with between forty-one and fifty pupils, only one class had more than fifty. Under the Education Act 1918, children under the age of fourteen could no longer be exempted from school and their employment in factories was now prohibited.[39]

A school for mentally defective children was opened at Nassau House in Old Road at Enfield Highway in June 1921, run jointly by the Enfield and Edmonton education committees. It was replaced, in 1939, by Durants School. Enfield set up a holiday home scheme for backward girls in 1922. It had been the practice to condemn such children to remain in the lower standards, among younger, brighter children, so inevitably they left school with a sense of failure. The new scheme placed them in a special domestic class at the age of twelve, where they did needlework, handwork and housewifery. Each year twenty-six of the girls were taken to an establishment at Herne Bay where they were allowed to run the place, doing the shopping, cooking, laying table, washing-up and making beds. Seventy-five per cent of these girls came from slum areas and they needed to be taught basic civilised behaviour, like eating decently and washing carefully.[40]

The problem of verminous children in elementary schools persisted. Dr Forrester, the schools medical officer, thought that there had not been much improvement; forty-three 'dirty cases' were reported in January 1924. A paper had been sent to each parent concerned warning that if the child did not return clean within one week, prosecution would ensue, but some of the children

214　St James School had been built in 1834. It was badly overcrowded in 1922, the toilets had no doors, infants taken short had to sit out in the rain. There was no staff room.

inevitably returned verminous.

It could be an uphill struggle to keep the children clean. 'After a bath in the freezing cold kitchen', recalled Richard Slater, who tells many an amusing story of his childhood, 'there followed a session with the "nit-comb" where my hair was religiously combed for about ten minutes over a metal tray. Any offending nits which appeared met an untimely end under my grandmother's thumbnail'. Then to bed, warmed by a house brick heated in the range oven and wrapped in a blanket.[41]

The cost of elementary education had risen dramatically since the beginning of the century; in 1901 the teaching of 9,009 children had cost £12,700, in 1930 the teaching of 9,062 cost £65,085. With the introduction of the Burnham scale, teachers' salaries had increased by 140 per cent compared with pre-war. They now had twelve weeks holiday with pay, three months full sick-pay and guaranteed superannuation. In April 1932 the teachers lost their representation on Enfield education committee, where they had been represented since 1929.[42]

So many houses were being built east of the Cambridge Road in 1933 that, to meet the needs of a greatly expanded number of children, Suffolks School was opened in January 1934. It drew 250 from Southbury School and 120 from St James School, which had become badly overcrowded. St James was a church school for girls and infants. Built in 1834, its three east rooms were very close to the noisy main road. Two of the classes were taught in one room with only a low moveable screen to separate them. There was no staff room, and although the head's study had been condemned as a classroom in 1909, from time to time it still had to serve for small classes. The girls' and infants' WCs were without separate doors and the infants' toilets were exposed to the rain. The extension of council housing in eastern Enfield gave rise to overcrowding at Eastfield and Chesterfield Schools. Many of the families which had moved into the new council houses were on the poverty line and they found great difficulty in paying the rents. The Children's Care Committee, formed as long ago as 1913, continued to provide free meals and boots; in the year ending March 1934 twenty-four thousand dinners had been provided and 490 pairs of boots.[43]

The government, by July 1936, met nearly half the cost of elementary education in Enfield; £79,374 came from the ratepayers, and £67,484 from the Board of Education. Overcrowding persisted at Chesterfield and Eastfield where some classes now contained fifty children. There was room at Suffolks, where they had places for two thousand, but had only 1,150 pupils; it lay however at some distance from the areas of greatest need. Temporary buildings at Eastfield were provided for four classes, some children at Chesterfield were accommodated in hired halls nearby and some were transferred to Suffolks. A site was acquired for a new school in Eastfield Road (Albany) and a further eight acres in Green Street for a junior and infant school (Brimsdown). Following the decision to erect 1,700 houses on the Aylands estate the education committee took steps to acquire a twelve-acre site for a school there.[44]

Problems were also created by developments around Enfield West where a school was planned in the Slades Hill area (Merryhills). Some residents at Grange Park were sending their children to Southgate schools. In middle-class areas the average number of elementary school children per house was 0.35, on council estates it was 1.54, at Grange Park it was 0.2, for many were sent to private schools. Another pressing problem facing the Enfield education committee in 1938 was the provision of school places for the children on Edmonton's thirty-

215. *There was considerable overcrowding at Chesterfield School in the Thirties. By 1936 there were classes of fifty, and some children had to be accommodated in hired halls nearby.*

acre housing scheme at Hoe Lane in Enfield where 354 houses were built.[45]

The authority's plan to meet its educational requirements up to 1943 looked likely to cost nearly a quarter of a million pounds. Albany School and clinic was completed by May 1939 and Brimsdown by September. Merryhills School had been built up to the eaves by the outbreak of the war and the Council sought permission to get the work finished. The Board of Education was assured that all the necessary loans had been raised and that the contractors had in hand most of the materials required. The site, it was argued, lay on the edge of open country and householders from areas thought to be more vulnerable to aid-raids were moving into nearby empty houses. No other school existed within one mile. After much heart searching, permission was granted to complete the school.[46]

It was estimated in 1919 that each child resident in the workhouse school at Chase Farm cost the ratepayers more than £1 a week, yet the children were undersized and, according to a doctor's report, compared unfavourably with children outside. They continued to receive their education at Chase Farm although poor-law schools were not recognised as an integral part of the education system under the 1918 Act. The Edmonton Board of Guardians was therefore within its rights when it made known that it did not intend to continue this educational work indefinitely. A conference was sought with the local education authorities within the Union. Enfield education committee was naturally much concerned as to who would pay for the education of workhouse children if they were sent to Enfield council schools. Eventually an agreement was reached by which forty boys and girls of ten years of age and over, and of promising ability, should be transferred, from January 1924 to the Chase Side and Lavender Schools. The clothing provided for the children was to be as varied as possible in order that they should not be too clearly distinguishable as paupers, yet, as the illustration shows (p.258), they were easily recognizable by their Norfolk jackets. The following year all the older children transferred either to Chase Side, Lavender or St Michael's Schools and by 1930 these schools were educating 180 Chase Farm children. Two of the boys moreover had been admitted to the Grammar School and one to the Central School. At Chase Farm the boys were still instructed in bootmaking, tailoring, baking and farm work. The farm there had thirty head of cattle, a thousand poultry and a herd of pedigree Berkshire pigs. All the footwear and other attire for the children was made on the premises. They had a swimming-bath, a hundred feet by thirty, which had been dug out by the local unemployed as a relief scheme in 1923, the building which housed it could readily be converted to a concert hall or gymnasium. With the decline in the number of inmates the cost of maintaining each child rose, reaching 30s a week in August 1929, according to the *Evening News*. At that time there was accommodation for 600 but there were only 336 children in the house. When the children left the institution at the age of fifteen they remained under the supervision of the Guardians until they reached eighteen. Some of them emigrated to Canada under the aegis of the Salvation Army.[47]

Middlesex County Council took over the powers of the Board of Guardians in March 1930 and the school was placed in the hands of the public health committee. There were still 371 children in the house in 1931 and educational work continued for the younger children, but when the infant teacher at Chase Farm retired during the following year, the committee decided to make no new appointment and to transfer all their remaining pupils to council schools. The number resident in Chase Farm was slowly reduced through the years 1934 and 1935 as the children were accommodated in scattered homes, each of which might house up to thirty. One such was Camden House in Chase Road Southgate, also number 10 Arundel Gardens in Winchmore Hill. Inevitably the existence of these homes gave rise to protests from the middle-class residents, who resented pauper children being dumped in decent neighbourhoods, nevertheless six more scattered homes were acquired in May 1934 at a cost

216. *Boys from Chase Side School 1926, the Chase Farm boys are recognisable by their Norfolk jackets.*

217. *Chase Farm boys' band c.1927*

218. *The choir at Chase Side Boys School in 1919 with the headmaster Harry Douglas Vincent and his wife who was the choir trainer.*

£6,700. Only children of less than three years old remained at Chase Farm in 1939 and on the outbreak of the war they were transferred to Whitewebbs. Thus Chase Farm School was progressively shut down and finally closed without ceremony. Chase Farm in 1939 became a hospital linked with the London Hospital.[48]

The two secondary schools in Enfield were full to overflowing in 1919, further accommodation was badly required but no extensions were made over the following five years. An inspector's report early in 1923 praised the high standards attained at the Grammar School but criticized the inadequacy of the building and its out-of-date laboratories. There were 350 boys at this time. The governors, in February that year, received £3,750 from the sale of Upper Edwards Hall Farm in Essex (it had been acquired in 1917) and with this money they purchased Colonel Somerset's former mansion, Enfield Court in Baker Street. The lower forms moved into the house early in the year 1925.[49]

The shortage of grammar school places persisted in Enfield. Middle-class parents who had sent their sons to preparatory schools with a view to entering them in the Grammar School, often found that there was no room even though they were willing to pay. A picture of the school under E. M. Eagles in the early Twenties is given by Hugh Jenkins (later Lord Jenkins of Putney, Arts Minister in the second Wilson government and Labour parliamentary candidate in

219. Enfield Grammar School about 1921 presented The Gondoliers. *There was obviously some difficulty, in an all-boys school, in finding suitable candidates for the female parts. I wonder how they do it now? The brothers Bill and Leonard Newman.*

220. *Enfield Grammar School football team 1919-20, the headmaster E.M. Eagles on your right. The school was overcrowded at the time, and there was a shortage of secondary school places. It was not until 1925 that the lower school moved into Enfield Court in Baker Street.*

Enfield West in 1950). It is from his autobiography *The Culture Gap* 1979.

'My parents', he says, 'insisted on paying the quarterly fee of £3 17s 6d at the Grammar School, although I had passed the examination, because dad said he did not want me held in contempt as a scholarship boy, but wanted me to get the same treatment as the sons of gentlemen, little aware that in the post-great-war period good masters were scarce and schooling quite appalling'. (Hugh Jenkins was writing about his childhood in Enfield; he was eleven in 1919.) 'The headmaster,' he went on, 'was a sadist and the walls of his study were lined with whips ranging from a huge cat o'nine tails to a tiny swagger cane. He would march up and down fingering them and taking down one or another, would thrash the air with a shuddering whistle'.

Sid Robinson, also a scholarship boy and at that time very obviously working-class and hard up, was at the Grammar School at the same time as Hugh Jenkins. He tells us, in his autobiography *Sid's Family Robinson*, that he was often caned, mostly for neglecting his homework, especially after he had inadvisedly in-formed the headmaster that his father thrashed him if he was caned at school, for upon receiving this information the headmaster felt safe from parental intervention and caned him more frequently than ever. Sid however, while agreeing that the standard of teaching was appalling, is sure that the working-class boys like himself were in no way treated worse than the paying pupils by the teachers. 'The teachers were gentlemen', he says, 'but they had been teaching too long'. Gertrude Williams who was at Enfield County School at that time also denies that the scholarship students suffered any discrimination.

One thousand sat the entrance examination in 1927 and although 125 passed there were only 90 vacancies. Those who obtained a place were given the opportunity to apply for a scholarship; parents had to give details of their financial circumstances. The Grammar School at this time received yearly £2,378 from fees (four guineas a term) and £2,460 from the County Council for free places. There were 490 boys and twenty-five teachers. Four hundred girls attended the County School at the end of the year 1928 and there were twenty teachers. Fees there provided an income of £1,390 and £3,519 was received from the County for scholarship places.[50]

The new Latymer extension in Haselbury Road was opened by the Duke and Duchess of York in October 1928, making Latymer the largest secondary school in the county; the work cost £67,000. A new secondary school was being built on the Cambridge Road at Bush Hill Park in 1929 for the Edmonton County School and extensions were being made at Enfield County. Higher education was also provided for boys at the Ponders End Technical Institute. The school had been opened by Middlesex in 1911 to provide pre-apprentice training for boys in the engineering trades. It offered a two year course in English, history, geography, mathematics, science, technical drawing and workshop training. There were 158 pupils in 1920, some from as far away as Hornsey, Tottenham and South-gate. A hundred boys competed in 1919 for the fifteen entrance scholarships awarded to elementary school children. In 1920, 150 boys took the entrance exam for fee-paying pupils (fees were £1 2s 6d a term) but it was possible to admit only eighty-four. Some of the boys on leaving entered the Royal Small Arms Factory or Woolwich Arsenal, as trade lads. The competition was stiff. In 1920, 160 candidates competed for only thirty-three places, yet of the twelve from Ponders End, ten were successful. The building in Ponders End High Street was

221. *The Ponders End Trades School opened in 1911 to provide pre-apprentice training for boys in the engineering trades.*

also used for classes, attended by RSAF apprentices in applied mechanics, machine drawing and experimental science, also for other evening and day classes.[51]

'It will be observed that there has been a considerable increase in the award of free places' (in secondary schools), said the chairman of the County education committee in March 1929. 'No child qualified for admission shall be debarred ... by reason of his parents' lack of means'. The proportion of free places in Enfield secondary schools in 1931/2 was 65.5 per cent, as against 54.3 per cent in the year 1929/30; 65.5 was much higher than the percentage for the country as a whole and moves were now afoot to curtail the number of free admissions in Enfield. Times were hard and a large number of local scholarship children, 323 in the previous year, had been withdrawn before they were sixteen. Secondary school pupils were divided into three categories; free place pupils (for instance those whose parents had one child and an income of not more than £4 a week, or £4 10s with two children), those who paid reduced fees according to their incomes, and those who paid the full fee which was fifteen guineas a year in 1932. The County Council, in January 1932, aimed to cut its expenditure by £3m and an economy committee recommended that the number of free places should not exceed forty-five per cent. A Board of Education circular in September that year announced higher fees at secondary schools. Middlesex, by 1934, was awarding 2,386 free places every year and 916 places at reduced fees; free places in the county were now reduced to 52.6 per cent of secondary school intake.[52]

At the Enfield Grammar School prize presentation in December 1936, held

222. The Grammar School was greatly extended before the Second World War. This alas involved the demolition of Enfield's once elegant Assembly Rooms.

in the Riding House at Enfield Court, it was emphasised that the school was in urgent need of a hall, a library, a science block and additional classrooms. An extension to the school was proposed; it involved, sadly, the demolition of 'the old building on the south side, at that time used as a science laboratory'. It was the former Assembly Rooms, the pride of eighteenth century Enfield. The foundation stone of the new school was laid by Sir Henry Bowles in May 1938. Fees in secondary grammar schools were abolished by the 1944 Education Act which transferred the control of all education from the local authority to the county council.[53]

Many working-class parents between the wars economised and deprived themselves to give their children a better education than they had received themselves. It was a development in society of the utmost importance, one which led to an increased mobility between classes. Many professional people who were born into working-class families in the 1920s owe a debt of gratitude to those self-denying, self-improving parents between the wars, who struggled to keep their children at grammar school and even, in a few cases, at university.

Notes to Chapter Four

1. *Gazette* 21 Ap 1921, 4 My, 27 Jl 1923, 18 Jl 1919, 6 Ap 1923, 8 Jl 1921, 14 N 1920
2. *ibid* 28 Ap 1922, 18 My 1928, 14 Ap 1922, 6 N 1925, 9 S 1927, 22 F 1924, 13 D 1929

3. *ibid* 30 Oct 1930, 31 Ja 1936, 2 My 1930
4. *ibid* 17 S 1937
5. *ibid* 5 Jl 1932, 9 D 1938, 4 Au 1939
6. *ibid* 15 My 1925, 22 Jl, 26 Au 1927, 9 N 1928, 16 Au, 20 D 1929
7. *ibid* 17 Oct 1930, 25 Oct 1935, 4 F 1938
8. *ibid* 19 Au 1921, 22 S 1922, 23 Ap 1923
9. *ibid* 28 Mr 1924, 4 Je 1920, 6 My, 5 Au 1921
10. *ibid* 24 Je, 9 S 1927
11. *ibid* 30 Ja 1931
12. *ibid* 22 Ap, 22 D 1922, 4 Mr 1927, 11 My, 29 Je 1928, 17 Ja 1930, 12 Ap 1935
13. *ibid* 12 My 1920, 19 My 1922
14. *ibid* 2 S 1921, 25 Jl 1924, 6 Au 1926, 27 My, 10 Je 1927
15. *ibid* 26 My, 21 Jl 1933, 9 Au 1935
16. *ibid* 20 F 1920, 26 F 1932, 6 Au 1937
17. *ibid* 17 Oct 1924, 20 My 1921, 26 Au, 28 Oct 1927, 23 Ap 1937, information R.Slater
18. *Gazette* 15 Au 1924, 12 Je 1925, 29 Ap, 22 Jl 1932, 4 Au 1933
19. *ibid* 11 Oct, 6 Au 1926, 17 Oct 1930
20. *ibid* 1 Mr 1929, 20 N 1931, 17 My 1935, 10 Ja 1936, 7 My, 16 Ap 1937
21 *ibid* 4 Oct 1929, 22 Ap 1932
22. *ibid* 13 F 1920, 11 Ap 1924, 16 Ja 1925, 1 N 1935, 32 Jl 1936
23. *ibid* 21 F 1919, 23 Ap 1923, 24 Je 1927, 21 F 1930, 4 Ap 1924
24. *ibid* 23 F, 2 Mr 1923, 30 My, 11 Ja 1924, 13 Ap 1928, 13 Je 1924, 3 Au, 14 S 1928, 9 Au 1935, 3 D 1937, 7 Ja 1938
25. *ibid* 10 My 1935, 5 Mr, 2 Jl 1937, 9 Je 1939
26. *ibid* 19 S 1919
27. *ibid* 14 N 1919, 20 Au 1920, 1D, 22 D 1922
28. *ibid* 2 My 1924, 5 Je 1925, 8 Jl 1927, 19 Oct 1928, 31 Jl 1931, 12 F 1932, 2 F 1934, 31 Ja, 5 Je 1936
29. *ibid* 25 Mr 1921, 23 N 1923, 30 Ja 1925, 30 Jl 1926, 6 My 1927, 31 Au 1928, 6 Mr 1929
30. *ibid* 1 Mr, 13 S, 25 Oct, 20 D 1929
31. *ibid* 13 F, 3 Ap 1931
32. *ibid* 31 Jl 1931
33. *ibid* 25 N, 2 D 1932, 8 Ja 1937
34. *ibid* 22 Ap 1921, 14 Mr 1924, 30 Mr 1923, 31 Oct 1930, 2 Mr, 12 Oct 1923, 13 F 1925, 26 N 1926
35. *ibid* 31 Jl 1925
36. Enfield LQ 1333, *Gazette* 17 Jl 1925, 19 Mr 1926, 28 Jl 1933, 22 Oct 1926
37. *ibid* 6 Mr 1931, 12 Ap 1935, 2 Jl, 17 D 1937, 23 D 1938
38. ED 60.172, ED 99.81
39. ED 19.180
40. ED 19.420
41. *Gazette* 1 F 1924, recollections of Richard Slater
42. *Gazette* Oct 1931, 22 Ap 1932
43. ED 99.81, *Gazette* 18 Mr 1932, 25 Oct 1935
44. *ibid* 31 Jl, 20 N 1936
45. *ibid* 2 N 1936, 5 Au, 21 Ja 1938
46. ED 16.704
47. *Gazette* 2 N 1919, 6 Ap, 27 Ap 1923, 30 Au 1929, 18 Ap 1930
48. M. Graham *Chase Farm Schools* EHHS 1974
49. *Gazette* 7 Mr 1919, 9 Ja 1925
50. *ibid* 1 Jl 1927, 29 D 1928
51. *ibid* 27 N 1928, 27 D 1929, ED 98.114
52. *Gazette* 1 Mr 1929, 30 Ja 1931, 29 Ja, 23 S 1932, 21 D 1934
53. *ibid* 4 D 1936, 26 N 1937

Chapter Five

Epilogue: The Approach of War

Twenty-one years separated the two world wars. Soldiers who returned home from the trenches, worn out but thankful in the autumn of 1918, were enrolled as air-raid wardens in the autumn of 1938. Small girls who sat down to their victory tea parties in 1919 saw their husbands off to the forces in 1939.

The end of the First World War was celebrated with joy tinged with sadness. Every street had its tea party, recalled Doris Shuttlewood. Families brought out their cups, plates and cutlery, their snow-white linen and damask tablecloths, long benches were borrowed from the schools, the trestles groaned with jellies, cakes, sandwiches …. Little girls donned white dresses and the boys who had sailor-suits wore them with pride … everyone had red, white and blue rosettes or bows'. There was a peace tea in the Market Place outside the main entrance to the Small Arms Factory and all the families in Government Row sat down at long trestle-tables. At Cosmos the young women held a victory social evening two days before Christmas 1918. There were many however, like Mrs Bennett of Bertram Road who, with three sons dead, had nothing to celebrate. Some wards at the North Middlesex Hospital remained occupied by half-forgotten men, broken in battle, who died quietly over the ensuing years at Edmonton or in some remote seaside resort like Pegwell Bay. The country yearned for peace and no more war. So strong was this longing that in the years between the wars

IN LOVING MEMORY
— OF —
OUR DEAR SON,
BEN COOK,
(Late Company Sergeant-Major, 7th Batt. Middlesex Regt.)

Who died at Pegwell Bay, Kent,
7th September, 1920,

AGED 27 YEARS.

Interred at Enfield Highway Cemetery.

223. *Company Sergeant-Major Ben Cook of the Middlesex Regiment and Titchfield Road. Badly wounded, he died of his wounds two years after the end of the war.*

224. The end of the Great War was celebrated with relief tinged with sadness. Every street had its tea party; here's the one in Titchfield Road in 1919.

225. ... and here's the one in Durants Road

weak governments were applauded as they made concession after concession to feed the strength and confidence of Hitler, Mussolini and the Japanese warmongers.[1]

It was not until the early Thirties that peace was seriously threatened. Some of our countrymen faced the threat with at least momentary realism. 'You can't stop war by disarming', declared Colonel Applin our local Member of Parliament in October 1933. His speech earned the disapproval of Aneurin Bevan

226. *Peace celebrations in the Town Park in the summer of 1919. The lady in the white dress next to the wagon is Mrs Edith Newman, the first woman councillor on the Enfield UDC.*

who felt that we should be a pacifist nation. Perhaps Applin's speech to his constituents on the Abyssinian crisis would have been more to Bevan's liking. 'Let them see to it', he told his audience, 'that they were not for war now, but for peace'. His constituents, alas, by and large, agreed. Frank Broad (the former member for Edmonton, Broad was out of Parliament in 1931-5) speaking in 1933, confidently asserted that there was no possibility of Germany arming so as to become a menace, for years to come. German National Socialists, in March 1933, paraded at Potters Bar with arms upstretched in tribute to the crew of the

227. *A peace meeting. All the major political parties were agreed, and the public mostly concurred, that in the face of the insatiable ambitions of Hitler, Mussolini and the Japanese warmongers, we of the decent democracies must negotiate. Here they all are: W. W. Henderson, Labour; Col. Applin, Conservative; H. Durrand Lang, Liberal; the vicar the Reverend Daisley in the chair and it looks like one of the Ridges peeping over his shoulder.*

airship shot down there in the First World War. The British Union of Fascists held a meeting outside the RSAF; it was given considerable (by no means adverse) publicity in the *Gazette*. One Sunday in November 1934 a dozen 'Christian' storm troopers took part in a service at St Paul's Presbyterian Church. Our local *Gazette* praised the movement as 'of a missionary character, working within the German protestant church', apparently unaware that the movement started in Catholic Bavaria. The peace ballot in Enfield, in March 1935, resulted in a strong vote in favour of dependence, not on tanks and aircraft to resist aggression, but on the League of Nations. An animated debate in the Council took place that July, on air-raid precautions. The following year the Council prepared a comprehensive scheme.[2]

Anti-Semitism, which was spreading like a foul plague across Germany, was also in evidence in North London. The Brookside Hard Court Tennis Club, in March 1937, refused membership to two Jews. The matter was raised by a Mr A. Gottfried, himself a Jew, who had been 'inadvertently admitted' and once in he presented a motion that the club should not discriminate by race or religion. His motion failed even to find a seconder.[3]

War began to look inevitable by the late Thirties. Eastern Enfield, with the RSAF, the power station, the reservoirs and widespread industry, was considered likely to be an important target for German bombers. The Enfield air raid precaution scheme was complete on paper by September 1937 but the Council was unable to take any practical measures until the government financial contribution was known. In October Enfield advertised for men over thirty to

NO WAR IN ENFIELD

228. The Enfield Gazette strongly urged everybody to keep their eyes shut so that they would not see the war coming. (Enfield Gazette 17 July 1936.)

act as air raid wardens and men over twenty-five to become auxiliary fireman. A draft emergency fire brigade scheme was adopted to cost £25,000. Recruitment however was slow; by January 1938 sixty applicants had come forward to fill the 830 places. Of the 2,600 volunteers required to man Enfield's ARP, only six hundred had enrolled by August 1938. Territorial recruitment for anti-aircraft and searchlight units made little progress.[4]

Then came the September crisis, which culminated in Chamberlain's visit to Munich. Suddenly the whole atmosphere was transformed, people expected immediate all-out war and were resolved to face it. Thousands queued for gas masks, trenches were dug in the parks, some fifty of them each capable of holding two hundred people; a scheme to deal with the expected wholesale casualties was organised. Notices were flashed on cinema screens warning people that they must attend various schools to be fitted with respirators; thousands queued on the Sunday to have their name, address and head size noted. The gas masks were distributed by lorry to various factories to be assembled and then rushed to the schools. Such was the urgency that distribution started at seven o'clock in the evening and by midnight forty thousand people in Enfield had been equipped to survive poison gas. Four hundred enrolled as air raid wardens and instruction was arranged to prepare them immediately for their duties. But then the crisis subsided, Chamberlain came home waving in triumph his agreement with Hitler. Instruction lectures were cancelled and trench digging stopped. Sunday was observed as a day of fervent thanksgiving, the churches were crowded. The atmosphere had changed again, apprehension replaced resolution.[5]

Civilian defence nevertheless had profited by the crisis; 1,372 volunteers had joined the ARP (801 men and 571 women) and 311 had applied to join the AFS. Yet Enfield three months later, still had only seven hundred wardens out of a

229. *The crisis of September 1938 brought an expectation of immediate war. The British people were resolved to defy Hitler. Primitive trenches were hurriedly dug in the parks, a few anti-aircraft guns were trundled out and millions of gas masks were issued. Then the Allied leaders again submitted, back from Munich came Chamberlain waving his piece of paper, and apprehension replaced resolution. The photograph shows the trenches on Library Green.*

230. *The crisis of September 1938, for a brief moment, forced us to look reality in the face, but not for long. Home came Chamberlain with his umbrella and the piece of paper. (*Gazette *7 October 1938)*

SO NOW WE'LL KNOW—!

231. *It was announced in March 1939 that 22,000 Enfield homes, where the man earned less than £250 a year (plus £50 for each child over two) were to get a free Anderson shelter* (Gazette *3 March 1939*)

requirement of eleven hundred. The main shortage was in the eastern half of the parish where only 185 had enrolled to protect a population of fifty thousand. The trenches in the parks were now full of water and, apart from the risk of children falling in, the danger had apparently subsided.[6]

But then the mood changed again. It became apparent that Munich was not a final settlement, that the Sudetenland was not Hitler's 'last territorial demand in Europe'. Preparation for war was reluctantly resumed. It was announced in March 1939 that 22,000 Enfield homes, where the man earned less than £250 a year (plus £50 for each child over two), were to get free Anderson air raid shelters. The local Territorial unit (B.Coy 7th Middlesex) by April was at nearly double its full wartime strength. There was a call for 450 women ambulance drivers and men were required for stretcher parties; Enfield would need seventy-five ambulances to deal with the vast number of casualties expected from German air raids. A letter from the Home Office in June required all councils to give priority to civil defence. Work on the Bullsmore Lane housing development was deferred.[7]

With memories of the Great War still fresh in people's minds, attack by poisonous gas was widely dreaded. 'Put your gas masks in your holiday luggage' advised the *Gazette* that August. A new anti-aircraft unit (the 48th Light AA Battery) a Territorial unit, was being formed for the defence of Enfield. ARP volunteers worked feverishly as Enfield's civil defence prepared for instant mobilisation; key defence points were manned day and night. Anti-aircraft units

DON'T "WAIT TILL THE CLOUDS ROLL BY"!

232. July 1939 and time for one last holiday (Gazette 21 July 1939)

PUTTING THE "JITTERBUG" IN HIS PLACE

233. 18 August 1939 and the cartoonist is still convinced that there won't be a war.

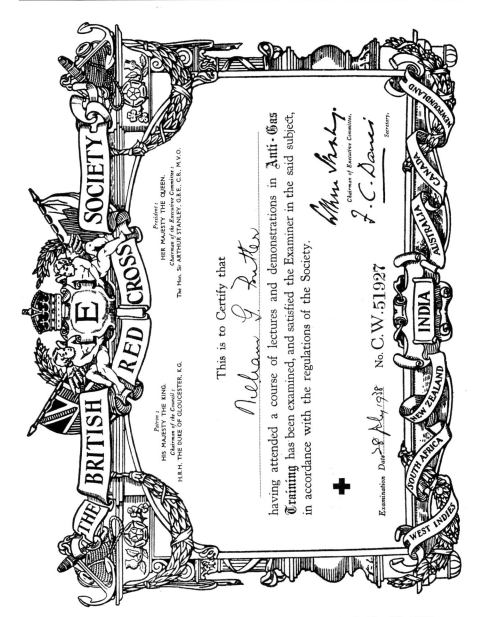

234. Memories remained of the suffering inflicted by poisonous gas in the First World War.

had taken up their dispositions by September. Frances Perry called for recruits for immediate service or training in the Women's Land Army.[8]

On 3 September people gathered around their radios to hear Neville Chamberlain announce the outbreak of war and afterwards came out to their gates to talk it over with their neighbours. All cinemas, theatres, dance halls and

235. Threshing corn on Parkside Farm, Enfield during the Second World War.

"LET'S KEEP SMILING."
A Series of Sketches depicting the lighter side of War.
No. 4.—"THE HOME AND AWAY FRONT!"

236. Nearly four thousand children were evacuated from eastern Enfield, but then nothing happened; there was a feeling of anticlimax, the evacuees drifted back home.

other places of public entertainment were to be closed until further notice. All windows which would show a light at night time had to be screened and all outside lights had to be turned off. Local shops did a roaring trade with black paper and black curtain material; there was a run on torches and batteries.

3,950 children living east of the Cheshunt branch line were evacuated in two convoys of eighty buses, each labelled with its destination. Two hundred children went to Cuffley and Northaw, six hundred to Harpenden, seven hundred and sixty to Hitchin, three hundred to Letchworth and others to Dunstable and Leighton Buzzard.[9] Thus the people resolutely prepared to face the onslaught of Hitler. The immediate aftermath was an anticlimax, perhaps even a disappointment, and I have left the telling of it to others.

Notes to Chapter Five

1. *Gazette* 3 Ja 1919
2. *ibid* 4 Oct 1935, 20 Oct, 17 Mr 1933, 10 Au 1931, 9 N 1934, 15 Mr, 2 Au 1935
3. *ibid* 12 Mr 1937
4. *ibid* 17 S, 29 Oct, 5 N 1937, 26 Au 1938
5. *ibid* 30 S, 7 Oct, 28 Oct 1938
6. *ibid* 2 D 1938, 2 Ja 1939
7. *ibid* 7 Ap, 28 Ap, 12 My, 14 Ap, 19 My, 2 Je 1939
8. *ibid* 4 Au, 1, 8 S 1939
9. *ibid* 8 S 1939

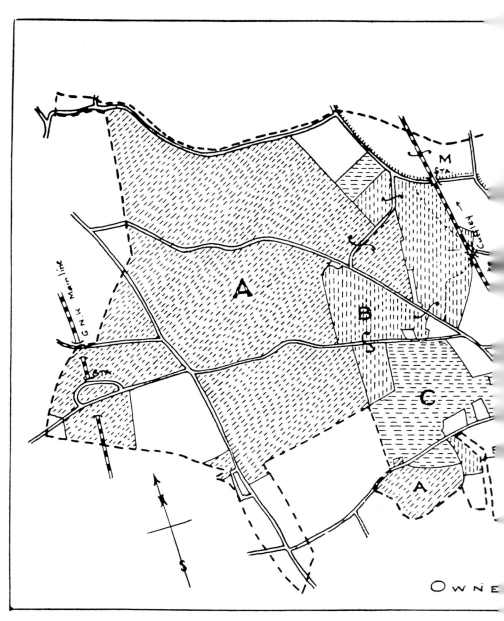

SCALE 1 M

Ownership Map

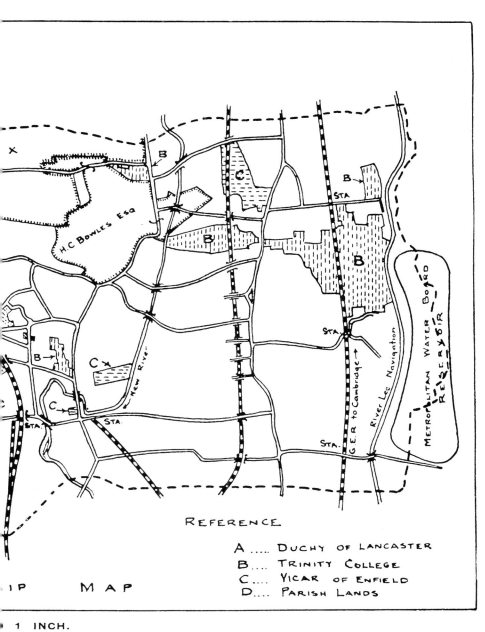

X

B

H.C. BOWLES ESQ

C

B

B

STA.

B

C

New River

STA.

B

C

STA.

STA.

STA.

G.E.R. to Cambridge

River Lee Navigation

METROPOLITAN WATER BOARD RESERVOIR

STA.

REFERENCE

A ..... DUCHY OF LANCASTER
B .... TRINITY COLLEGE
C .... VICAR OF ENFIELD
D .... PARISH LANDS

IP   MAP

1 INCH.

nfield, 1911.

Bibliography

Headings used in bibliography

Middlesex	buildings	poor law
Enfield	charities	religion
Enfield Chase	co-operatives	shops
Bush Hill Park	education	sport
Hadley Wood	epitaphs	theatres and cinemas
Winchmore Hill	industry	transport
agrarian history	parish registers	war
archaeology	place names	water supply

Abbreviations used in bibliography

EHHS Edmonton Hundred Historical Society
EAS   Enfield Archaeological Society
EPS   Enfield Preservation Society
LMAS London and Middlesex Archaeological Society
Trans transactions
ed   editor
JRG   Jewish Research Group of EHHS
J   Journal

Bibliography

Mostly selected by Graham Dalling

MIDDLESEX
Lysons, D. The environs of London. 1811
Robbins, M. Middlesex. 1953

ENFIELD
Avery, D. The Tudor Hundred of Edmonton: evidences and survivals. EHHS, 1968
Burnby, J. G. L. Drovers and tanners of Enfield and Edmonton. EHHS, 1988
Dalling, G. Enfield in the time of Charles Lamb. Charles Lamb Soc. Bulletin, new series 34, 1981
Doree, S. Domesday Book and the origins of Edmonton Hundred. EHHS, 1986
Hardy, P. Hints for the benefit of the inhabitants of Enfield. 1809. *The duties of an overseer*
Hodson, G. and Ford, E. A history of Enfield. 1873
Pam, D. O. Elizabethan Enfield. EHHS, 1975
Pam, D. O. Protestant gentlemen: the Wroths of Durants Arbour. EHHS, 1973
Pam, D. O. The rude multitude: Enfield and the Civil War. EHHS, 1977
Pam, D. O. Charles Lamb in Enfield and Edmonton. Enfield Libraries, 1972
Pam, D. O. ed. The castle of antiquaries, our local story in verse. Enfield Libraries, 1980

Phillips, P. Upon my word I am no scholar. EHHS, 1982. *Describes Enfield Wash in the mid-eighteenth century.*
Recollections of old Enfield. 1910, reprinted EHHS, 1983
Robinson, S. Sid's family Robinson, 1990
Robinson, W. The history and antiquities of Enfield, 1823
Roe, W. J. Tottenham, Edmonton and Enfield historical notebook. 1952
Tuff, J. Historical, topographical and statistical notices of Enfield. 1858
Victoria County History of Middlesex, vol.5. 1976 *Includes Edmonton Hundred*
Whitaker, C. W. An illustrated historical account of Enfield. 1911, reprinted EPS, 1965

ENFIELD CHASE
Madge, S. J. The Domesday of Crown Lands. 1938
Pam, D. O. The story of Enfield Chase. EPS 1984
Thompson, E. P. Whigs and hunters: the origins of the Black Act. 1975

BUSH HILL PARK
Ford, J. W. A sketch towards the history of the neighbourhood. 1904
Haigh, D. Old Park in the Manor of Enfield. 1977
Hoy, D. From fields to flats. 1985

HADLEY WOOD
Clark, N. Hadley Wood: the background and development. 1968

WINCHMORE HILL
Cresswell, H. Winchmore Hill: memories of a lost village. 1912
Dumayne, A. Fond memories of Winchmore Hill. 1990
Pam, D. O. Southgate and Winchmore Hill. Enfield Libraries, 1982
Regnart, H. G. Memories of Winchmore Hill. 1952

AGRARIAN HISTORY
Allan, M. Tom's weeds: the story of Rochford's. 1970
Avery, D. Manorial systems in Edmonton Hundred in the late medieval and Tudor periods. EHHS, 1963
Burnby, J. G. L. John Sherwen and drug cultivation in Enfield. EHHS, 1973
Burnby, J. G. L. and Robinson, A.E. And they blew exceeding fine: Robert Uvedale, 1642-1722. EHHS, 1976
Burnby, J. G. L. and Robinson, A.E. Now turned into fair garden plots. EHHS, 1983. *Contains a biographical dictionary of local nurserymen.*
Lewis, T. and Pam, D. O. William and Robert Cecil as landowners in Edmonton and Southgate, 1561-1600. EHHS, 1974
Pam, D. O. The hungry years: the struggle for survival in Edmonton and Enfield before 1400. EHHS, 1980.
Pam, D. O. The fight for common rights in Enfield and Edmonton, 1400-1600. EHHS, 1974
Middleton, J. View of the agriculture of Middlesex. 1798.

ARCHAEOLOGY
Dinn, J. Excavations in Enfield 1977/9. Trans LMAS v.31, 1980. *The Palace Gardens site.*
Enfield Archaeological Society. The site of Elsynge Hall. 1968
Gentry, A. Excavations at Lincoln Road Enfield, 1974-6. Trans LMAS v.28, 1977
Gillam, G. Prehistoric and Roman Enfield, a summary of the … archaeology. EAS, 1973
Renn, D. F. A bridge framework from Camlet Moat, Trent Park. Trans LMAS v.21, 1967

BUILDINGS

Colvin, H. M. ed. History of the king's works, v.4, 1485-1660 pt2, 1982. *Contains Camlet and Elsings or Enfield House*

Doree, S. Trent Park. 1974

Doree, S. The Sassoons of Trent Park. Heritage I, JRG, 1982

Edwards, J. The story of Capel. 1985

Enfield Preservation Society. Enfield's architectural heritage. 1977. *Illustrated guide to the buildings of Enfield, Edmonton and Southgate.*

Enfield Preservation Society. A portrait of Gentleman's Row. 1986

Jones, I. K. and Drayton, I.W. The royal palaces of Enfield. EAS, 1984

Royal Commission on Historical Monuments. An inventory of the historical monuments of Middlesex, 1937. *Buildings before 1714.*

CHARITIES

Hardy, P. An account of the charities and estates belonging to the parish of Enfield, 1834. *Includes plans of charity property.*

Weld, H. C. An account … of the charities belonging to the parish of Enfield. 1895.

Dalling, G. and Westaway, J.D. The Hundred Acres Charity. 1983

CO-OPERATIVES

Smith, H.C. Co-operation in Enfield. 1932

EDUCATION

Ambrose Fleming School. Jubilee edition of the magazine. 1961.

Collicott, S. Enfield School Board. EHHS, 1985

Edmonton County School. Fifty years of us. 1969

Enfield County School Old Girls Assn. Golden jubilee magazine. 1959

Marshall, L. B. A brief history of Enfield Grammar School. 1958

Middlesex County Council. Higher education in the administrative county of Middlesex. 1907

Morris, J. A. A history of Latymer School at Edmonton. 1975

Raglan School, 1928-1949. 1949

Sturges, G. W. Schools of the Edmonton Hundred. 1949

Taylor, R. W. A history of a school. 1968 *The Enfield British School*

Whitbourn, F. Lex, being the biography of Alexander Devine, founder of Claysmore School. 1937

Williams, R. T. A history of St Andrew's School Enfield Town. 1983

EPITAPHS

Cameron, H. K. The brasses of Middlesex, pt8: Enfield. Trans LMAS v.19, 1957

Cansick, F. T. A collection of curious and interesting epitaphs in the churchyards of Hornsey, Tottenham, Edmonton, Enfield, Friern Barnet and Hadley. 1875 *Many now lost or no longer legible.*

INDUSTRY

Hall, P. G. The industries of London since 1861. 1962

Martin, J. E. Greater London: an industrial geography. 1966

Enfield Archaeological Soc. Industrial archaeology in Enfield. EAS, 1971

Enfield District Manufacturers' Assn. Industries of Enfield. 1947

Brickmaking

Bass-Walker, P. Gabriel's opt for modernisation. British Clayworker, Feb. 1972

Roenisch, P. That was brick making. London's Industrial Archaeology, I, 1979 *Part of a tape recording by Frank Purse*
A useful work on this subject, by S. Beadle, will be published 1994 by EHHS
Electrical
Belling and Co. The Story of Belling, 1912-1962. 1962
Belling, Lee Ltd. Golden Jubilee, 1922-72. 1972
The pageant of the lamp. 1949 *The story of Ediswans*
Electricity Supply
North Metropolitan electric power supply and tramways. Electrical Review, v.55, no. 1898, 1904
North Metropolitan Electrical Power Distribution Co. The Enfield Electricity Works. 1907.
North Metropolitan Electric Power Supply Co. The Brimsdown 'A' generating station. 1939
Firearms
Amalgamated Union of Engineers and Foundry Workers. Some account, to 1935, of the Enfield Lock branch. 1970
A short history of the Royal Small Arms Factory is in preparation by Middlesex University
Ames, E. The Enfield arsenal in theory and history. Economic J. Dec. 1968 *The mid-19th century re-organisation*
Bowbelski, M. The Royal Small Arms Factory. EHHS, 1977
Min. of Defence. British rifles: a catalogue of the Enfield pattern room. 1981
Reynolds, E. G. B. The Lee-Enfield rifle. 1960
Robinson, A. E. and Burnby, J. G. L. Guns and gunpowder in Enfield. EHHS, 1987. *The origins and early history*
Gas Industry
Merrison, H. W. A brief account of the Tottenham and District Gas Company's first hundred years, 1847-1947. 1947
Tottenham and District Gas Co. Ponders End Works. 1949
Mills
Wright and Sons Ltd. The story of a family business. 1963

PARISH REGISTERS
Middlesex Parish Registers. Marriages 9 vols. 1909-1938 *Enfield marriages, 1550-1837 in v.5*
Lewis, T. People and parish registers. EHHS, 1979

PLACE NAMES
English Place Name Soc. The place-names of Middlesex. 1942
Dalling, G. A guide to Enfield street names. EPS, 1982

POOR LAW
Richardson, S. I. A history of Edmonton Poor Law Union, 1837-1854. EHHS. 1968
Graham, M. The Chase Farm Schools. EHHS, 1974

RELIGION
Mude-Smith, R. The religious life of London. 1904 *Based on a survey of church attendances*
Pam, D. O. Late medieval religion in Enfield, Edmonton and Tottenham. EHHS, 1968
Roman Catholic
Avery, D. Popish recusancy in the Elizabethan Hundred of Edmonton. EHHS, 1968
Vaughan, H. J. J. Our Lady of Mount Carmel and St George: a parish history. 1992

Church of England
Christ Church, Cockfosters: 125 years. 1967
Clutton, H. R. The parish church of St Mary Magdalene, Windmill Hill. 1970
Dalling, G. Enfield's railway king: David Waddington and the great pew controversy. *A violent episode 1853-4 at St Andrew's Church*
Hoy, D. From fields to flats: a history of Bush Hill Park and St Stephen's Church. 1985
Koch, E. H. A. Forty Hill church and parish. 1935
Lamb, C. The parish church of St Andrew. 1969
Ross, B. The story of St John the Baptist Church, 1857-1957. 1957

Nonconformist
Knight, G. Nonconformist churches in Enfield. EHHS, 1973

Baptist
Enfield Baptist Church from 1867 to 1967. 1967
Totteridge Road Baptist Church, 1868-1968. 1968

Methodist
Williams, R. T. Enfield Town Methodist Church. 1978
A scholarly history of Ponders End Methodist and Baptist churches by P. Charters is in preparation.

Society of Friends
Edwards, I. L. 1668, Middlesex village to suburb of London: 250 years of the Winchmore Hill Meeting. J. of the Friends' Historical Soc. v.35, 1938

United Reformed Church *(formed 1973 by the amalgamation of the Congregational and Presbyterian churches)*
Gould, F. J. and Day, J. R. History of Christ Church Enfield. 1975
Stribling, J. S. History of Christ Church Enfield. 1917
St Paul's Presbyterian Church. The semi-jubilee of St Paul's, 1902-27. 1927

Evangelical
Noble, H. C. The first eighty years, 1897-1977: a history of the Enfield Evangelical Free Church. 1977

SHOPS
Kensey, M. F. Grout's of Enfield Ltd. 1975
Pearson's Enfield Ltd. The Pearson story: 75 years of independence. 1978

SPORT
Enfield School Sports Assn. ESSA jubilee 1896-1958. 1958
Cockfosters Cricket Club: a history of the first hundred years. 1973
Enfield Golf Club, a centenary history, 1893-1993. 1993
North Enfield Cricket Club. One hundred years to remember … 1886-1986. 1986
Winchmore Hill Cricket Club: the first hundred years 1880-1980. 1980

THEATRES AND CINEMAS
Sully, H. B. A short history of the cinemas in Middlesex, 1910-1965. Middlesex Local History Council Bulletin, 8. 1964
Gillam, G. Theatres, music halls and cinemas in the London Borough of Enfield. 1986

TRANSPORT
Buses
Blacker, K. C. London's buses, v.1 The independent era, 1922-34. 1977
Railways, general
Jackson, A. London's local railways. 1978

Great Eastern
Allen, C. J. The Great Eastern Railway, 5th ed. 1968
Dalling, G. All stations to Enfield Town. Enfield Libraries, 1986
Hill, J. Buckjumpers, gobblers and clauds. 1981. *The author was an engine driver based for many years at Enfield Town.*
Treby, E. The Edmonton, Cheshunt line, Railway Magazine, March 1958
Great Northern
Grinling, C. H. The history of the Great Northern Railway, 1845-1922, 1966 *Substantial references to the London suburban area*
Hodge, P. The Hertford loop. 1976
Lake, G. H. and Weight, R. A. H. The Wood Green, Langley Junction line. Railway Pictorial and Locomotive Reviews, Aug. 1949
Young, J. N. Great Northern suburban. 1977
Goode, C. T. The Hertford loop line. 1984
Piccadilly
Lee, C. E. Sixty years of the Piccadilly. 1966
Jackson, A. Piccadilly line golden jubilee. Railway World, Nov. 1983
Jackson, A. and Croome, D. Rails through the clay: a history of London's tube railways. 1962
Roads
Dearman, W. C. Up and down the Hertford Road. EHHS, 1980
Ordish, T. F. History of metropolitan roads. London Topographical Record v.8, 1913, *London turnpike roads from 1826-1872*
Pam, D. O. The Stamford Hill, Green Lanes Turnpike Trust, EHHS, pt1, 1963, pt2, 1964
Tramways
Smeeton, C. S. The Metropolitan Electric Tramways v.1 Origins to 1920, v.2: 1921-1933. 1986
River Lea
Burnby, J. G. L. and Parker, M. The navigation of the River Lee, 1190-1790, EHHS, 1978
Denny, M. London's waterways. 1977 *Contains a chapter on the Lee Navigation*
Pam, D. O. Tudor Enfield: the maltmen and the Lea navigation. EHHS, 1970
Smeaton, J. Report of John Smeaton, engineer, upon the new making and completing the navigation of the River Lee ... to the town of Hertford. 1766.

WAR
Enfield Urban District Council. Enfield victory celebrations: official programme. 1946
Gillam, G. Enfield at war, 1914-18. EAS 1982
Gillam, G. Enfield at war, 1939-45. EAS 1985

WATER SUPPLY
Barry, S. Some notes concerning the growth and development of water supply and storage in Chingford. Chingford Historical Society, 1975
Metropolitan Water Board. Chingford Reservoir, inauguration by King George V 1913. *Details of unique Humphrey pumps*
New River
Gough, J. W. Sir Hugh Myddelton, entrepreneur and engineer. 1964
Berry, G. C. Sir Hugh Myddelton and the New River. Trans. Hon. Soc. of Cymmrodorion, 1956
Rudden, B. The New River: a legal history. *More a history of the New River Company*

All the works listed are available in the Enfield local history collection at the Town Hall, Green Lanes, Palmers Green.

Subscribers' List

London Borough of Enfield
The Worshipful the Mayor of Enfield

Bishop Stopford's School at Enfield
Capel Manor Primary School
Carterhatch Junior School
Chace School
Eastfield Primary School
Edmonton School
Eldon Junior School
Enfield County School
Firs Farm Primary School
Galliard Primary School
George Spicer School
The Latymer School
St Andrew's C.E.Primary School
St Ignatius College
St Michael's C.E. Primary School
St Paul's C.E. School
Worcesters Primary School

Addington, Mr & Mrs E.W.
Allen, Joan
Allum, Mrs N.
Andrews, Geoffrey L.
Andrews, Mrs Vera
Appleby, Dr E. Calvert
Artiss, Mr & Mrs E.F.
Atkins, Patricia
Austin, Michael, BSc, FIBMS
Authers, Ellis W.
Badger, Mrs Iris A.
Bagley, Mrs K.
Ball, Mrs Anne
Barber, Paul J.
Barbour, Margaret S.
Barker, Mr R.L.
Barnard, Katherine and Alan
Barnard, Richard A.C.
Barnes, Alan, CBE, MA
Barnsley, Lynwen & Mike
Barry, Joseph H.D.
Barton, T.H. and V.B.

Baruch Mrs P.
Bayford, Mr Frank
Beadle, Donald
Beadle, Miss
Beale, T. Edward, CBE, JP
Beard, R.E.
Beaumont, Jack, MBE
Bedford, Miss M.A.
Beetlestone, Florence
Benjamin, Jenny
Bennett, Mr D.J.
Bennett, Herbert F.
Berkeley, Mrs Sonja
Bevan, S.H. & G.B.
Biggs, Mr A.J.A. & Mrs M.J.
Bignell, Victor & Janet
Bird, Mr M.V. & Mrs H.C.
Birley, Mr & Mrs C.D.
Blake, Mr J.H.
Blaskett, S.R.J.
Boardman, Mr Fred T.
Bocock, Marian
Bolden, Keith F.
Bone, Mr & Mrs F.M.
Booker, S.
Booth, Mr S.H.F.
Borner, Mr L.C. & Mrs J.
Bouffler, L.E.
Bougnague, Mr P.
Boutell, Mr C.J.
Bowie, Val
Bowyer, Mrs Vera
Brewer, Ray
Brock, Mrs M.M.
Brown Terry
Browning, Miss Sheila
Bruce, J.A.G. & R.E.B.
Bruin, Mrs E.R.
Buckle, Mr Allan T.
Budd, Miss Valerie
Bull, Graham & Lynn
Bull, Mr & Mrs L.H.
Bull, Pamela M.

Bulling, Sarah Jane
Bullock, Alan
Burke, Mrs Doreen M.
Burrell, Mr & Mrs R.S.
Bushell, Mr & Mrs R.D.L.
Butler, Frank
Butler, Miss I.G.
Butterick, Mr P.W.F.
Byron, Pat
Campbell, Sue + James
Cannon, Mrs Mary
Capp, Alan
Carnaby, Miss Lilian G.
Carr Mr & Mrs K.T.
Carr, Ronald F.
Carter, Henry and Valerie
Carter, Mr & Mrs J.W.R.
Carter, Terry & Eileen
Cattermole, Leonard
Cattermole, Shirley
Chamberlain, Mrs C.A.
Chamberlain, Marian and Neville
Chaplin, Edgar
Chapman, Eddie
Chapman, Eric
Charge, S.P., MA
Chase, Mr R.
Chase, Mr Roland F.
Cherry, Mr & Mrs J.
Christen, Leta Christina
Christmas, Frederick G.
Churchill, Mrs Ruth
Clark, Miss B.D.
Clark, D.
Clark, Mr George
Clark, V.E.
Clarke, Geoffrey T.
Clarke, Mr R.P.
Clarke, Mr Roger J.
Clifton, James
Cockle, Mr D.
Coleman, Mr & Mrs K.L.
Collie, Mrs Rita
Combe, Andrew, Christine, David
   and Stephen
Comyns, Mary C.
Conrich, Gilda & Robert
Cook, Christine & Russell
Coote, Major A.D.

Coote, Stephen
Coote, William Raymond
Corbett, Robin B.
Cordell, Mr J.R.
Cornwell, Jean
Corper, Mr Philip
Cotton, Shirley & Albert
Couzens, Mr & Mrs A.E.
Cowley, Miss Winifred E.
Cox, Helen May
Cracknell, Mr M.E.
Cracknell, Peter M.
Cracknell, Mrs Robert
Cranfield, I.
Critchlow, Frances and Eugene
Crofts, J.W. & E.
Croughton, David W.
Crutchley, George + Joyce + Michael
Cufley, David R.
Cufley, Ronald R.
Dane, Peter D.L.
Daniels, Dorothy
Darling, Mrs N.W.
Davies, Mr J.Ewart
Dawe, Richard D.
Dawson, Mr Cecil
Day, Erik
de Warrenne, Anna
Deacon, Mr M.John
Deamer, J.R.
Deer, G.A.E.
Deering, Peter H., JP
Delvin, Stuart
Dennis, Reg
Dewell, Mrs E.
Dixon, Mr D.A., (Headmaster)
   Carterhatch Junior School
Dormer, R.J.
Dorrington, Albert & Beryl
Doust, Mr P.
Draper, Mr & Mrs R.J.
Dumayne, Alan
Dye, Mrs Doris
Ebbels, Mrs D.
Eddington, Mr Roger
Eden, Joyce Rosana
Edwards, Mr John E.
Edwards, Mr & Mrs
Egan, C. & J.

Elkin, Mr Roger
Ellis, Andrew
Ellis, Mrs J.M.
Ellwood, Mr & Mrs R.F.
Elmes, Sylvia
Everett, Arthur H.
Fairclough, K.R.
Fairhurst, David
Farquharson, Carole
Farrant, Frieda F.
Farthing, Mr & Mrs M.G.
Featherstone, Laurence
Featley Mr Kenneth
Featley, Mr D.G.
Fenn, Stephen R.
Ferguson, Mr R.J.
Finkel, Mrs Jeanette
Fisher, David, Paula & Zebaria
Fishpool, Claire
Fleming, Mrs Hazel
Fletcher, Mrs A.L.
Fletcher, Mr & Mrs K.E.
Flitter, Miss J.R.
Flitter, Joyce
Ford, B.
Ford, Miss Jane
Foret, Mr Raymond
Foster, Edna
Fox, Miss V.M.
Francis, Mr S.W.
Frear, Brian
Freer, Mrs P.A.
French, Mr Sidney W.
Frost, L.W. & M.E.
Gale, P.B.
Ganderton, Mr Colin
Ganderton, Mrs Margaret C.
Gardner, Brenda
Garrett, Mrs O.
Gay, Ken
Gee, Miss G.
George, Leslie & Jean
Gething, Mr & Mrs J.
Gibbons, Paul P.
Gibbs, John G.
Gibbs, Mr & Mrs R.A.
Gilburt, Stephen
Gillam, Geoffrey
Gitter, Susan and Simon

Gleeson, Geof
Glick, Mrs Marjorie
Goaman, H.F.
Godfrey, K.H.
Gould, Mr & Mrs John
Goulding, Mr T.G.
Gower, Paul J.
Gowers, Mr J.S.
Gowers, Mr R.
Gravell, Mr T.J. and Mrs B.R.
Grayston, Cllrs. Brian & Sheila
Green, John
Greening, Alan
Groom, Audrey E.
Grubb, Miss G.
Guiver, Dr Ian M.
Guttridge, Mr N.V.
Hackney, Mr D.J.
Hackney, Mrs V.L.
Hall, Arthur
Halstead, Miss Margaret B.
Hamer, Miss Doris
Hammond, David H.
Hampton, Janet
Hancock, Frank + Jean
Handley, Graham and Barbara
Hands, Roger & Joan
Hardy, E.F.H.
Harper, Mr J.W.
Harris, Mr & Mrs H.J.
Hartridge, Mr R.J., MA, MSc(Econ)
Hastings, Leonard Wm.
Hawkes, Mrs Lily
Hawkins, Graham & Sue
Hayes, Miss J.
Head, Mr R.L., ARIBA
Heanes, Mrs Nina
Henderson, Dr L.W.
Hicks, Graham
Hicks, Mr & Mrs R.A., Adrian &
  Louise
Higgins, Mr D.J.
Hill, Mrs P.
Hillsdon, D.J.
Hoare, Roger
Hobbs, Mr & Mrs S.W.
Hodge, Mr P.R.
Holland, Mrs B.A.
Holland, Miss P.A.

Honeyball, Mr & Mrs G
Hopkins, Miss Joyce
Hopwood, Jeff
Hornby, B.F.
Hoult, Constance
Howell, Mr E.H.
Howell, L.
Hoy, Mr & Mrs D.L.
Hoy, Ian C.
Hudson, David J.
Huggett, Mr Malcolm C.
Hughes, Mr & Mrs K.J.
Hulley, Mr J.R.
Humphrey, Mr S.C.
Hunt, Mrs Barbara M.
Hunt, Mr & Mrs W.C.
Hutchings, William N.
Huxley-Robinson, Kenneth, BA,
    MPhil
Irons, J.F.
Jachim, Mr & Mrs J.
Jackson, Cllr. John, JP
Jacob, Arthur & Edna
Jacobs, Mrs S.J.
Janes, M.J.
Jeeves, David H.
Jenkins, Mrs Gwen
Jenkins, Mr J. & Mrs P.
Jephcott, Christopher and Ursula
Jewell, M.F.
Johnson, Mr & Mrs B.C.
Johnson, John C.
Johnstone, Miss Kirsty
Jones, Mr David S.
Jones, Mr E.E.
Jones, Ian K.
Jones, Ken & Chris
Jones, Miss Peggy
Jones, Peter and Jean
Judd, Evelyn
Kean, Miss Joyce E.
Kearney, John
Keeble, Len
Kelly, Kay
Kemp, Mr Anthony I., FRICS
Kerridge, Mr J.F. & Mrs J.M.
Kevan-Marcelo Mrs Janet
Keyte, Mr & Mrs C.
King, Mrs Eileen

Kingdon, Ron
Knowles, Dr Wendy A.
Kolter, Jill and Peter
Lambe, Mrs C.A.
Lambourn, Mr E.H.
Lancaster, Mr M.T.
Lancucki, Mrs J.M.
Lancucki, T.S.J.
Landsman, Dr A.H.
Lane, Mrs E.
Lane, Miss M.C.
Langley, Mr & Mrs J.B.B.
Langridge, Mr L.W.
Langston, Mr & Mrs P.A.
Law, Mr & Mrs C.
Lawrence, Mr Leslie N.
Leftwich, Darren, BA, PGCE, FRGS
Leighton, M.B.E.
Letchford, J.A.
Levy, Pamela
Lister, Peter
Little, Mrs D.
Love, Philip
Lowe, Bob
Lowe, Mr & Mrs D.
Lowe, Ms. E.
Lowen, Mr S.J. & Mrs P.
Luxton, Mr Martin C.
Luxton, Richard J.
Luxton, Mr T.
Macfarlane, Gordon
Mallaburn, Beryl
Malleson, Mr & Mrs R.P.
Malone, Colin
Manning, Mr E.S.
Mantell, Mr G.A. & Mrs A.C.
Mantle, Anita and Robert
March, Mr David F.
Martin, Bob
Martin, Mr R.W.
Mason, Mr H.S.
Matthews, Mr Paul R.
Maul, Mrs Elaine
May, Mrs Margaret I.
McEleney, J.
McGowan, Stuart
Mellor, Mrs J.B.
Middleton, Mrs Barbara
Mills, Stuart D.E. & Cope, Carol

Mooney, David, MA
Moore, Mr B.B.
Moore, Mr & Mrs Fred
Moorhouse, Mrs D.J.
Morris, M.A.
Mortimer, Mr Anthony T.
Morton, B.D. and L.M.W.
Mott, Mr J.L.
Moulden, Jack L.
Munday, Mr D.B.
Murdoch, Miss M.
Mussett, Mrs Frances
Nafzger, Alan
Needham, Christine and Derek
Newens, A.S., MEP
Newman, John Bissett
Newton, Mr & Mrs Brian
Nicholls, Mr Jeffrey H.
Niehorster, Mrs A.J.
Nix, Harold
Noble, Harold & Sheila
Oakman, Mr R.D.
Oliver, Barry M.
Orr, Phyllis
Othen-Price, Joseph
Page, Mrs Barbara
Page, R.S. & P.J.
Pain, Tom & Cherry
Pam, Mr Joseph J.
Parker, Mrs Gwendoline Rose
Parker, M.A.
Pattison, M.A.
Pavey, Mr & Mrs D.R.
Peach, John C.
Pearce, Kathleen M.
Pearl, Mr & Mrs C.J.
Peffer, Mr M.T.
Pennell, Mr T.R.
Pepper, Mrs Lyn S.
Perham, Mrs Heather
Perman, David
Perrins, Terence
Perryman, Cllr. Peter
Pickard, Mr B.R.
Pinkham, Miss M.J.
Pizzala, Sheila
Platt, H.W.
Plumb, Mr Jack
Pointer, Mr and Mrs C.L.

Pond, Mrs J.M.
Ponsonby, Mrs Rose
Porter, Valerie Jean
Poulton, W.
Prentice, Mr R. & G.
Price, John Rea
Pritchard, Mr & Mrs Harold
Pritchard, Mr & Mrs Peter
Proud, O.E.
Prudames, Anne
Purssell, Mr A.W.
Puttock, Kay & John
Ramsbotham, Leonard
Rash, Mr C.S.
Read, Marjorie B.
Read, Mrs Norah E.
Read, Mr W.N.
Redfern, Mr S.
Reed, Mr & Mrs H.J.
Reed, Mr Nick
Regester, LLB, Dr P.T. & Mrs R.M.
Reid, Graham & Jennie
Reid, Mrs Helen
Richards, Jill & James
Richardson, Brian & Margot
Richardson, Mr & Mrs D.
Richardson, James
Richardson, Mr S.I.
Richart, Iris
Ricketts, Betty
Ridge, Dr R.B.L.
Ridgewell, Mr W.L.C.
Ridgway, Mrs H.
Robbins, Dr R.M.
Roberts, Mr P.H.
Roberts, Ronald & Jacqueline
Robinson, A.L.
Robinson, Miss J.O.
Robinson, Sid
Rolfe, Eric
Rolph, Fred
Rondeau, Stanley
Rooke, Peter
Rosewell, Eric & Joan
Rowe, John A.
Rowley, Mrs Joy
Rubenstein, Dr I.D.
Ruskin, Douglas
Rye, Mr Bernard O.

Rye, Mr Derek J.
Rye, Mrs Hazel E.
Rye, Mr Michael J.
Rye, Mr and Mrs P.S.
Ryman, Ernest
Sanders, Mr & Mrs C.C.
Sandilands, Mr Roy
Sargent, A.E.
Sargent, Irene
Saunders, S.C.
Say, P.I.
Scarles, Thomas A.
Schofield, Miss Kathleen M.
Seaborne, Mrs F.D.
Searle, Mr & Mrs P.
Sedgwick, Mrs Dilys
Seeley, Mr & Mrs R.H.
Seeley, Mr & Mrs V.F.
Sellick, Olive
Setterfield, Mr William
Sewell-Alger, Mr P.A.
Sharkey, Doctor & Mrs Joseph
Sharman, Betty
Sheppard, A.G.
Shotter, Mrs Dorothy
Simmons, Amy and Stan
Simons, Sally, Christopher, Thomas
   & Sarah
Singleton, Jean & Ron
Skilton, Alan J.
Slatford, Kenneth
Sluter, Mr F.A.
Small, Miss Jean
Smart, Mr & Mrs Derek
Smart, Philip J.
Smith, Betty
Smith, Donald
Smith, Hilary
Smith, Hilda
Smith, Hildegard and Eric
Smith, Len & Rita
Smith, Mrs Marie Anne
Smith, Mark
Smith, Monica
Smith, Pat and Peter
Smith, Mr Philip Francis
Smith, Mr & Mrs R.L.
Smith, Sue
Smith, Mr & Mrs T.G.

Smith, Irene & Stanley
Soma, J.
Somerville, Stephen
Soutar, Mrs B.
South, Mr & Mrs N.
Spiegel, Margaret M.
Spray, Zygmunt
Stamp, Mrs Doreen
Standbrook, Stanley & Audrey
Stanford, Dennis W.
Stanford, Ivy and Eric
Staunton, Mr Lee
Steele, A.
Surtees, H.K., C/Eng, Figase,
   Miplante, Finste
Sutton, Thelma
Swinson, Mr C.
Symons, Ivan P.
Tait, W.J.
Talbot, Mr F.S.B.
Taylor, Dr A.R.
Taylor, Lynn
Taylor, M.P.
Taylor, Michael A.P.
Tether, Pamela
Theobald, J.F.
Thompson, Mr & Mrs E.G.A.
Thompson, Jacky
Thomson, I.J.
Thorn Ted & Betty
Tibbatts, Mr & Mrs K.
Tillbrook, Mr & Mrs C.J.C.
Tilling, Mrs J.
Tollady, Mr C.A.
Tolliss, Mr R.F.
Toms, Alan E.J.
Tott, Anne & Trevor
Toussaint, Miss Alice
Tridgell, Mr & Mrs F.P.
Triggs, Miss S.E.
Trojanowski-Winchester, Mr & Mrs
Trussell, Mr D.G.
Try, Miss G.B.
Turnbull, P.
Turner, Mr John D.
Tuson, John F.
Tyler, Mr & Mrs E.T.
Tyrrell, T.G.
Vacher, Robert and Alison

Valentine, Graham
Vaughan, Mrs T.M.
Vickers, Mr D.T.
Voisey, Mr Roger J.
Wade, Mr Dennis
Wainwright, Mr & Mrs P.
Walby, Janet
Walker, Brian & Pat
Walker, Colin & Anne
Ward, Mrs Kathleen
Warren, Audrey
Warren, Mr B.
Warren, Professor F.L.
Waters, Mr Terence H.
Watson, G.W.
Watson, L.M.
Watson, Vera
Wayland, Mr & Mrs A.
Webb, G.I.
Webb, Patrick A.
Welsh, Sylvia B.
West, Marion and Richard
West, Peter D., BA, LRAM
Wetherall, Emma J.
Whatmore, Mr Rhys D.
Whitaker, Mr & Mrs J.
White, Mr David J.

White, Mrs J.M.B.
White, Miss Joan
White, Peter & Irene
Whitehead, David
Wick, Mr Donald
Wick, Mr Ian
Williams, Colin D.
Williams, Dr Molly T.
Williamson, Dr J.
Willis, William R.
Wilson, Alan G.
Wilson, Mrs M.
Winch, Mr B.S.
Wing, Mrs C.E.
Wolfson, Leslie R.
Wolton, John & Joan
Wood, Gladys E.
Woodfield, Mr & Mrs W.T.
Woodroffe, Mr & Mrs S.E.
Woods, Brian and Gillian
Woods, H.G.
Woolgar, Mrs Gwen
Woolveridge, H.T.
Worrall, Mr Edward S.
Wortley, Stephen
Wright, Mr & Mrs John H.
Young, M.R.

Index to Volume Three